Praise for *No Way but F*

No Way but Forward is a remarkable achievement. By way of his decades-long involvement in Gaza, and now particularly through the deep narration of the lives of these three families, Brian Barber reveals how we continue to survive; he shows our happiness, our sorrow, and what we dream. Overall, this book underscores the need for justice, dignity, and peace . . . and it demonstrates that sometimes humanity fails to insist on these for everyone.

—Yasser Abu Jamei, Director General, Gaza Community Mental Health Programme

A poignant labour of empathy and dedication to truth—Tolstoyan in span, meticulously researched. It will be a classic on Gaza alongside Sara Roy's *The Gaza Strip*. Historically, a priceless record of a Gazan era obliterated since Oct. 7 and a worthy memorial to it.

—Walid Khalidi, Senior Research Fellow (ret.) of the Center for Middle Eastern Studies, Harvard University; author of *From Haven to Conquest*, *All That Remains*, and *Before Their Diaspora*

Brian Barber has done what, to my knowledge, no one else has done: follow three Gazan families over three decades and document their lives in great and intimate detail. In doing so, Professor Barber has given us a work of immense beauty and humanity, an unassailable refutation of the dehumanization and unseeing to which Palestinians have always been subject. Rather, he shows us that we are Palestinians and Palestinians are us; their dreams and aspirations are ours and ours, theirs. An invaluable and much needed contribution to the literature on the Israeli-Palestinian crisis. Absolutely essential. A gem.

—Sara Roy, Associate of the Center for Middle Eastern Studies, Harvard University, author of *The Gaza Strip, Silencing Gaza,* and *Failing Peace*

[An] engaging narrative [with] stories that defy Western narratives of Palestinian youth. . . . A powerful look into occupied Gaza through the lenses of three ordinary young men.

—*Kirkus Reviews*

Barber's methodical and beautiful work charts [Palestinians'] everyday lives, the small things that make up a human being's passage on earth—in Gaza. This is not a lecture, or a book focused on the political issues—it is about humanity, how it continues to grow, how people actually live. This is a life's work: an urgent, vital and precious life's work that needs to be read by as many people as possible. *No Way but Forward* is the most accurate depiction of the struggle—but also joy that Palestinian families in Gaza had managed to find, in a backdrop of constant war.

—Janine di Giovanni, Executive Director, The Reckoning Project; award-winning author and journalist

No Way but Forward is hard to put down. Amid the violence and destruction of occupation and war, Brian Barber brings his readers into the lives of three families living in Gaza. Politics shape their world, but Barber succeeds in illuminating the daily experiences and emotions that transcend the boundaries of geography and culture. It is a wrenching lens that lays bare the simple truth of our common humanity.

—Anne-Marie Slaughter, CEO, New America; author of *Renewal* and *The Chessboard and the Web*

As someone raised in Gaza, living in exile, and mourning the wartime deaths of two dozen family members, I fully relate to the concept of "no way but forward." In his intimate narrative of three families courageously persevering despite Israel's decades-long occupation, siege, and current genocide, Brian Barber has captured the essence of my story and that of all two million plus citizens of Gaza.

—Ahmed Alnaouq, writer, journalist; co-author of *We Are Not Numbers*

A heart-rending and powerful book. Professor Brian Barber opens our eyes and hearts to the grim realities of the life—and death—of Gazans, describing with great sensitivity their upbringings, strivings, successes, failures, and tragedies under Israeli oppression.

—Jeffery D. Sachs, University Professor of sustainable development, Columbia University; author of *The End of Poverty* and *A New Foreign Policy*

Brian Barber interweaves intimate personal and family narratives from Gaza within the wider context of colonial oppression, military occupation, siege, death, and destruction. In the life stories of his three protagonists, Barber shares with us their determination to live in dignity, to fulfil their aspirations for family life and, above all, for freedom. In the context of the ongoing genocide in Gaza, these remarkable testimonies, and the subsequent heart-rending WhatsApp exchanges with the author, stand in marked contrast to the racism and dehumanisation so disgracefully applied by Israel and the West to the population of Palestine. A beautiful, deeply moving, and essential book.

—Avi Shlaim, Emeritus Professor of International Relations, University of Oxford; author of *The Iron Will* and *Israel and Palestine*

Barber carefully excavates and weaves together a narrative of life, of dreams and hopes, of love and humanity, as he traces three families making lives for themselves in the Gaza Strip, under the most oppressive of regimes. *No Way but Forward* brings us into the intimate homes of the protagonists, calling on us to share every moment of joy and sorrow, every victory and loss, every aspiration and disappointment, so that by the end, we know these families like they are our own. We become one with them, as Barber holds our hands, and calls on us to witness how their lives have unfolded across generations, shaken by colonial violence and hate, but still grounded in the indomitable hope for justice.

—Tareq Baconi, writer; author of *Hamas Contained*

Brian Barber has spent more time on the ground in Gaza than almost any outside observer. He writes with great clarity and empathy about life there, told through the stories of three men and their families that he has chronicled over decades, stories that have taken on even more resonance after the Gaza War that followed Hamas's attack on Israel on October 7, 2023. If you are trying to understand what life is like for ordinary Gazans, this book is essential reading.

—Peter Bergen, Vice President, New America; author of *The Rise and Fall of Osama bin Laden*

Brian Barber's keen research eye and his empathic heart combine to capture the richness of the daily lives of Palestinians in the Gaza Strip amidst the chaotic living conditions caused by geopolitical disputes largely outside their control. *No Way but Forward* attests to the resilience of the human spirit. The world must see this book and the sooner the better. It grabbed me and hasn't let go.

—Harold D. Grotevant, Emeritus Professor of psychology,
University of Massachusetts Amherst

In this tour de force book, Brian Barber deftly conveys Gaza's history and cultural practices by taking us into the lives of three men who grew up in refugee camps and endured the brutal reality of occupation and repeated military onslaughts as they persevered with their education and struggled to keep hope alive . . . Their stories are a testament to the humanity, kindness, tenacity, and decency of a people who have over the years been so thoroughly demonized by Israel and the West and denied all their human rights. Barber's book is both an invaluable window into pre–October 7th Gaza and an affirmation of the dignity of a society whose obliteration those of us fortunate enough to know Gaza now mourn.

—Nancy Murray, President, Gaza Mental Health Foundation

Palestinians have been viewed through a Jewish Israeli gaze, defined as the "terrorist," the "less civilized," the less deserving of international sympathies and understanding. Brian K. Barber offers an antidote to this prejudiced, inappropriate way of thinking in his new book, *No Way but Forward.* Barber writes with a sensitive understanding of Gazan life, politics, and culture, describing the lives of these three individuals, creating a clear picture of their deep humanity and challenging the rhetoric of our times.

—Alice Rothchild, physician, activist, filmmaker; author of
Condition Critical and *Inspired and Outraged*

NO WAY BUT FORWARD

Life Stories of Three Families in the Gaza Strip

Brian K. Barber

ISBN:
E-book: 978-969-589-281-7
Paperback: 978-969-589-282-4
Hardcover: 978-969-589-283-1

Cover design © Brian K. Barber. The author took the photograph in east Khan Younis, Gaza, in 2017. The tree shows that life still goes on amid impoverished circumstances. The writing on the outer wall of the house celebrates the marriage of an individual named Omar. For the author's many other photographs of Gaza taken during the decades covered in this book, see https://bkbarber.com/palestine-2/.

FOR Sharif Sharaf, Abu Ali Hillis, Eyad el Sarraj, Ahmed Abo Abed, and Bruce Chadwick—all dear friends and colleagues. May they rest in peace.

FOR the thousands of Palestinians, especially Gazans, with whom I have interacted personally, to all other Palestinians, and to all oppressed peoples around the world.

Table of Contents

Map of the Gaza Strip

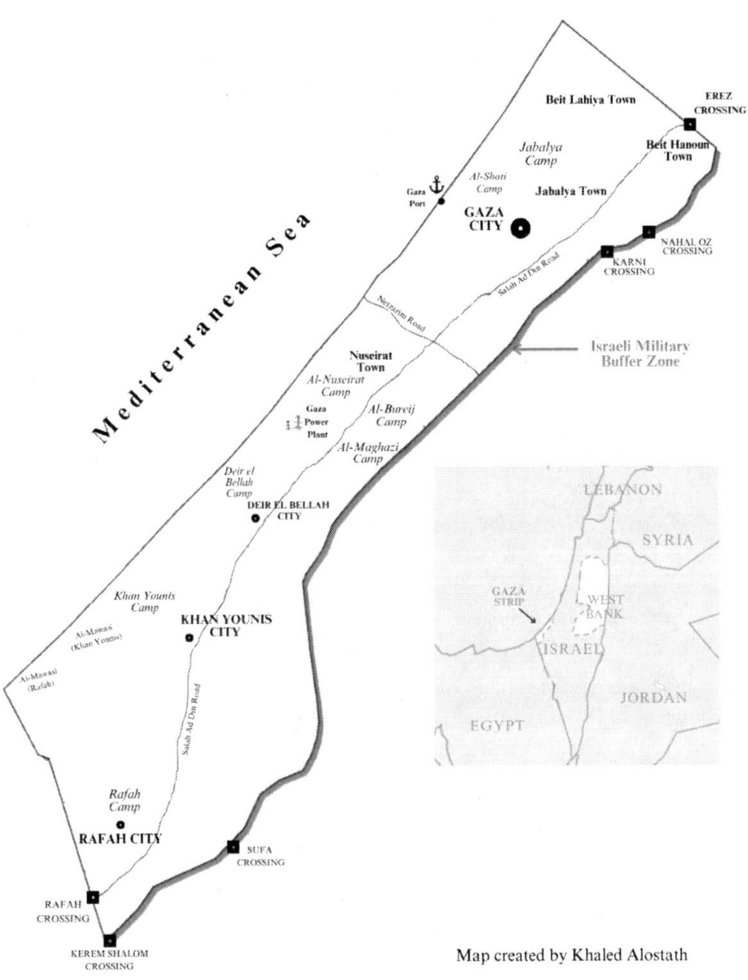

Map created by Khaled Alostath

Even the darkest night will end and the sun will rise.

—Victor Hugo, *Les Misérables* (1862)

Our souls are filled with pain, sorrow, and tears we can no longer shed . . . Each day brings a new story, a worse reality than the one before . . . yet as long as we have breath the dream endures. (January 5, 2024)

Resilience and determination to live with dignity burns within us. And with each passing day, hope is somehow maintained and the will to move forward grows despite all the hardships. (April 5, 2024)

—Khalil's twenty-three-year-old son,
Mohammed Abu Shammala

Introduction

No Way but Forward is a set of stories—deeply human accounts—of three young men and their eventual families. All three were born after the Israeli military occupation of the Gaza Strip that took force in 1967, and they have lived the entirety of their lives under its control. Throughout the occupation, they have faced violence, humiliation, and the loss of loved ones. They have also confronted seriously dwindling freedom of movement, basic resources, and economic opportunity. Moreover, they came of age during a historic six-year uprising against the occupation (the first *intifada*; see below), which the Gazan population, especially young people, engaged in actively.

Yet along with their parents, wives, and children, they have persevered in making an honorable life for themselves, with the fullest measure of happiness that conditions permit. In short, each of these three young men has been driven by the most classic of Palestinian maxims: that when one is confronted with an obstacle or setback, there is nothing to do but move *forward*.

Crucially, the book chronicles how these three individuals and their families are managing during the fierce, ongoing Israeli bombardment that followed the shocking Hamas attack on southern Israel on October 7, 2023.

Hammam (hah-MAHM), Khalil (khah-LEEL), and Hussam (hoo-SAHM)—who, incidentally, have never met—are ordinary people living in an extraordinary context. In seeing their day-to-day reality, we recognize ourselves—our own interests, struggles, dilemmas, joys, and pains. This daily reality encompasses anxiety about school exams and disappointment about failure, the satisfaction of getting a job and receiving a promotion, the fear and stigmatization of infertility, the thrill of experiencing the birth of a child, and the agony of learning about a cherished mother's cancer. Readers will get lost in such familiar human drama—only to be awakened by the realization that it's all playing out in tiny, oppressed Gaza, of all places.

No Way but Forward is not a treatise on history, politics, or economy, as are most of the dozens of important English-language books on Gaza. For a list of some of them, see Appendix 1. Nor is it a book about the Palestinian-Israeli conflict. Rather, it is a set of stories about everyday life in a grim and sorely misunderstood corner of the globe—tales of the extraordinary determination of ordinary people who are trying to forge a good and dignified life. These narratives are gripping, instructive, inspiring, tragic, and universally relevant as tales of survival, endurance, and hope.

Gaza is so misunderstood and maligned by outsiders because relatively few of them have gone there—and even fewer have stayed long enough to learn about the culture and the values of its people. Thus Gaza's first tragedy is that despite this ignorance, most people—whether politicians, diplomats, journalists, or everyday citizens of other countries—feel authorized to weigh in with firm declarations about who Palestinians are, about what they do or don't deserve, and about what they do or don't have the right to want, hope for, or achieve.

Discovering Gaza

"Are you sure you want to go there? Isn't it too dangerous?" went the refrain from colleagues and friends when, as a young assistant professor in the spring of 1995, I announced that I was planning to go to Gaza on my own to continue the sociological and psychological research that our academic teams had been conducting on Palestinian families in the West Bank and East Jerusalem for the past two years. Their alarm was justified if one believed the propaganda. For years, the Israeli media had been referring to the Gaza Strip as a "hellhole" full of "hornets."[1]

We researched and found that more than 80 percent of articles in five major US newspapers that had "Gaza" in the article title paired the name with violence or terror. Even the many Palestinian colleagues and friends I had made the previous two years in the West Bank and East Jerusalem couldn't help dispel these negative characterizations, since most of them had not been to Gaza for several years.

But I had already been inoculated against the nonsense that inexperienced pundits expounded about Palestinians as angry and vengeful people. Instead, my colleagues and I had found the thousands of Palestinians we researched and interacted with in the West Bank and East Jerusalem to be uniformly warm and engaging. The professional literature on mental health was equally misguided. Instead of a youth population psychologically disabled by continuous exposure to violence over the previous six years, we documented a population with healthy self-esteem, social cohesion, and hopes for a peaceful future.

---

[1] Amira Hass, *Drinking the Sea at Gaza: Days and Nights in a Land under Siege* (New York: Metropolitan Books, 1996).

On a spring morning in 1995, my taxi left Jerusalem and traveled ninety minutes southwest through Israel to the Gaza Strip. We passed verdant plains and drove on paved four-lane roads with modern traffic signals. Eventually, the driver pulled off the main road and drove west on a rough dirt road until we soon arrived at a set of rudimentary huts fronted by an asphalt pathway blocked by a horizontal white barrier. The driver dropped me off and wished me a safe journey. I figured it would not be wise to duck under the white bar, and so I waited. Eventually, the bar began a jerky but eerily silent ascent.

I went forward with some trepidation. Wordlessly, an Israeli soldier approached. I handed him my passport, and he motioned for me to wait on an old bench outside one of the huts. After several minutes he exited the hut, gave me my passport, and returned to his office, saying nothing. I assumed that I could proceed and did so, just as the education official from the United Nations Relief and Works Agency for Palestine Refugees in the Near East (UNRWA) had instructed me by phone to do: ever forward until you see a white car with blue UN markings. The path leading away from the huts was dusty and rocky, repeatedly clogging the little plastic wheels of my carry-on suitcase.

The spring weather was pleasant, and I took a rest for a bit, noting how silent the scene still was. Far off to the left, I could see farmers driving donkey carts, caring for their irregular fields. To the right, what looked like an abandoned factory appeared. I walked forward until I saw the gleam of the car, waiting some two hundred yards—"no-man's land"—past the Israeli checkpoint. Standing next to the vehicle, Ahmed, assistant to the head of the UN education system in Gaza, greeted me warmly. Over the course of our twenty-minute drive to Gaza City, he talked proudly about his eight children and how much he enjoyed working for UNRWA.

Endless paradoxes confronted me during the drive. On the western horizon, I saw the ugly, gray cinder-block monstrosity of the Jabalya refugee camp housing ninety thousand people; then on the eastern horizon, I saw charming green farmland. In the distance, marring the otherwise brilliant blue of the Mediterranean, I saw the foul stain of raw sewage pouring openly into the sea from the al-Shati refugee camp north of Gaza City.

A bizarre combination of modern but dilapidated diesel trucks and sedans speedily wove their way on torn-up roads between horse-drawn wooden carts clip-clopping feverishly ahead. The carts carried cargo ranging from enormous, overspilling stacks of yellow potatoes to rebar twice the length of the carts themselves, to entire large families. The cacophony of traffic noise and masses of people contrasted with the silent expanses of the pastures and orchards. And from dusty schoolyards, thousands of bubbly young students flooded the already jammed streets in their ill-fitting uniforms. Many were walking hand in hand—girls with girls, boys with boys—eager to get to their homes in Gaza City or their respective refugee camps to eat the afternoon meal.

The following day, UNRWA education officials gave me a tour of the whole Strip; you can drive its length in less than an hour and its width in twenty minutes. The contrasts persisted: We drove past dense, sprawling groves of orange trees and date palms; strings of drab factories; and gorgeous stretches of pale sand teased by the white froth of small breaking waves from the vast Mediterranean.

We visited numerous schools, most of them in the eight refugee camps across the Strip. The camps themselves revealed paradoxes. Narrow, sandy pathways with rivulets of raw sewage trickling into seepage ponds wove between identical unplastered cinder-block structures that were topped with tin or black plastic fifty-gallon water cisterns, with rebar stretching upward awaiting new floors for the sons once they've married. Yet these structures were also peppered with shiny, modern satellite dishes.

Through an interpreter, I spoke to many small classrooms packed with fifty or more students who were every bit as well-behaved as their counterparts in the West Bank and East Jerusalem in the dozens of classrooms I had visited there. As I was leaving a classroom, one young man stood up tall and respectfully implored: "Please go home and tell the world that we are not all terrorists." At another school a young girl penned a note in English and handed it to me shyly as I left her classroom:

> By the name of God, Dear Sir,
>
> You are welcome here in Gaza. Your small country. Me and by the name of my friends thanks you for visiting our school, and I hope that you will enjoy this visit. We are very pleased to see you here with us as Palestinians who like to meet foreigners and talk with them in order to tell them about our country. Finally, I wish you will enjoy your time in Gaza and will think of repeating this visit.
>
> Yours, Samira Abusalim

An administrator took me aside at another school and expressed essentially the same gratitude for the visit and the hope that I would come back.

In short, I observed no hellhole and encountered no swarms of hornets in Gaza. I felt totally comfortable, and with few exceptions, I have returned there since that 1995 visit, typically twice a year for weeks or months at a time. I was in Gaza in March of 2020 when the coronavirus began to hit hard, and I took one of the last remaining flights out of Tel Aviv back home. Once the pandemic subsided, I was able to renew my permit from the Israeli Defense Forces (IDF) to enter Gaza. I scheduled myself to enter on October 15, 2023. Entry became impossible beginning October 7.

Historically, the name *Gaza* has referred to two entities. First, across the nearly six thousand years of its recorded history, it has referred primarily to the ancient port city of Gaza, one of the world's oldest cities on record. Gaza City was the chief center of the frankincense trade as early as 500 BCE, as well as the commercial center for many other products. In the late fifth and early sixth centuries AD, the city was famous for its fairs and theaters, as well as for its school of rhetoric, which was at the time the basis of all higher education.

So important was Gaza in Roman times that it had its own calendar. The inscription on one coin minted in Gaza around the beginning of the first millennium BCE reads: "The city of the Gazaeans is sacred, and an asylum and autonomous, faithful, pious, brilliant, and great."[2] Five hundred years later, Antoninus Martyr wrote: "Gaza is a splendid and beautiful city; its men most honest, liberal in every respect, and friendly to the pilgrims."[3]

The history of Gaza City reads like a Who's Who of famous personages: Rameses I, Ramses II, Ramses III, Samson, Saul, David, Solomon, Alexander the Great, Plutarch, Pompey, Caesar, Herod, Jesus, Antony, Cleopatra, Porphyry, Omar ibn al Khattab, and Hashim ibn Abd Manaf (great-grandfather of Muhammad), among many others. Alexander lost ten thousand men conquering Gaza. Napoleon was injured there. It took General Edmund Allenby, commander of the British Egyptian Expeditionary Force, three days to capture the city at the end of World War I.[4]

---

[2] Martin A. Meyer, *History of the City of Gaza: From the Earliest Times to the Present Day* (New York: Columbia University Press, 1907), 159.

[3] Quoted in Meyer, *History of the City of Gaza*, 69.

[4] Gerald Butt, *Life at the Crossroads: A History of Gaza*, 2nd ed. (Nicosia, Cyprus: Rimal Publications, 2009), chap. 1.

The name Gaza also refers to the territories north, east, and south of Gaza City's boundaries—territories that have fluctuated across the shifting regimes of Egyptians, Canaanites, Philistines, Assyrians, Seleucids, Greeks, Romans, Israelites, Fatimids, Babylonians, Persians, Ottomans, and others.[5]

The Gaza Strip

The Gaza Strip[6] is a rectangular territory at the southeastern bend of the Mediterranean Sea directly above Egypt. The approximately 40 square mile area (between 7.8 and 3.4 miles wide and 28 miles long) was demarcated at the end of the 1948 war between Jewish and Arab forces that led to the establishment of the State of Israel. The armistice agreement designated Egypt as the administrator of this new Gaza Strip.[7]

The years following the establishment of Israel were full of deadly violence between Palestinian infiltrators from Jordan and the Israeli military. By 1954 Gaza had become caught up in the same incursion-retaliation dynamic, but more so in 1956 when Israel, supported by Britain and France, launched a war in response to Egypt's nationalization of the Suez Canal. For four months Israel occupied the Sinai Peninsula, including Gaza, withdrawing only under heavy US pressure.[8]

In the 1967 Arab-Israeli War (also known as the Six-Day War), the Israeli military seized the Gaza Strip and the Sinai Peninsula from Egypt. It also took control of the West Bank and East Jerusalem from Jordan, as well as the Golan Heights from Syria. In 1978–79 Egypt and Israel reached a peace agreement, lubricated by the US promise to provide billions of dollars of aid annually to each nation. Under the terms of the agreement, Israel withdrew from the Sinai Peninsula. Egypt had insisted that the Israeli military also withdraw from the West Bank and Gaza, but Israel refused to include the Palestinian territories in the agreement. Thus the West Bank, the

---

[5] Butt, *Life at the Crossroads*, chap. 5.

[6] Consistent with customary usage, I have used "Gaza" interchangeably with "the Gaza Strip." Although Gazans refer to Gaza City simply as Gaza, I have retained "City" to avoid confusion.

[7] Sara Roy, *The Gaza Strip: The Political Economy of De-development*, 3rd ed. (Washington, DC: Institute for Palestine Studies, 2016), chap. 1.

[8] Ian Black, *Enemies and Neighbors: Arabs and Jews in Palestine and Israel, 1917–2017* (New York: Grove Press, 2017), chap. 9.

Gaza Strip, and the Golan Heights remained—and still are—Occupied Territories.[9]

Immediately following Israel's occupation of Gaza in 1967, senior Israeli leaders—prime ministers, defense ministers, and others—began discussing ways, some admittedly cruel, of emptying Gaza of Palestinians or drastically reducing their population, with the end goal of some of the plans to annex Gaza to Israel: for example, by using military force to transfer Palestinians to the Sinai or Jordan; by demolishing or evicting them from their homes; by depriving Gaza of enough water to destroy its agriculture; and by otherwise ensuring a low standard of living in Gaza to encourage emigration.[10] Sara Roy has thoroughly documented Israel's deliberate and systematic "de-development" of Gaza's economy since 1967 to ensure that it can't support itself.[11]

Before Israel's occupation, Gaza—with a population of three hundred thousand Arabs, two-thirds of whom were refugees—had thriving citrus and agricultural industries that were supplemented by a merchant and tourist trade with Egypt, whose residents traveled there to enjoy the beaches and the duty-free shops. But already by 1970, Israeli forces were imposing strict curfews and had destroyed hundreds of houses. Some were describing Gaza as a "battlefield and a sewer, [the] capital of despair."[12] In 1971 Israel began developing Jewish settlements in Gaza.

---

[9] Black, *Enemies and Neighbors*, chap. 11; Rashid Khalidi, *The Hundred Years' War on Palestine: A History of Settler Colonialism and Resistance, 1917–2017* (New York: Metropolitan Books, 2020), chap. 3; Avi Shlaim, *The Iron Wall: Israel and the Arab World*, updated ed. (London: Penguin Books, 2014), chap. 6.

[10] Ofer Aderet, "'We Give Them 48 Hours to Leave': Israel's Plans to Transfer Gazans Go Back 60 Years," *Haaretz*, December 5, 2024, https://www.haaretz.com/israel-news/2024-12-05/ty-article-magazine/.premium/we-give-them-48-hours-to-leave-israels-plans-to-transfer-gazans-go-back-60-years/00000193-9716-dac2-add3-b75e12d30000.

[11] Roy, *Gaza Strip*.

[12] "*Gaza 1970: A City Besieged*," *The Facts about the Palestine Problem*, Arab Women's Information Committee, Beirut, Lebanon, supplement, April 1971, 3–4.

The First *Intifada*

The term *intifada* ("uprising" or "shaking off") was first used to describe the 1987–93 Palestinian uprising against the Israeli occupation, a rigid military-governed control that had already been in place for more than twenty-five years when I arrived in Gaza. Because the three young men in my narratives were born under this occupation and came of age during this historic uprising, it is important to lay out some of the details of what happened.

By design, the 1967 occupation controlled the political, economic, and cultural domains of Palestinian life. This control included Israel's suppression of Palestinian legal, civil, political, land, and water rights; Israel's forceful treatment of Palestinians through its "Iron Fist" policy of using collective punishment, arbitrary harassment, arrests, curfews, torture, and home demolitions to respond to resistance; Israel's economic exploitation of Palestinians, including controlling the service infrastructure of the West Bank and Gaza, confiscating Palestinian land and water resources, exploiting and degrading Palestinian labor, holding the Occupied Territories as a captive market, and restricting external trade.[13]

The occupation meant Israeli control of social and financial institutions, including banks and trade unions, and the repression of culture and ideology. That repression included licensing all publications; censoring the media; destroying Arabic historic sites; expunging the word *Palestine* from all textbooks and maps; forbidding the use of the four colors of the Palestinian flag (green, white, red, and black) in any publication or artwork; changing the names of towns, hills, and streets from Arabic to Hebrew; and prohibiting festivals, exhibits, and public lectures.[14]

The repression of Palestinian rights created a tinderbox ready to explode—and that's exactly what occurred on December 9, 1987, the day after an Israeli truck driver crashed into a line of cars and vans filled with men from Gaza returning from their day work in Israel. The funerals for three of the four Palestinians who died in the accident quickly turned into massive demonstrations fueled by rumors that the crash had been deliberate. Protests continued the next day, leading to direct confrontations with Israeli soldiers, who attempted to restore order by firing tear gas and live ammunition into the crowds. However, this military response only increased

[13] Roy, *Gaza Strip*, chap. 6.

[14] Khalidi, *Hundred Years' War*, chap. 5.

Palestinian anger. Protests soon escalated and spread to the West Bank and East Jerusalem. What appeared initially to the Israeli military and government as little more than normal unrest developed into an unprecedented six-year struggle of almost daily conflict. The potency and duration of the outburst surprised everyone: Palestinians, Israelis, and those outside the conflict.

This first *intifada* is still distinguished by the massive participation of young people, with historic rates that vastly dwarf any other documented rebellion in the world. Throughout the movement, more than 80 percent of young men and 50 percent of young women and parents took part in one or more activities: demonstrating, throwing stones at the IDF, burning tires to obscure pathways, rushing raw onions to demonstrators to relieve the stinging of tear gas in their eyes, distracting soldiers, and so on. A sizable majority of young male Palestinians and a significant minority of young female Palestinians had their homes or schools raided or were verbally abused, hit or kicked, shot at with bullets, humiliated, or forced to witness others being humiliated by the IDF. Twenty-five percent of young men were detained or imprisoned.[15]

When I first visited the Gaza Strip in 1995, the population comprised 1.4 million Palestinians. The vast majority of them were Sunni Muslim Arabs, and roughly 1 percent were Arab Christians, mostly Greek Orthodox. About 30 percent of this population consisted of native Gazans (Palestinians who had been there since before 1948, as well as their descendants), who were living in cities, towns, and villages. Approximately 70 percent of the population were refugees who had been expelled by Israeli forces or fled their homes in pre-Israel Palestine and their descendants. About two-thirds of these Gazans were living in eight refugee camps that housed between twelve thousand and ninety thousand people.[16]

The newly formed UNRWA set up these camps after the 1948 war. They were originally tent encampments, but when Israel would not allow the refugees to return to their homes, more permanent structures were built, first out of adobe and some years later (and to this day) out of locally manufactured cinder blocks.

---

[15] Brian K. Barber et al., "Whither the 'Children of the Stone'? An Entire Life under Occupation," *Journal of Palestine Studies* 45, no. 2 (2016): 77–108, https://doi.org/10.1525/jps.2016.45.2.77.

[16] Roy, *Gaza Strip*, chap 1.

In 1993 the population of Gaza also included four thousand Jews, who had begun arriving in 1971 and lived in sixteen (originally 18) settlements that took up at least 25 percent of the land in the Strip.[17] These settlements were fenced off and guarded by thousands of Israeli soldiers. Most settlers worked day jobs in Israel and used Jewish-only roads to get in and out of Gaza. The IDF ran all major institutions in Gaza. In 2005, to concentrate its military resources on the West Bank, Israel forced these Jewish settlers to leave Gaza and redeployed its forces across the border fence with Israel.[18]

The Narratives

All the scenes in this book were told to me by the individuals themselves, and I have rendered them into narrative prose. Although I have not invented any scene, I have sometimes taken the liberty of embellishing the context to include elements of the culture and the feel of Gaza as I know it. On some occasions I was with Hammam, Khalil, and Hussam as the scene actually unfolded. Otherwise, I selected the scenes that they nominated as the most defining moments of their lives. Because I did not meet these men until they were in their early twenties, the narratives about their earlier lives come from their memories of what happened, what they thought, and how they felt. All three men have read their entire narratives and have confirmed that my text represents their experiences vividly and authentically.[19]

I did not decide to write this book until I was well into my empirical research on Palestinian youth—specifically, understanding youth activism and how sustained conflict with Israeli forces affected them. One method of our research was to conduct intensive group and individual interviews with

---

[17] Roy, *Gaza Strip*, 176.

[18] Andrew Sanger, "The Contemporary Law of Blockade and the Gaza Freedom Flotilla," in *Yearbook of International Humanitarian Law—2010* (vol. 13), edited by Michael N. Schmitt, Louise Arimatsu, and T. McCormack, 397–446 (The Hague, Netherlands: T.M.C. Asser Press, 2011). https://doi.org/10.1007/978-90-6704-811-8_14.

[19] Readers will note some inconsistency in the coverage of events, both among and within the three narratives. Several factors led to these discrepancies. On some of my visits, not all three men were available for an interview. Because of their exhaustion with the difficult circumstances in Gaza, sometimes they were not able to elaborate on their answers to my questions. And more generally, the three men's memories vary in specificity and vividness. I have provided pronunciation guides for the names of the main characters: Hammam, Khalil, and Hussam, as well as their wives and parents.

hundreds of young men and women.[20] Thus I did not select these three men in advance to profile for the book. I chose Hammam, Hussam, and Khalil in 2014 on the basis of several factors, including their availability for frequent interviews across the decades, their diversity of personality and approach to resisting the occupation, and their fluency in English.

I conducted all the interviews in English because my Arabic is not good enough for complex conversations. When I didn't fully understand what someone meant, I asked him or her to repeat that portion of the story in Arabic, and I had those sections translated into English. On the few occasions when I am part of the narratives, I refer to myself as "I" or "me," and my protagonists refer to me as "Dr. Barber," "Dr. Brian," or "Brian," depending on when the interaction occurred and how formal the person was being.

My three protagonists are male. In this orthodox Muslim culture, it is not acceptable—either then or now—for a man to have access to a woman's private thoughts and experiences. For example, I can't wander along the camp alleyways with a woman and have her narrate her memories, meet her at a coffee shop or privately in her home for an extended interview, or probe her perspectives as intrusively as necessary to elicit personal nuance and complexity.

Nevertheless, I have gained extraordinary access to women—mothers, wives, and daughters—which I have earned through my regular presence and the trust it has built between me and all three men's family members. As a result, in the homes of my protagonists (and many other Gazan homes), contrary to custom, women did not retreat to their private spaces when I arrived but instead join our social encounters in the public rooms. Also, they welcomed me into the kitchen and bedrooms to play with the children, exhibiting a rare openness to a foreign man. Even though they felt awkward, they sat for extended interviews with me for this book with other family members present.

More than ever, people depersonalize Gazans as numbers: as quantities of the impoverished, the injured, and the dead. Lost in that sterile rendering is the pulsing vibrancy of humanity, of being alive and sentient. Hammam,

---

[20] See Appendix 2 for a list of my research teams' publications that involved Palestine. Our work began when I was an associate professor of sociology at Brigham Young University (1994–2001) and continued when I was professor of child and family studies and founding director of the Center for the Study of Youth and Political Conflict at the University of Tennessee (2001–17).

Hussam, and Khalil are mindful, complex individuals who merit our attention not just because of how they process traumatic experiences, but because of how they make their lives work during those vast interim periods: the hours, weeks, months, and years in between the dramatic moments, when the outside world wakes up and temporarily shows interest and sympathy.

Given the ongoing catastrophe in Gaza and its essential role in the world's most intractable conflict, it's hard to imagine that anyone on earth has not heard of this small strip of land. The publicity almost always stereotypes Gaza as a pathetic and vile place and its people as angry and vengeful. It is not, and they are not.

During my early years doing research in Gaza, I often took small groups of visitors inside the Strip. They were students, professionals, Christians, and Jews. Initially, I prepared a list of points to make so that these visitors understood certain essential aspects of Gaza—the place and the people. I quickly learned, however, that I didn't really need to say anything beyond the major facts. The observable realities—the injustices, the harsh living conditions, the quality of the people, and so on—spoke for themselves. After visiting Gaza for just a half a day, every single person had changed. Common responses included "I had no idea how things really are here," "My whole attitude to this conflict has changed," and "I'm so grateful that I could see for myself."

Throughout my life I have learned, grown, and changed the most when I have engaged directly with a situation or culture. My most significant example of this personal and professional transformation is my response to Gaza. In *No Way but Forward*, I try to take you there—and I hope that like all the others I've taken to Gaza in person, you will also emerge with greater knowledge and deeper feelings about the place and its people; about their perseverance and resourcefulness; and about the irrepressible drive of all Palestinians for dignity, human rights, self-determination, sovereignty, justice, and the opportunity for their children to receive an education and for their families to live in peace.

PART 1

THE NARRATIVES

Hammam
The Social Man

Becoming a Man

(1980, age five)

Little Hammam (hah-MAHM) al-Faqawi (al-fah-KAH-wee) straightened his shoulders and looked straight ahead. All of five, he felt spiffy, decked out in his *mariun*, the uniform young boys wore to kindergarten: a red robe like a dress, worn over trousers, with pure white shoes and socks. He was delighted about his clothes but much more so about the day itself. If only his father were there to share the excitement. For Hammam, the first day of kindergarten—September 1, 1980—was a crucial day, as it was for every Palestinian child. In a culture that regards education as vital, it was "the first step of the ladder of life," as the saying goes. Hammam's mother, Fatima, age twenty-five, walked her first-born son to the door of the house.

In 1948, when the State of Israel was created, roughly 700,000 to 750,000 Palestinians were expelled from or fled their homes and more than 400 Palestinian villages were destroyed in what Palestinians refer to as the *Nakba* (catastrophe), some 250,000 of the refugees ended up in the Gaza Strip.[21] At the end of 1949, as it became clear that Israel would prevent the refugees from returning to their original homes, the United Nations created the United Nations Relief and Works Agency for Palestine Refugees in the Near East (UNRWA). Since then, this agency has been responsible for the medical, relief, and educational (through ninth grade) needs of all Palestinian refugees in Gaza and the other regions of their exile, mainly Jordan, Lebanon, and Syria. Over the years the initial tent residences evolved into adobe and then into cinder-block structures.

Khan Younis is the second-largest refugee camp of the eight camps in the Gaza Strip. It is attached to Khan Younis City, Gaza's second-largest city. The camp extends to within approximately three kilometers of the Mediterranean. By the early 1990s, the camp housed approximately 43,000 residents. Together, Khan Younis and the Rafah refugee camp on the Strip's

---

[21] For some of the many historical accounts of the *Nakba*, see Ian Black, *Enemies and Neighbors: Arabs and Jews in Palestine and Israel, 1917–2017* (New York: Grove Press, 2017), chaps. 7, 8; Rashid Khalidi, *The Hundred Years' War on Palestine: A History of Settler Colonialism and Resistance, 1917–2017* (New York: Metropolitan Books, 2020), chap. 2; Walid Khalidi, *From Haven to Conquest: Readings in Zionism and the Palestine Problem Until 1948* (Washington, DC: Institute for Palestine Studies, 1971), introduction; Avi Shlaim, *Iron Wall: Israel and the Arab World*, updated ed. (London: Penguin Books, 2014), chaps. 1, 2.

southern border with Egypt constitute what is known as the Southern Camps. Four smaller camps, known as the Middle Camps—Deir el-Bellah, al-Maghazi, al-Bureij, and al-Nuseirat—had populations ranging from 12,000 to 35,000 residents at the time. The Middle Camps are situated between Khan Younis and the northern part of the Strip, where there are two additional camps: al-Shati, appended to the northernmost part of Gaza City had a population of approximately 52,000, and Jabalya, even farther north with a population of approximately 67,000.[22]

Khan Younis means "the Inn of Younis," named after Prince Younis Dawadar, who built a military fort there in 1387 to protect pilgrims traveling to Jerusalem or Mecca. Napoleon reportedly used the fort when he conquered Gaza in 1799. These eight camps house approximately two-thirds of Gaza's Palestinian refugees, which by 1980 consisted of the original refugees who fled to Gaza in 1948 plus two generations of their descendants. The other third of the refugees plus their descendants live in the villages, towns, and cities of the Strip, along with the original Gazan Palestinians whose ancestors inhabited these population centers before the influx of refugees. By the early 1990s, Gaza's Palestinian population, refugee and nonrefugee, was approximately one million, the vast majority of them Sunni Muslims, with approximately 1 percent Arab Christians, mostly Greek Orthodox.[23]

Like so many aspects of Palestinian life, the geography of the Strip is paradoxical. The camps are in fact densely packed: Some demographers estimate that Jabalya, where the *intifada* began, is the most densely populated place in the world. Yet when Hammam was growing up, some 50 percent of the Strip was unpopulated agricultural land or sand dunes. The agricultural regions included vast groves of orange, guava, mango, olive, and other trees; fields of strawberries, other fruits, and flowers that were cut and exported; and all sorts of other produce, especially on the eastern edge of the Strip bordering Israel, where the soil is most fertile. Gaza is also dotted with trees, ranging from enormous date palms spread across the Strip, often swaying in the wind, to acres of fragrant eucalyptus trees in southern Gaza.

In the 1990s approximately 25 percent of the Strip was settled by approximately five thousand Jewish Israeli citizens, who lived in sixteen

---

[22] Sara Roy, *The Gaza Strip: The Political Economy of De-development*, 3rd ed. (Washington, DC: Institute for Palestine Studies, 2016), 15–16.

[23] Roy, *Gaza Strip*, 15.

isolated and heavily guarded enclaves.[24] Most of these Jewish settlers commuted daily to their jobs in Israel on Jewish-only roads. The refugees in the Khan Younis camp came mostly from Jaffa, one of the world's most ancient seaports.[25] For centuries, Jaffa has been famous for its oranges.[26] The city is now a suburb of Tel Aviv.

Hammam's father, Fuad (foo-AHD), was born in Jaffa right before the 1948 Palestinian exile. By the time Hammam was born, the refugees in Gaza had long since given up any real hope of returning to their homes, although many held onto the keys to their houses as agonizing memories. At one point in Hammam's childhood, his mother and grandmother (Fuad's mother) took him to visit the family home in Jaffa. His grandmother wanted to at least see—and show Hammam—the home that she, her husband, and Fuad had been forced to leave in 1948, when Jewish soldiers stormed the city during the war that led to the creation of the State of Israel. The locks had been changed, of course, and when the current Jewish residents of the house heard his grandmother's explanation that this was once her family's home and they simply wanted to see it, they were polite. But the visit was awkward.

The al-Faqawi home in the Khan Younis Camp was the ubiquitous modern version: locally manufactured cinder blocks held together by too few sticks of rebar, which invariably extended a few meters above the corrugated lead roofs, anticipating the next level of the home. Once Hammam got married, the family would build that new floor for his apartment, and then one for every other son, finances permitting. The only direction to expand in a refugee camp is up. The al-Faqawis had more money than most of their neighbors because Fuad, Hammam's father, was fortunate enough to be employed as an English teacher at an UNRWA elementary school. Thus at their home, unlike the neighboring homes, the sandy floor was laid with large tile squares, the openings in the walls had doors and windows in them, and they had a thick iron door so heavy it threatened to bring down the cinder block itself.

Fatima (FAH-tee-mah), Hammam's mother, was beautiful—short and trim, with a clear olive complexion and jet-black hair that she kept tucked

---

[24] Roy, *Gaza Strip*, 17.

[25] *Encyclopedia Britannica Online*, s.v. "History of Tel Aviv–Yafo," accessed December 19, 2024, https://www.britannica.com/place/Tel-Aviv-Yafo/History#ref978342.

[26] Charles Issawi, *An Economic History of the Middle East and North Africa* (New York: Columbia University Press, 1982), chap. vii.

under her head scarf. Hammam studied her face as she handed him a lira, a small Israeli coin, so that he could buy himself a snack at school or on the way home. Because she betrayed no sign of worry, he relaxed. He clutched the worn coin in his little fist as she kissed him. Enthusiasm in her voice, she sent him along his way: "Now you are a man, my son! Now you are starting your life!" Fatima and her mother-in-law had decided not to accompany Hammam to school that day, a deliberate lesson intended to help the boy learn confidence in this, his first major step toward manhood. They may not have appreciated how painful it would be for Hammam to be the only boy alone at school.

Arab societies are highly patriarchal, even more so in less developed, religiously conservative regions such as Gaza. Thus men and sons—particularly a family's eldest son, like Hammam—are celebrated, especially in public, while women reign in the home and in the classroom. In Palestinian culture being or becoming a "man" essentially means being or becoming a "good person." For male and female Palestinians, to be a good person means to maximize education, maintain and build family, and oppose the occupation in individualized ways.

Fatima sounded so happy, seemed so confident. Yet his father wasn't there. Hammam tried to put that absence out of his mind and relax. After all, he was intimately familiar with the way to school. In fact, like all his friends, he had long ago memorized the trek from his home to anywhere in the sprawling refugee camp. His little feet, often bare, had already added to the millions of steps that, over the nearly twenty years of the camp's existence so far, had packed down the beach sand that formed the ground of its labyrinth of narrow alleys.

Hammam felt brave and proud as he walked to the school building on his own. He was eager to begin his life, to take this first step on a journey that would be unambiguously calibrated and validated by educational achievement: kindergarten, elementary school, secondary school, and university. There are few vagaries in Palestinian ambitions, and to be highly educated is Ambition No. 1. Hammam understood that education was the pathway to manhood, and he was happy to finally be setting off.

Hammam knew all the neighbors who lived in the homes he passed on his way to school. In fact, many of the crusty adobe or powdery cinder-block structures housed his extended family—his clan.

When UNRWA built the refugee camps, it had done no advanced planning, and thus Hammam's journey took him through the irregular maze of narrow alleys between the high walls of the homes. He was used to the stench of the raw sewage that drained from the camp's homes into these alleys and then trickled into seepage ponds—and periodically, he skipped over the sewage rivulets that bisected the sandy pathways. Although this was the dense residential area of the camp (the commercial area was on the outskirts), foot traffic was relatively sparse. Few people loitered, especially so early in the morning, except for the occasional young child balancing plates of fresh hummos and crispy falafel drenched in olive oil, whose intoxicating, spicy aroma cut through the less pleasant smells. Barefoot or sometimes wearing decrepit flip-flops, these children paid no mind to dirtying their feet; they concentrated only on not spilling their family's meal.

Just yesterday Hammam had been one of those small children—but today he focused on his kindergarten outfit, occasionally stopping to brush the sand off his pristine white shoes and socks. As he made his last turn before crossing the unpaved road that separated the school from the camp, he passed "Candy Man." Dressed in full traditional garb—dark gray *gallabiyya*, black-and-white checkered *keffiyeh*—the kind, elderly man balanced himself precariously on a cracked plastic chair outside his small food store. Hammam had never stopped to buy anything there because he'd never had money. But today he clutched the tiny coin his mother had given him and decided that he would return to visit the man on his way home from school.

For now, however, what mattered was getting to school.

When he arrived, the schoolyard was already filled with people. Some children were crying as their parents left. Hammam told himself that he was too old for tears, yet he couldn't help noticing that every other child's father was present. Stumbling amid the throng, he felt terribly alone. Everyone seemed to be staring at him, and he imagined them asking, "What's wrong with that boy?"

As he squeezed his way through the crowd, he overheard one father say to a teacher about his son: "Take good care of him, please. Help him feel relaxed. Be good to him. We very much hope that he becomes a good man." Hammam wanted very much to be a good person too. But could he, without his father? He stood alone, and a wave of sadness began to erode his bravery. He made himself think back to his mother's encouraging words that morning. She was behind him, he knew. And if his father were here, he would be too, he convinced himself.

The family farewells ended. The children stood in the schoolyard awaiting their room assignments. Hammam wondered where he'd have to go in this somewhat peculiar building, with two classrooms at the bottom of a small hill and the third classroom up the incline.

"Hammam Fuad al-Faqawi! Upper class!" boomed the voice of the head teacher, Mrs. Fatiha. Hammam dutifully made his way up the steps. It didn't take long, though, before his sadness returned. He didn't know a single child in that classroom. And the teacher . . . well . . . he didn't like her at all. She was shouting. She even hit one of the children!

Suddenly he couldn't help himself; to his shame, he began to cry. This teacher would not do! This classroom was not for him! Genetically equipped with Fatima's directness, he ran out of the classroom and found a teacher in the hallway who seemed nice—at least she wasn't shouting—and declared, "I refuse to be in that class!"

"Why, my dear boy? You have a good teacher there," she replied.

Hammam couldn't stop himself—he began crying again.

"No! Never, never!" he exclaimed. "I hate that class!"

He remembered seeing a distant relative—a young girl whose home he had visited in the past—in one of the lower classrooms. He hardly knew her, but that little glimpse of familiarity was enough. He wanted that classroom. And he asked for it. The teacher, whom he would later come to know as Mrs. Mubina, assented.

But it was what Mrs. Fatiha, the head teacher, quietly said to Mrs. Mubina that made all the difference to Hammam: not just on that day but for the rest of the year . . . and beyond. "This boy's father is a brave man. He is in prison. This is why Hammam has come on his own. Please help him."

Fuad had been imprisoned by Israeli forces right after Hammam's conception. Unlimited detention, often without specific charges, or imprisonment adjudicated by a military tribunal were prime tactics of the Israeli Defense Force (IDF) to deter Palestinian activism against the occupation. To illustrate the magnitude of these favored measures of prevention, some estimates put the number of Palestinians detained since the occupation at 800,000.[27] When charges were brought, the list was endless: for example, raising a Palestinian flag, publishing anything that combined the four colors of the Palestinian flag, criticizing the occupation, engaging in any form of resistance against the occupying soldiers. Fuad had just joined

[27] "Palestinian Prisoners and Their Conditions inside the Israeli Prison," State of Palestine Ministry of Foreign Affairs and Expatriates website, January 23, 2019, https://www.mofa.pna.ps/en-us/mediaoffice/ministrynews/palestinian-prisoners-and-their-conditions-inside-the-israeli-prison.

the resistance. The day after he joined, he was caught up in a sweep and charged with planning to kidnap Jewish settlers to use as bargaining chips for the release of Palestinian prisoners.

At his young age, Hammam did not have any political awareness. All he knew was that for the first five years of his life, he could see his father only on arduous, monthly visits with Fatima. In fact, Fatima had been a mother for just a week when she made her first visit to see Fuad. She took the bus with baby Hammam, leaving Khan Younis at 7:00 a.m. and arriving half an hour later in Gaza City at the large prison there, a former army base encircled by barbed wire that would come to be known as the Ansar II prison. Both she and the infant shivered uncontrollably in the cold as they waited at the prison gate. They weren't allowed to enter until 7:00 p.m. At that time, they saw that twenty prisoners had been assembled, each man behind a window in a cubicle facing the corridor. The windows—made of thick, scratched and faded plexiglass—were small, about two square feet each.

Fatima didn't know any of this procedure. She had thought that they could sit with Fuad and talk, and that Fuad could hold Hammam. But she could only press her palm against the window and mouth, "How are you?" She raised Hammam up so that Fuad could see him through the window. Just twenty-four at the time, Fuad later recalled being mesmerized by the sight of his firstborn, experiencing those indescribable feelings of a parent meeting the first baby he had helped create. He was a father now, a huge step on his road to manhood. He inspected every feature of Hammam's face with awe, but also with a deep pain because he couldn't hold his son. Fuad's grief overwhelmed his joy. After all the traveling and waiting, Fatima was allowed only twenty minutes to visit her husband. Given how tortuous the ordeal of visiting was, Fatima made the journey just once a month for the next five years.

Now satisfied with his new classroom, Hammam began to feel comfortable in his new school environment. His courage came flooding back. He realized that he had been wrong to think he was alone. Here were teachers who would care for him, who respected him . . . and his father. He was proud of his ability to manage this first step into manhood. The morning raced by, and he was surprised when the old metal plate that served as the school bell was struck three times. His first day of school was over.

On his way home, Hammam went directly to Candy Man. He had always dreamed of tasting the delicious chocolate he had heard the man sold. Hammam pulled out the lira and showed it to the old man. The coin was exactly enough for a little stick of milk chocolate, as though his mother had somehow known it was precisely what he'd want after school. And the candy tasted better than anything he'd ever eaten. The luscious taste still filled his mouth when he rounded the last corner and saw his house. His grandmother was sitting out front. "Welcome home!" she yelled. "You are now a man!"

Hammam smiled proudly. "Thank you, Jidditi (grandmother)." He quickly opened the front door to find his mother. There she was, sweeping the salon.[28] She threw down the makeshift broom—a brittle date palm frond—and threw open her arms. Matching her enthusiasm, Hammam jumped into her embrace. "Tell me about your day, my son. What did you do?"

Throughout that first year of school, Mrs. Fatiha continued treating Hammam with devotion. She'd always greet him in the morning with a huge smile and ask, "How are you today, my young Hammam?" She'd wash his hands and face and give him food from the cart. He wondered, but wasn't sure, whether she gave him such special attention because of his father's plight. Maybe she was just kind; she seemed good to all the children.

Hammam was so much her favorite that it seemed to Hammam that Mrs. Fatiha structured the final day of kindergarten around him. This was a day he would remember the rest of his life, with everyone eager for the great party to start. They had finished their first year! Mrs. Fatiha announced loudly, "Hammam will begin this celebration!" She had coached him to carefully open the ceremony by reciting the *Surat al-Fatihah*—the first chapter of the Holy Quran. Literally, the chapter title means "The Opening." It is seven brief verses that essentially constitute a prayer for guidance and are recited in full at each of the five daily prayers, as well as at the opening of important events.

Hammam's mother and grandmother were seated proudly in the front row. Hammam was nervous—and he wondered whether he would be if his father were here with him. He shook off the stress and began the recitation just fine. Then suddenly he faltered, but Mrs. Fatiha rescued him, just as she had on day one. She had positioned herself behind the lectern where he stood, with just a frayed bed sheet serving as a curtain between them. She

---

[28] *Salon* (sah-LONE) is the Arabic word for the room where people receive guests in their home. It is typically the first or front room of the house. In smaller houses it also serves as the room for meals. Its root is the French word *salon*, a room or hall for receiving guests for intellectual and literary gatherings. In the narratives I use both "salon" and "front room."

was able to whisper the forgotten portion of the prayer, and he repeated it with a delighted smile.

When he had finished reciting the *Surat al-Fatihah*, Hammam jumped off the stage and ran into the arms of his loved ones. Another child's father offered them a can of black shoe polish, which is often used to ceremonially mimic a beard or a mustache on a young boy's face. But his grandmother waved it off, proclaiming: "The son of a brave man is a man whether he has a mustache or not!"

There it was again—another reference to his hallowed father. Such homages nevertheless served to sustain a connection, however ethereal, between him and his absent father. In some ways he felt that his life was full yet not complete, rich yet lacking something. He had begun his journey to manhood—to become a good person—and had proudly done much of the work on his own. He had crucial anchors: his mother, his grandmother, Mrs. Fatiha. But still, something essential was missing. It was simple: Hammam longed for his father. And in some ways, he always would.

Hamman thought to himself: Now I will wait for my father to get out of prison. Then a new life will begin.

The Lamb

(1981, age six)

Seated front row center, Hammam was not surprised when his father's friend Salim opened the classroom door unannounced. He had been prepped the night before: The day of his father's release from prison was upon them. Awash with excitement and delight, Hammam also worried about missing school. His teacher for this first year of elementary school was old and extremely tough. Hammam did not want to incur his wrath and be marked absent.

After a short discussion with Salim, Hammam's teacher bellowed:

"*Yalla*, Hammam! *Goom*!" Get up and go, Hammam! "And don't bother coming to school tomorrow. For that matter, don't come the following day either. You are the son of a brave man. He is fighting for our freedom! Stay home and enjoy this time with your father."

After Hammam changed clothes, they began the thirty-minute trek to Gaza City, with Salim driving a rickety, dusty, white Peugeot. One of Hammam's uncles sat in the front passenger seat; two other relatives were in the back with Hammam. No one was concerned about how they'd fit his father into the already full car. They'd just do it.

It was well known where Fuad would emerge from the prison, and Salim parked the car ten meters or so across from that eastern door. They waited, perhaps a half hour, until the small green door opened unceremoniously. Two soldiers exited, slowly followed by Fuad. Short and with a medium build, Fuad had no belongings—just the brown trousers and beige shirt he was wearing. They could have been one hundred meters away and still have known that it was Fuad because of his prematurely white hair, the signature characteristic of al-Faqawi men. In less than two decades, Hammam's hair would follow suit.

Eyes wide open and shaking a bit with nervousness, Hammam stood transfixed as they exited the car to greet his father. *Am I really going to be with my father now*? He waited shyly for the relatives to hug and kiss Fuad multiple times on each cheek—and then again and again. Fuad finally reached down and picked up his young son, making a bowl for him with his arms and holding him close. This was their first ever embrace, and they lingered, hearts pounding. There was no need to speak.

The approximate date of Fuad's release had been known for months, allowing the family to prepare his homecoming. Hammam wanted to do something special for his father. And he was certain that doing so would discourage his relatives and neighbors from simply dismissing him as that pesky little first grader. He didn't want them to think of him as Hammam, the young boy, but instead as a man. Finally, the idea came to him while he was eying the sheep that his grandfather—Fatima's father—raised and sold. (Fuad's father had passed away in the 1970s.) He recalled the custom of slaughtering a sheep to celebrate the return of a loved one after a long absence. *That's what I'll do*, he thought with confidence. Everyone would be impressed, his father above all. He began inspecting his grandfather's flock until he found a lamb that he thought would be just right—still small, it would be perfectly fat in time for the celebration six months away.

Hammam revealed his ambitious plan to his grandmother (Fatima's mother). She passed it on to her husband. "Okay, Hammam, you can have that lamb if you want it," said his *jiddi*, his grandfather. "But how are you going pay for it?"

"I promise you, Jiddi, I promise I'll feed it and take care of it," replied Hammam, full of expectation. "And I'll save all of the money I can to pay for it."

True to his promise, Hammam fed and watered his lamb daily. He made a special effort to find grass and corn leaves to make sure the animal would grow as big as possible. He also fed his little green plastic piggy bank with the coins his mother gave him to buy sweets. Every day for six months, he pushed them into the slot until he couldn't stuff in any more coins.

Finally, on the day before his father's homecoming, Hammam took the packed piggy bank to his grandfather and slammed it against a wooden table; it exploded, scattering the worn coins everywhere. "Here is the money I've saved to pay for the lamb, Jiddi. I know it's not enough, but I did everything I could. Please accept this. I've done my very best, and I've worked very hard." To Hammam's relief, his *jiddi* nodded with approval. Hammam felt so proud. He knew his relatives and neighbors would honor this effort. He had done his duty as the first son. He felt like a man.

During the homecoming celebration, he heard his father's voice: "Hammam, where are you?"

"I am here, Father. What would you like?"

"I was told you bought a lamb for me. Is that correct?"

"Yes, Father, I did."

Hammam went to the stable, tied an old piece of rope around his lamb's neck, and guided the animal to his father. "Here, Father, this is for you."

Later that day, snuggled deep in his father's lap, Hammam took in the scene. An enormous number of cars were parked every which way. It seemed as if throngs of people from the whole Gaza Strip had streamed into the canvas greeting tent that had been erected on a parcel of land his grandfather owned east of Khan Younis. There would have been no way to welcome this size of crowd in the camp. Until this moment Hammam knew only intellectually that a hero receives a homecoming, a tradition that he had heard about but never witnessed. Now he understood on an emotional level how much it meant to everyone to have Fuad back.

It could not have meant more to anyone than it did to Hammam. He fell asleep in Fuad's arms, finally feeling whole and thinking that life would now really begin for him. Fuad felt the same. So many years of absence. Both would spend the rest of their lives trying to compensate for that void.

Jerusalem

(1982, age seven)

Fuad's return made all the difference to Hammam. He no longer felt the void that had plagued him since he could remember. The father–first son relationship in Arab society is precious (as is the mother–first son relationship). Finally, he had his father with him.

For his part, Fuad felt raw pain that he had deprived his son during the most formative period of the boy's life. This agony was constantly amplified by the drawings Hammam made after Fuad's release; he drew a prison, a prisoner, a fence, and soldiers in every single one. Fuad could think of no other way to make it up to Hammam than by gifting him everything possible. He bought every toy he could afford, gave him extra treats, and kept Hammam with him constantly. Some people criticized him for spoiling Hammam, but for Fuad, these gifts were nowhere near satisfactory compensation.

"I want to take you to Israel tomorrow, so you can see the Noble Sanctuary in Jerusalem," announced Fuad one morning, referring to the Dome of the Rock and the Al-Aqsa Mosque, located in East Jerusalem on a flat elevated plaza that Jews call the Temple Mount. "Oh, please, Baba!" replied Hammam, jumping up and down with delight.

Gaza gets surprisingly cold in winter, so Hammam dressed in gray wool pants, shirt, and sweater. Fuad drove the decrepit Peugeot with Hammam squeezed between him and one of Fuad's friends, with three more in the back seat—all fellow elementary school English teachers and all essentially uncles to Hammam. Fuad had returned to his teaching job after being released from prison.

One leaves Gaza through the Erez crossing at the northern border with Israel. There were no paved roads then, just a single rocky path. In those days the crossing was made up of ten or so concrete-filled barrels of various colors. Five Israeli soldiers, some of whom looked to be teenagers, were huddled around a wood fire that was burning in half of an old oil barrel. They were laughing and smoking, with their rifles—which seemed to be as long as their bodies—lying to the side. One soldier waved for Fuad to stop. "Where are you going?" he asked calmly. "To Jerusalem," Fuad replied. "You may pass," said the soldier. It was easy at that time: no request to see their IDs, no inspection of person or vehicle.

Hammam took little notice of this process. He was dying to see Israel and Jerusalem, in particular, and to this day remembers his father's announcement: "You are now passing into Israel!" This was the greatest adventure of his life; he was entering a world that had previously existed only as faint images in his head. Immediately, he noticed that the roads were wider, newer, and paved, with green trees lining both sides. For the first time in his life, he saw traffic lights and needed Fuad's explanation as to what they were and how they worked. There seemed to be endless miles of lush, green fields flanking the road. He'd never seen so much green. Except for the fields and orchards, Gaza was a dusty and sandy bit of land.

An hour into the ninety-minute drive, the road began its windy 740-meter climb. Hammam asked his father, "Where is Jerusalem, Baba? Are we near?"

"You will see it very soon, my son!" replied Fuad. The higher they climbed, the more trees Hammam saw—and they were huge. Gaza has tall, skinny date palm trees and a multitude of fruit trees, but they are nothing like these towering beauties.

Once they were in Jerusalem, they went to the Noble Sanctuary, where they prayed at the Al-Aqsa Mosque, just across the sanctuary from the Dome of the Rock. Both are deeply significant Islamic monuments that Hammam had seen only in postcards. He had never even seen such large buildings. Gaza had numerous mosques, but they were miniscule compared with these grand structures. Hammam, Fuad, and his father's friends removed their shoes, placed them in the shelves provided at the entrance to the mosque, and walked silently inside over the thin carpets. Hammam was awestruck by the cavernous mosque. It felt like a tremendously important place.

After they visited the Al-Aqsa Mosque, they went to view the Dome of the Rock more closely. They didn't enter—it isn't always open—but from the outside the shrine was stunning. It seemed precious, its blue and gold gleaming in the morning sun. Nothing else in sight matched the colors of this massive structure, with its huge, perfectly shaped dome.

Once they had climbed down from the Noble Sanctuary, Hammam's little feet danced across the ancient cobblestones of the Old City, a roughly one-square-kilometer area of East Jerusalem whose towering walls were erected in the mid-1500s by Suleiman the Magnificent, the Ottoman sultan who was the second ruler of Jerusalem. At the junction of Al-Wad Street and the narrower Via Dolorosa, leading steeply up to the Christian Quarter, they saw a procession. "Who are those people?" asked Hammam. One of them was waving incense, and others were carrying placards with two photos.

"These are Christians," Fuad explained, "and those are depictions of Miriam and Issa" (Mary and Jesus).

Later, as they left the Old City through the famed Bab al-Amud (Damascus Gate), the northernmost-facing of the city's eight gates, Fuad pointed out the little wooden pushcarts with two front wheels and two long handles that were packed with freshly baked *ka'ak*. It was that delicious light brown, crunchy, horseshoe-shaped bread covered with sesame seeds that his grandparents sometimes brought back to Gaza from their visits to Jerusalem. Naturally, Hammam wanted to buy some. Fuad obliged, gave him some shekels, and told him to also ask the man for some of the hard-boiled eggs he had on the cart. They sat on the curb and ate their lunch. Later, when they had returned to the car, Fuad said that he had forgotten something and would be right back. Shortly afterward, he reappeared with a gift for Hammam. It was Hammam's first digital watch.

The whole visit to Jerusalem was almost more than Hammam could take in. To this day, he vividly remembers many of the details, mostly how "very, very, very happy" he was spending time with his father and "uncles" in a beautiful and sacred place. In addition to his own enjoyment and wonder, Hammam was excited that he could now explain to his classmates at school and to other people in his Gaza refugee camp what Israel and Jerusalem were like.

He could not have known then that he would never see Jerusalem again.

Even though Hammam didn't get to travel, he was able to meet people from other places. Fuad had been promoted from elementary school teacher to an area representative of UNRWA. In this position Fuad received many international visitors, typically leaders of various nongovernmental organizations (NGOs) from Scandinavia or Italy, sometimes even Japan and the United States. Hammam delighted in touring them around his refugee camp.

He would begin the tour with a viewing of his own menagerie of animals crammed in the tiny courtyard in front of their home: chickens, rabbits, a goat, and a sheep. Then he would lead visitors off to the nearby cookie plant, where he cleverly secured samples from the affable owner. Next he would show off the seemingly ancient, barely mechanized olive oil workshop, whose dirt floor was drenched with decades of dripped, pungent oil and covered with mounds of now-blackened olive pits. Finally, Hammam would display the camp's not-much-more-contemporary *khubz* (pita bread) bakery. It was dusty with flour all around the squeaking conveyor belt that escorted the small, flat, round loaves to the stone oven, which puffed them to the point of near explosion but then delivered them browned and flat again, the whole process permeating the air with its delectable aroma.

The Tire

(1989, age fourteen)

During the six-year-long *intifada* (1987–93), but also to a lesser extent beforehand, the IDF often implemented monthlong school closures and strict curfews, as well as carrying out frequent school raids. Students were afraid to go to school because they were worried that they'd be stopped or detained.

Before the *intifada* began, Gazans and patrolling soldiers had interacted awkwardly. Sometimes soldiers even handed out treats to the young kids. But there had also been terrifying moments. One of those incidents occurred when Hammam was ten, and he has not forgotten it. Soldiers had surrounded his elementary school, and some of the braver kids had yelled at them: "So, you think you are men? Then come and fight us!" The taunt succeeded, and the soldiers charged. Many of the boys tried to escape over the ten-foot stone wall, which was irregular enough to allow them to scale it quickly. The soldiers were on to them but arrived too late to catch the kids who had climbed the wall, dropped to the other side, and escaped down the street to the left. For whatever reason, Hammam lingered for a few minutes and then finally tried to escape by running in the opposite direction down a narrow camp alley. Three soldiers grabbed him, threw him onto the ground, and began kicking him over his whole body, including his groin. The lead soldier struck Hammam repeatedly in the face with his walkie-talkie.

The school was near his home, and when Fatima and two of his aunts heard the commotion, they ran to the scene just in case Hammam had been involved. When they reached Hammam as the soldiers were beating him in the alley, the soldiers then started kicking and beating the women with their billy clubs, breaking one of Fatima's fingers. One soldier told another to throw Hammam into the jeep. Busy dealing with the fracas, the second soldier told the first soldier to do it. Sensing their distraction, Hammam kicked one of the soldiers in the stomach and fled down the alley. They began shooting at Hammam with rubber bullets: three shots. Hammam heard a bullet whizz by his ear. Unfortunately, one of those bullets hit a pregnant woman who was standing by her front door, and she eventually lost the baby. The three soldiers left Fatima and his aunts in the alley and chased Hammam—but burdened by all their gear, they couldn't catch him.

Aside from that frightening incident, Hammam avoided trouble. Even before the *intifada* erupted, he had decided firmly that he would never become directly involved in the confrontations. He had suffered greatly during Fuad's imprisonment, and he wanted to keep off the Israeli military's blacklist so that he would never be absent from his own children's lives. Instead, during the *intifada* he undertook many behind-the-scenes tasks, such as bringing onions to relieve the stinging from the tear gas that burned the protestors' eyes, stacking up piles of stones, caring for the wounded, distracting soldiers, and visiting the homes of those who had died. Sometimes his friends teased him for taking this stance. Stone throwers were real men, they blustered. Hammam would always say: "There are fighters and politicians. I want to be a political man who makes peace."

One morning early in the *intifada*, when Hammam was fourteen, an IDF squad stopped him as he was bicycling to town to have copies of some papers made for his grandfather. They pointed to a burning tire and ordered him to fetch something to put it out with. Knowing that refusing would bring disaster, Hammam complied: He set his rickety bike aside, found a weathered pail, filled it with water from a small well, and doused the thick flames. Feeling troubled and uneasy, he abandoned his errand to make copies and mounted his bicycle to return home to his family.

But the soldiers had other plans for Hammam. They pulled him off his bike and forced him into their nearby jeep. Soldiers from a lookout atop a nearby building had radioed down that Hammam was the boy who had set the tire on fire. Hammam pleaded: "No, I was just going to make a photocopy."

"And the tire?" they charged.

"I didn't do it," he implored, to no avail. The soldiers didn't hurt him, but they took him to the police station.

When Hammam arrived at the station, a plainclothes officer demanded his name—and upon hearing it, he accused Hammam of wanting to cause them problems. "No, I'd never do such a thing! I never did anything to you!" Hammam replied. The officer slapped his face and told the others to transport him to the military headquarters in Khan Younis city.

There a female officer, perhaps in her early twenties, set on him: "You were throwing stones at the Israeli army. You were lighting tires." As two other soldiers held him by his clothes, she kicked him repeatedly between his legs and then hit him in his stomach, neck, and face. "Why are you doing this to me?" protested Hammam with every little breath he had. "I have done nothing to you!"

Witnessing the incident, a Palestinian woman waiting to travel south to Egypt ran up and protested: “Why are you doing that? He’s a young boy; he’s just a child.” The officer ordered her to sit down and drop the subject—that is, unless she wanted them to withdraw her application for a long-sought permit to go to Egypt. The officer returned to booting Hammam, and the two soldiers also started beating him with their hands and nightsticks.

When they were finished, they took the bruised and trembling boy back to the police station, where the original soldiers began to blindfold and cuff him, presumably to take him to the nearby jail for detention. Hammam pleaded, “I never did anything. You know that. You found me on my bicycle and told me to put out the fire. I did that for you. Why are you lying?” Finally, the soldiers seemed to relent: “Okay, okay, okay,” they said and handed him over to a police officer, who wrote down something in Hebrew. Hammam was sure it was a formal charge of having burned tires and thrown stones.

The police officer then asked Hammam how his father could be reached. They didn’t have a phone in their camp home—but it wouldn’t have mattered anyway, since all of the lines to the camp had been cut. Hammam remembered the phone number of an uncle who lived in the city, outside the camp. The officer allowed Hammam to call him. He told his uncle about his detention and asked him to find his father and send him to the police station. When Fuad arrived, the main officer reiterated the accusation. Hammam again denied it forcefully. The officer called him a liar, but this time he didn’t beat him. Instead, he was permitted to go home after Fuad had paid a fine of five hundred shekels, more than a month’s salary.

Failure

(1993, age eighteen)

The family was growing. Hammam now had two sisters, Hana and Hadeel, and two brothers, Hani and Wasseem. He devoted hours every day to help Fatima care for them all. Eventually, two more sisters would arrive, Wafa and Heba. Hammam had sailed through elementary school and was well-known as one of the top students in secondary school. That success came with hard work, and although he faced extreme pressure ahead of the infamous college qualifying exam, no one doubted that Hammam would attain the highest marks. He was compulsive about his preparations, often skipping sleep. Fuad and Fatima supported him further by hiring private tutors for all the subjects in the exam.

The *tawjihi* (tahw-JEE-he) is the Arab equivalent of the British General Secondary Education Certificate Examination. A grueling, twenty-one-day exam taken after the final year of high school, it covers Arabic, English, math, physics, biology, chemistry, computer science, earth science, social science, and religion. The exam is so difficult that an average score of 51 percent across the subjects is a passing grade. Hammam had chosen the scientific track over the social studies track. The scientific track was especially rigorous, but it was mandatory for anyone who wanted to be an engineer or a doctor. Although only the top students chose that track, no one was surprised at Hammam's choice, because for a long time he had proudly made it known that he planned to become a doctor. Everyone expected him to score at least an 85 on the exam.

Education is of supreme value to Palestinians. It has strong roots in Islam and has become ever-more crucial as the most effective way to succeed and survive under the increasingly restricted opportunities for Palestinian autonomy. As in the West Bank and East Jerusalem, the literacy rate in Gaza has always been 95 percent or higher. School enrollment is similarly high. Virtually all students complete primary school, large majorities complete junior high school, and most boys and girls complete high school.[29]

Failing the *tawjihi* would bring deep personal and family shame. Failure meant no chance of going to university, something that all Gazans want to

[29] For details, see the Palestinian Central Bureau of Statistics website: https://www.pcbs.gov.ps.

do. However, preparing for the exam was particularly difficult this year because the *intifada* was in full boil, and the IDF was imposing frequent school closures and curfews.

At that time, Arab countries would not accept a Palestinian student with an Israeli certificate for graduate study because since 1967 the Israeli military had controlled all institutions in Gaza. The Palestinian Liberation Organization (PLO), the umbrella organization for Palestinian political parties, established an agreement with Egypt to score and certify the exams.[30] That meant that the completed exam booklets were driven to Egypt across the Rafah crossing on Gaza's southern border. They were processed in Arish, the closest Egyptian town to Gaza, and then returned to the students' schools. Students took the exam at a location other than their home school, and they were randomly assigned seat numbers in various classrooms.

The procedures were complicated and rigid, and the volume of students overwhelmed the system, making it impossible to proctor all exams. Some students in the classroom where Hammam was assigned to take the exam had somehow gotten hold of the answers. Like prisoners who had learned the patterns of their guards, they found out when the Egyptian proctor would show up, and before he arrived each day, they took the opportunity to copy answers from the answer key to their exam sheets. At that time, young Palestinian men felt empowered because of their heroic role in fighting Israeli soldiers. Perhaps they felt entitled or even invincible. Hammam refused to participate in the cheating. To him, such dishonesty was unacceptable, even shameful, for a Palestinian.

Somehow the proctor had gotten word of the cheating. One morning he arrived at an unusual time, even scaling the school wall instead of entering through the main gate. He took the class by surprise and caught the offending boys red-handed. Furious, the proctor made the split-second and irrevocable decision to fail the students for that day's exam. Dramatically, he exclaimed: "Students from seat 1 in classroom 1 to the last seat number in classroom 4 fail, every single one of you."

Hammam trudged home, devastated. A failed day of the exam could have a catastrophic impact on his overall score. Close to frantic, he told his parents what had happened, and they tried to calm him down. Perhaps, they suggested, the proctor had made his dramatic declaration just to scare the

[30] For more about the PLO, see "Khalil: The Defender of Human Rights," note 54.

students. Hammam went to a respected official at this school. "What happened, Abu Jamal? Can it really be true that good students have failed?"

"My dear son," replied Abu Jamal sorrowfully, "I don't know what to tell you. The decision is final. You failed."

Hammam felt abused by this injustice, but he realized that there was nothing to be done. He would solve the problem himself, he decided, with extraordinary scores on the remaining exams. And he did just that. Thus he was certain that he had passed the overall exam. He had done the calculations himself. But when the results were taped on the classroom door, his name was on the list of those who had failed! An earthquake of shock and anger erupted in him. "This is wrong, completely wrong!" he shouted over and over again. He raced home, every blood vessel in his face nearly exploding, tears streaming down his face, and his eyes streaked with red. "Baba, I swear to you that I passed this exam! I swear it! Look, here are all my exam scores."

It was just as obvious to Fuad that Hammam had passed. There had to have been a mistake in calculating the average, and final, score. Fuad went immediately to the Egyptian official in charge of the exam. He pleaded urgently: "Look, it's obvious that this final score doesn't align with the true average of the individual exams!" Fuad said. "Please correct this mistake! I beg you, please. Failing this exam, especially unjustly, will destroy my son and my whole family!"

Staring intently at the documents, the Egyptian official's brow creased, and his eyes squinted a bit, as if he could understand the problem and its severity. He asked Fuad to return the next day to give him time to carefully investigate the situation. That night none of the family slept well. Hammam rocked between tears and anger, but he eventually calmed himself with the certainty that this was simply a mistake that would be corrected quickly.

Fuad and Hammam went the next morning at the appointed hour, unnerved but confident that the problem had been solved. The official's face looked uncomfortable, but his eyes seemed determined. "Fuad, we have done a full examination of Hammam's test results. You are correct. There was a mistake; it was a transposition of numbers on one of the exams," he explained. Both Fuad and Hammam nearly jumped with relief. But the official continued: "Regrettably, there is nothing we can do about it now. The scores have been recorded. Hammam will have to repeat his senior year and then retake the exam."

Fuad protested, "No! No! This cannot be! He passed the exam! How can he fail if he passed?" Falling on deaf ears, his indignant protests turned to supplication: "Please, sir, I beg you, won't you make an exception in this case? You know how shameful it is to fail the *tawjihi*."

The official simply replied, "No, I'm sorry." Fuad then pleaded for Hammam to be allowed to retake the exam. He would do it immediately. Making him repeat his entire senior year of high school before he could retake the *tawjihi* would be so cruel. "No, that is not possible," said the official. "I'm sorry."

Bitter but resigned, they trudged home in the day's heat. Hammam felt like he was burning in hell. He had worked so assiduously to prepare to be a doctor. And then this cursed Egyptian system betrayed him. He was innocent, just like he had been when the soldiers falsely accused him of setting the tire on fire. He felt deflated.

Back home, he was immediately smothered by family members and soon by friends who had heard the news and wanted to comfort him. They went round and round with assurances that it was not his fault, that the system had failed him. Do not worry, the family will be fine, don't take it personally. But Hammam didn't want to talk. He had failed—and at that moment, he feared that he had lost everything of value in his life and had forever sullied his family's name. No sentiments could assuage him; no words could capture the degree of fury he felt toward the Egyptians; no words could come close to adequately capturing the depths of his anguish. He lay down on the straw mattress in the courtyard, feeling as though he were sleeping on nails.

The next year was the worst year of his life so far. He had no fears about passing the year and the exam, of course. He was a top student. What pained him the most was the loss of his cohort of buddies. They had all passed the first time and were now off at university with no time to play around anymore. Hammam felt so alone, so insignificant, so inadequate. Hardly needing to study, he spent his time mostly tending to his animals and helping Fatima care for the other kids. At the end of the school year, he took the *tawjihi* again.

His score: 85 percent.

A New Bottom

(1994–1998, ages nineteen through twenty-three)

After passing the *tawjihi* earlier that year, Hammam had immediately enrolled in a bachelor of arts program at Al-Azhar University in Gaza City. He knew no one there. Some of his high school cohort of friends hadn't passed the *tawjihi* and thus didn't make it to a university; others who had passed went to a different university. Fortunately, his kind and easygoing personality had always drawn people to him, and he formed a group quickly.

After the *tawjihi* ordeal, he had become apathetic about studying. There were basically two broad groups of students at the university: those who worked diligently at their studies, and an "irresponsible" group that did not. Hammam and his new buddies—all smart—fell comfortably into the second group. Hammam was majoring in English because after the exam nightmare, he had shifted his goal from being a doctor to becoming a teacher, like his father.

And life for Hammam went relatively smoothly during his university years. His family was doing well. He had six younger siblings now. He had good chums. The *intifada* had been over for a year, and Hammam was satisfied with the end result. In 1993 Yasser Arafat (widely known as Abu Ammar) had arrived in Gaza from exile in Tunisia to run the newly established Palestinian Authority (PA), the fruit of the secret negotiations in Oslo, Norway, that had put an end to the *intifada*. As part of that agreement, Arafat would have limited authority to govern Gaza (and the distant city of Jericho) as the first of several anticipated steps toward gaining fuller autonomy for the Occupied Territories. For Hammam, prospects seemed bright. They were on track to achieve an independent Palestinian state.

"*Wa—alay—kum—a—sa—lam, ya—sha—bab*!!!!!" bellowed Hammam to his buddies in his trademark cadenced bravado as they gathered at their usual meeting spot at the entrance to the university. "Peace be upon you, guys!" The group of four buddies had met just outside the university gates, after checking the lists to see if they had passed their fourth year in college and would thereby receive their BA diplomas.

Hammam saw his name on the list of the students who had failed the capstone course. Full of lazy, self-deluding rationalization, he told himself: *Well, I survived failing the* tawjihi. *That didn't turn out so bad after all.* Khalas! *Enough! I will just do it again.* Like his outward speech, Hammam's inner pep talk was full of bravado: *Well,* mish mushkila! *No problem!* And, he thought, it would be all the easier because he would not have to repeat the year alone. His best mates—Zakaria, Sameh, and Yassin—were in the same fix. They had all had failed enough classes to guarantee a repeat senior year. *So,* yalla*! We'll do this together! And we'll have more fun in the process!*

Thick with this cynicism and swagger, Hammam asked the group, "So, how did you all do? Huh?" (wink, wink, wink). About to bluster on with some empty talk about how they'd all do fine together over the next year after failing, Hammam barely heard their decidedly hushed reply:

"Well, brother. It seems that we passed."

Once Hammam had grasped what they said, his stomach seized up, and his mind froze. "Say again? No way! You failed subjects just like I did! How could you have passed and not me?"

"Yes, Hammam," they replied, "we don't understand it either. We are so sorry, brother."

Hammam flailed against this unthinkable outcome as he began to grasp its reality. Yet again, he would be abandoned by friends to manage life on his own.

As his buddies left him to determine the next steps in receiving their diplomas, Hammam reeled, no longer able to manage his cavalier, outward persona. Nothing short of an earthquake of terror had beset him. It felt essential, catastrophic, as if the wave he had been riding joyfully had somehow crested abruptly and slammed him flat against a rocky shore—dispatched to the searing, somehow primal, sands of failure . . . and loneliness.

He stumbled to the large tree in the courtyard of the university. As if its shade could ease his searing mind, he leaned his back against it and slid bumpily down its rough trunk. The courtyard was busy with students and faculty dashing back and forth, but his world was a dark silence. He wanted to cry but could not; his mind was too busy knocking thoughts around. Unlike with the *tawjihi*, there was no injustice to soften the blow of this new failure. He knew that he was completely responsible for this outcome, and he thought: *Failure has become my permanent friend. It accompanies me with every step I take.*

He excoriated himself for his laziness and for prioritizing enjoyment. Inside, he felt demolished. He knew he needed to change, and he yearned to.

He was now twenty-one years old and still making big mistakes. But he didn't know how to alter his path.

And what about his parents? He hadn't told Fuad and Fatima about the courses he'd failed, but he knew he couldn't lie to them about this grand failure.

After a half an hour or so of agonizing, the deeply sobered Hammam decided to go home. He found a seat in one of the group taxis that were headed to his Khan Younis camp. Although Hammam hadn't smoked a single cigarette all day, he began chain smoking, struggling to figure out how he could change. Once the taxi arrived in the center of the camp, he walked directly home, putting on his best face for the people he passed along the way.

Hammam's siblings were either in school or outside playing. After entering the house, he went directly to the office that doubled as his bedroom. He could hear Fatima in the back of the house and hoped she wouldn't realize he was there. He just wanted to change clothes and disappear. But his mother did hear him and came to the door of the room. "Is something wrong, Hammam?" she asked.

He shot back, "Nothing. I'm going out."

Without any direction in mind, just a desperate need to keep thinking, Hammam ended up pacing Gaza's main road south to Rafah. After an hour, with his mind somewhat cleared, he went to his trusted Uncle Ziyad's house in Khan Younis city and confessed the terrible story to him. Characteristically, his uncle was matter of fact, asking only what he planned to do.

Hammam asked for a pen and some paper and began to write three lists. On the right side of the page (Arabic flows from right to left), he began listing all the reasons he had failed. In the middle column, he listed his strengths. In the left column, he wrote what he planned to do to become the new person, the changed person, that he was craving to be—more desperately now than ever before.

At the end of his analysis, Hammam concluded that he had to do three things to survive this crisis. First, and in his mind most importantly, he would no longer allow Fuad to pay for his education. Given his failure, Hammam reasoned, it would be unfair to use money that could otherwise be spent on Hani and Wasseem, his two younger brothers, who were now beginning college. Second, he would no longer lie and hold things back from his parents—or anyone, for that matter—because he believed that a mature man should be honest in all things. Finally, he vowed to no longer prioritize his friendships and the time spent frivolously socializing. Hammam was pleased with his three-part plan, and he felt confident that he could start a new life by following these principles. Now he was ready to talk to his parents.

Scared to tell Fatima, who wore her emotions on her sleeve, Hammam decided to confess to his father first. Fuad was more reserved, and with Hammam he always behaved as much like a friend as a parent—someone his son could confide in. Two days after Hammam had finalized his plan at his uncle's house, he chose the moment to tell Fuad his secret while they were walking together in the camp.

"Baba, I have made a big mistake. I hate myself for it, and I really want to change," he began. Fuad listened passively to the difficult story, but Hammam sensed disappointment through his silence. With great earnestness, Hammam continued to lay out his plan, promising his father that he was totally committed to making these changes.

Fuad replied, "Hammam, I'm sorry, but at this stage I just don't believe that you will do it."

Hammam responded, "Baba, I understand why you say that. I really do. But please, just give me one more chance, and if I fail again, you can say that I'm no longer your son."

Fuad replied, "Well, we shall see."

Privately, Fuad knew how upset and humbled Hammam was, and he was impressed with the effort he had put into analyzing his problem and committing to a plan to rectify it. Although he didn't tell his son, Fuad felt that this failure might prove to be a transformative moment in Hammam's life. He didn't doubt that Hammam would be more honest and would prioritize his studies in the academic year he had to repeat. But he knew that Hammam would need help in accomplishing the first part of the plan: landing a job to be able to finance his own education.

To that end, Fuad asked Hammam to go back and see Abu Hani, a friend of Fuad's who ran a small trading business out of Gaza City. Abu Hani had approached Hammam the year before, seeking an interpreter for his business, but Hammam had turned him down because he didn't want to add the workload to his academic studies (and his social life with his buddies).

Abu Hani welcomed Hammam and gave him a job immediately. He and his business partner, Mohammed, were both illiterate and desperately needed someone like Hammam to represent them in various business dealings. To spare him the rides on crammed buses to get to his classes in Gaza City, they lent him their nice company car. The car had VIP plates, allowing it to drive through the Erez crossing to Israel and the West Bank, and soon Hammam was assigned to deliver and pick up items. In those days prices were often cheaper outside of Gaza, so Hammam would regularly pick up sunflower seeds, sunflower oil, lentils, cheese, jam, and other items, as well as execute trading documents. Abu Hani and Mohammed were delighted with Hammam's dedication to the work, and they told Fuad.

Apart from the business aspect of their relationship, Hammam's two employers sincerely wanted to facilitate his education. They were completely flexible about giving Hammam time off to attend all his lectures and take care of his other school responsibilities. And with gratitude and appreciation, Hammam was true to his commitment to take his education seriously. He attended every lecture and never left early. He went directly to his seat at the broken wooden table, packed among thirty-eight students in the drab classroom, never looking around or socializing. He was changing and was determined to do things right this time. Overall, he was gaining a feeling of empowerment from being a reliable and skilled businessman while also studying assiduously to get his degree. He was making tremendous progress at addressing his deep guilt at having failed the previous year. In one interview, Hammam told me that by failing, he felt that he had "committed a crime unto" himself.

Life's First Victory

(2000, age twenty-five)

On December 29, 2000, Dr. Hassan gathered the five students sitting for the final English exam in a small, windowless classroom with six wooden desks. He sat at the front desk, and the five students—three young men and one young woman—sat at the ones facing him. The exam, consisting of ten white pages stapled together, was in the "American style": one hundred multiple-choice questions on English grammar to be completed in two hours by filling in answer bubbles with a pencil. Success on this exam would clear Hammam to graduate with his BA in English. It would not be easy. Dr. Hassan was famous for his rigorous tests.

Hammam had gotten along well with Dr. Hassan throughout his years at the university. As a teacher, he was easygoing and liked to have fun with his students.

Outside the exam room, Dr. Hassan saw Hammam and said, "Enter to graduate!"

"I studied hard, Dr. Hassan. I really did because I need to finish," said Hammam. Once all five students were seated at their desks, Dr. Hassan passed out the exams and began the clock.

Hammam was tense and put everything out of his mind as he proceeded through the questions, completing them at the ninety-minute mark. He signaled to Dr. Hassan that he had finished. Dr. Hassan shot back, "Review your answers!"

Hammam replied, "I'm exhausted! I can't concentrate anymore!"

"Review your answers," repeated Dr. Hassan with even more emphasis.

Hammam did the most thorough review he could and was sure he'd done his best. Still, he was incredibly scared, given how much was riding on the result. He had worked so hard to right his life and fulfill his promises to Fuad and Fatima. As he handed the exam to Dr. Hassan, Hammam was so anxious that he was afraid he might piss his pants. When Dr. Hassan left the exam room and went to his office to grade Hammam's test, the other students said to Hammam, "This is a really hard exam!" Hammam replied, "Review your answers!"

The door to the office had two tiny windows. Hammam pressed his face again one of them and watched Dr. Hassan making a mark next to each of his answers. Hammam began counting: "One, two, three, four, five, six . . .

breath . . . seven, eight, nine, ten . . . *breath*." At some point he lost track. All he needed were fifty-one correct answers to graduate, but he needed many more than that to graduate with honors. He waited for what felt like an eternity. Eventually, Dr. Hassan turned his head toward the door, saw Hammam's face squashed against its window, and waved for Hammam to enter the office.

This was the real moment of truth. Passing the exam would be the final evidence Hammam had successfully changed his life. Another failure would kill him.

Dr. Hassan's face was deadpan. As Hammam approached his desk, trembling, the professor smiled wryly and said, "Well, Hammam, it seems that you have passed."

Hammam yelped with excitement. He jumped up onto the desk, crying and shouting. "I passed! My God, I really passed! I achieved my dream! I kept my promise to myself and to my family. I have changed my life! I have achieved my first victory!" He yanked the cell phone out of his pocket and dialed Fuad. "Baba, I did it! I passed!"

He gave the phone to Dr. Hassan so that he could verify the passing score. "Peace be unto you, Fuad," he said. "I'm delighted to confirm that Hammam has passed the exam and is now ready to graduate."

Fuad, seated at his desk in the school office, shielded his own tears. He had hoped so much that Hammam would be successful. It had been a long road for Hammam to correct his life's trajectory. Fuad felt a warm rush of pride in his firstborn's achievement. He excitedly called Fatima.

Hammam still refers to this moment as the first victory of his life. He began thinking seriously about his future and about how to reach his greatest dream: to become a teacher. And, crucially, he thought about what he needed to do to become independent from his parents.

Shada

(2000, age twenty-five)

Truth be told, Hammam had not lost all his impulsiveness. During his final year at the university, he developed a crush on a classmate. He was past the age when most men married, and frankly, his hormones were raging. Contrary to tradition, in which parents take the lead in arranging all aspects of a marriage, Hammam had audaciously proposed to Sawsan one day in class. He had consulted with his father the day before but knowing that Sawsan was not likely to accept such a nontraditional approach, Fuad had agreed to the proposal. Sawsan was shocked by Hammam's unorthodox and improper approach, and she responded, "You haven't even finished college!"

"But maybe you could wait six months," Hammam countered.

"No," she said finally. "I want to marry a man who is successful." Hammam shrugged off her rejection.

When Fatima got word of this situation, she realized that it was time for her to start searching for a wife for Hammam. After some deliberation and discussion with other mothers in the camp, she decided that Hammam would marry Shada (SHA-dah), a distant cousin. When she informed Hammam of this decision, he was actually quite pleased. He already had fond feelings for her because when he was five, he had accompanied her mother to the hospital for Shada's birth.

Shada supported the idea, but only under two conditions. First, the marriage had to be completely traditional. She was aware that the al-Faqawi family wasn't always big on tradition, and she didn't want them to cut any corners. Second, she was in her first year of university, and she wanted to get her bachelor's degree before they had children. Hammam was fine with the first request, and he agreed eagerly to the second. He believed that education was important for everyone, not just men. In turn, he promised her that once she finished, he would start graduate school.

After their marriage the following year, they made the agonizing decision to leave their family homes in the Khan Younis refugee camp and get an apartment in Gaza City, where Shada was in school and Hammam worked. It was only sensible, but never—not even for a single night—had either of them been away from their family. Both were frightened, and neither knew if they could make it work, emotionally or financially. Hammam had stayed true to his commitment to stop taking money from Fuad. His salary was low, but if they lived extremely frugally, he thought they could make it work.

When Shada and Hammam were engaged to be married in 2000, the second *intifada* broke out in Jerusalem. Many triggers had brought about the onset of this renewed fighting, but the most public one was the entry of then–Prime Minister Ariel Sharon into the Al-Aqsa Mosque located in the Noble Sanctuary complex (what Jews call the Temple Mount). No previous prime minister had entered the mosque since 1967, when Israel had agreed that the nation of Jordan would have full authority over the sanctuary. Palestinians in Jerusalem erupted in stone throwing at what they perceived as a desecration of their holy site. The IDF responded with hundreds of thousands of rounds of rubber bullets, tear gas, and live ammunition. The violence spread quickly through the West Bank.[31]

Palestinian public resistance to the occupying Israeli forces during the first *intifada* consisted mainly of throwing stones, setting tires on fire, and lobbing some Molotov cocktails. This second iteration of the struggle was radically different. Militant Palestinians had by then accessed many forms of armaments that they used to fight the Israeli military, and over the five years of this struggle, various political factions conducted hundreds of suicide bombings. For its part, the IDF relentlessly attacked the West Bank with tanks and fighter planes, encroaching heavily into the territory.[32]

There was little violent confrontation in Gaza during the second *intifada*, but the already heavy presence of Israeli forces was augmented. New checkpoints were set up. The Abu Holi checkpoint essentially divided the Strip in two and severely impeded the daily lives of Gazans and the operations of aid and humanitarian organizations. The checkpoint was often closed. Sometimes people were allowed through in either direction without much interference, but at other times, they were immediately forbidden and sent back. Alternatively, Gazans were made to wait for many hours and then either allowed or forbidden to cross.

Abu Holi had a powerful emotional effect on the people. In their efforts to visit their families on weekends, Hammam and Shada were always nervous about whether they'd be able to cross—and if they were allowed, whether they'd be allowed to cross back in the other direction and return to their studies and work in Gaza City.

---

[31] Black, *Enemies and Neighbors*, chaps. 21, 22.

[32] Black, *Enemies and Neighbors*, chap. 22.

They could afford only a single-room apartment in one of Gaza's prototypical cinder-block structures with no heating, cooling, or insulation. During the cold Gaza winters, the couple snuggled together under a pile of thick, colorful acrylic blankets from Egypt. Gaza has no central heating. Some families used dangerous kerosene heaters, but they were too expensive for most people.

It was a rough year, but Shada was able to complete her bachelor's degree in business management. They stayed in the bare apartment in Gaza City for another year. Then a long-awaited opportunity arose. Long before 1948 Hammam's grandfather had purchased a piece of land to the east of Khan Younis. This was the parcel where the family had welcomed Fuad home from prison, when Hammam had given his father the lamb. Fuad and Fatima had been waiting throughout their entire marriage to build their own house outside the refugee camp. By the time Hammam and Shada were married, they had completed the skeleton of that cinder-block house. It had four levels, and after discussion among the family about preferences, they decided that the ground floor apartment would be for Hani and his family, the second level for Fuad and Fatima, the third level for Hammam and his family, and the fourth level for Wasseem and his family. Fuad and Fatima's daughters would live with their parents in the second-floor apartment until they got married and went to live in their husbands' homes.

When Hammam had graduated two years earlier, he'd continued to work at the trading company until he received an offer to work for an international relief agency. Desperate not to lose Hammam, the head of the trading company offered to double his salary. As tempting as that counteroffer was, Hammam was eager to work more directly to help his people and to achieve a respected status among them. Both the deprivation he experienced in not having Fuad with him in his early years and his failures during high school and college had left him insecure, constantly striving to prove his worth.

Hammam stayed at that relief agency for a year and was then delighted to receive a one-year offer to work as a researcher for the Al Mezan Center for Human Rights, one of Gaza's most respected civil society organizations. He enjoyed the work, especially the personal relationships he developed with other staff members. However, in late October 2003 he received his dream offer, and he quickly accepted a job as an elementary school teacher at a boys' school near his family's new home in eastern Khan Younis. The salary was low, but it was a permanent government job. Finally, he had stable employment. And best of all, he would be entering the same field—teaching—that Fuad had started his career with as a young man.

After Shada finished her bachelor's degree, the couple moved into Hammam's family home. One of Shada's conditions for marrying Hammam had been that she would get her undergraduate degree before they had children. And Hammam had promised that he would not begin graduate school until after they had their children. But it had already been two years since Shada had graduated, and she still hadn't gotten pregnant. They decided together that Hammam should enroll in a master's degree program. He would take classes in the evenings and on weekends so that he could continue his work as a teacher at the boys' school. The kids loved him because he was so personal with them. During break periods he was always in the schoolyard checking in on how each boy was doing, especially those whose families were the poorest. Before long, the school promoted him to head teacher (principal).

Both Hammam and Shada felt deeply relieved to move out of their little apartment in Gaza City. They would no longer be separated from their families, and they wouldn't have to waste money on rent anymore. They now sorely needed cash to help outfit their apartment in the new house. Initially, their new quarters were even less comfortable than their apartment in Gaza had been—because the new place didn't yet have glass installed in the window openings. There were many nights when they felt as if they would freeze. Over the next year, Hammam was able to have glass windows installed, and they saved enough money to buy some furniture. Their home began to feel comfortable, and the couple was happy. But something important was missing from their lives.

Who Will It Be?

(2006, age thirty-one)

As they had agreed, once Shada got her bachelor's degree nearly four years prior, the couple started trying to have children. But she still hadn't gotten pregnant. Both Hammam and Shada were increasingly stung by the constant whispers: "Why don't they have any children? What's wrong with them? It's their duty, and they should have had them long ago." It began to be extremely painful.

At this point everyone assumed that the problem was with Shada. But a doctor convinced Hammam to get himself checked out. Sure enough, the physical problem turned out to be his, and a simple operation fixed it. Shada quickly became pregnant, ushering in the most blissful time of their lives. They would cuddle at night and caress each other, recounting their achievements to date: Both had completed their undergraduate degrees, Hammam had a stable job that he loved, and they had a home of their own that was now furnished. They were eager to take the next vital step of having children.

After Shada had gone into labor and they were at the hospital, Hammam had fallen asleep in the hallway outside the delivery room. (It wasn't customary for husbands to be in the labor and delivery room.) It was late at night, and he was awakened by a couple of gentle taps on his shoulder and the soft but intense voice of the obstetrician. "Hammam, my dear brother, I'm afraid there's a problem."

Hammam snapped alert, his widened eyes and pursed lips betraying anxiety. This was new territory for Hammam; he had never faced a serious medical issue, and he began to fear the worst. His voice broke when he asked, "Please tell me. What is it, doctor?"

"There is a complication such that I don't know if I'll be able to save both Shada and the baby," the doctor replied. "I am afraid I must ask you to make a horribly difficult decision. Which one will you have me save?"

Suddenly, Hammam felt as if all the air had been sucked out of the hallway, which was bare except for a row of plastic chairs. His mind whirled frantically. *What kind of question is that?* he thought. *Who could possibly make such a horrible and brutal decision? Could anything be more unfair?*

But after some minutes, his mind cleared enough for him to make a firm decision. "If this awful moment comes, doctor," he said, "please save

Shada." Much more than simply his wife, Shada was his soulmate, his prime confidant. He sought her consultation on every matter he faced. He couldn't live without her. Yes, it would be an awful thing to lose a child—their firstborn—but he realized that he and Shada would have more children if Allah wanted it to be so.

After he told the doctor his decision, he bent over in the chair and wept. How horrible this moment was. *Why us? We have worked so hard and sacrificed so much. I had turned my life around and become a good man. Why this now?* No one wanted a child more than Hammam, but he began preparing himself to have to wait.

After what seemed like an age, Hammam spotted the doctor approaching from the far end of the hallway, which was now mostly dark because of the late hour. Hammam shot up from his chair. As the doctor got nearer, coming into focus as he passed under each occasional overhead light, Hammam could see his sweaty brow and hair beneath his surgical cap. He could see the doctor's wrinkled surgical gown, stained with some blood. He cleared his throat but could not find his voice to ask what had happened. Now directly in front of him, the doctor placed his hands gently on Hammam's shoulders:

"My dear brother, I was able to save Shada," he said gently. Hammam nearly collapsed with relief. "And," continued the doctor, "praise be to almighty God, I was also able to save the baby." Grabbing Hammam more firmly by the shoulders to prevent him from falling, the doctor then drew him into an embrace and said: "You are a father, Hammam. Please come see Shada and your son."

Hammam was not allowed to enter the room yet, but he could see Shada through a viewing window. She was exhausted but gave him a satisfied smile when she saw him. A nurse then brought the baby to the window. Hammam inspected every inch of his son, mesmerized by the wonder of this treasured addition to his family.

The next day Hammam and Shada gave their boy a name. Fuad, of course.

Troubling Times

(2006, age thirty-one)

Fuad was born in 2006, a year that proved to be crucial for Gaza's future. The second *intifada* had essentially ended the previous year. In February 2005 the Israeli government under the leadership of Prime Minister Ariel Sharon took two major actions vis-à-vis the Palestinians. First, his cabinet approved a substantial extension of the concrete barrier in and around the West Bank that Israel had begun building three years earlier, during the second *intifada*. Second, Israel forcefully removed all Jewish settlers from Gaza, and the substantial military presence that had guarded these settlers was then redeployed to Gaza's border with Israel.[33]

In June 2006 a five-month series of battles between Palestinian resistance groups and the Israeli military broke out. The inciting incident for this renewed conflict was the capture of Israeli soldier Gilad Shalit by the Islamic militant group Hamas.[34] Operation Summer Rains, as the IDF labeled its bombing and ground attacks on Gaza, was intended to stop rockets from being launched into southern Israel and to secure the release of the soldier. By early October neither goal had been achieved, yet 256 Palestinians had been killed and 848 injured, while 2 Israelis had been killed and 31 injured. During the offensive, the Israeli Air Force bombed Gaza's only power plant in the middle of the Strip. It would take months for it to be repaired.[35]

Long-awaited Palestinian elections were held in January 2006. During the previous thirteen years after the Oslo Declaration had established the

---

[33] Donald Macintyre, *Gaza: Preparing for Dawn* (London: Oneworld Publications, 2017), chap. 3.

[34] Tareq Baconi, *Hamas Contained: The Rise and Pacification of Palestinian Resistance*, Stanford Studies in Middle Eastern and Islamic Societies and Cultures (Stanford, CA: Stanford University Press, 2018), 116. Hamas is an acronym for *Harakat al-Muqawama al-Islamiyya* (Islamic Resistance Movement). Hamas, an Islamist and nationalist movement that is an offshoot of Egypt's Muslim Brotherhood, was founded in December 1987 when the first *intifada* began. See Sara Roy, *Hamas and Civil Society* (Princeton, NJ: Princeton University Press, 2011), chap. 2; Baconi, *Hamas Contained*, chap. 1. There is evidence that Israel helped create Hamas to counter the PLO's more secular approach to resistance. See Mehdi Hasan and Dina Sayedahmed, "Blowback: How Israel Went from Helping Create Hamas to Bombing It," *Intercept*, February 19, 2018, https://theintercept.com/2018/02/19/hamas-israel-palestine-conflict/.

[35] United Nations Office for the Coordination of Humanitarian Affairs (OCHA), "Gaza Strip Situation Report, 10 October 2006," https://www.ochaopt.org/sites/default/files/GazaStrip_10Oct06.pdf.

Palestinian Authority under the leadership of Yasser Arafat, life had not improved for Gazans. They were ready for a change. Hamas was created in 1987 with the encouragement and support of the Israeli government, whose intention was to fracture Palestinian unity. Although for years its members had been effective elected leaders at the municipal level in Gaza, Hamas had not yet entered a general election.[36]

Hamas did exactly that in January 2006—and to everyone's surprise, it garnered a higher percentage of the popular vote than Fatah, the political party of the Palestinian Authority, and it therefore won dramatically more seats in the Palestinian Legislative Council. After President Yasser Arafat died in 2004 during an Israeli siege of the Fatah compound in Ramallah, Mahmoud Abbas (Abu Mazen) had been elected president of the Palestinian Authority in 2005. The government was now split, with a Fatah president and a Hamas legislative council. The two parties quickly formed a unity government, but the coalition proved problematic, and by October major skirmishes between Fatah and Hamas forces had begun. This fighting ushered in a ferocious civil war in Gaza. By the summer of 2007, Hamas had expelled Fatah forces and gained complete control inside Gaza.

Even though the 2006 legislative council election was certified as fair,[37] Israel, Egypt, and the United States refused to recognize a Hamas government. By November 2008 Israel and Egypt, with US backing, effectively sealed off Gaza indefinitely by establishing extreme restrictions on people entering and leaving the Strip; forbidding exports from Gaza; reducing its energy supply; and restricting its imports of food, fuel, and aid to the bare minimum. This blockade (also referred to as the siege) still remains in effect.

These were troubling years for Hammam and his family, as well as for all families in Gaza. The civil war between Hamas and Fatah kept them in their homes as much as possible, out of fear of being hurt during the chaotic violence. The crippling effects of the siege would soon be felt.

---

[36] Baconi, *Hamas Contained*, 76–77.

[37] National Democratic Institute for International Affairs (NDI), *Final Report on the Palestinian Legislative Council Elections*, January 25, 2006 (Washington, DC: National Democratic Institute for International Affairs, 2006). https://www.cartercenter.org/resources/pdfs/news/peace_publications/election_reports/Palestine2006-NDI-final.pdf.

Mukhtar

(2007, age thirty-two)

At ten in the morning, Hammam received his first call of the day, just as he was beginning to enjoy some playtime with his children: "*Mukhtar*, come quickly!" The caller explained that tensions had been high during an important practice match for an upcoming soccer competition. Sharif, a member of Hammam's family, and Ali, not part of the family, started having words. At first it was just bad-mouthing, but soon it escalated. Someone ran to Ali's house and told his family about the fight. One of his family members then went to the soccer field with a bicycle chain, which he gave to Ali, who struck Sharif with it, lacerating his forehead. Sharif's friends took him to the hospital. Seventeen stitches.

Hammam had a special position regarding such disputes. A year after young Fuad's birth, grandfather Fuad appointed Hammam to be his deputy. Fuad was the *mukhtar* for his family's branch of the large Barbach clan. The title means "the chosen one" in Arabic, and the position is essential in the traditional Islamic social organization and management within many Arab societies (as well as Turkey and Cyprus). The role of a *mukhtar* varies, but he is considered essentially a tribal chief, judge, village leader, or town mayor. This culturally sanctioned role—the conflict manager-in-chief for his branch of the clan—is traditionally passed down from first son to first son. It was therefore fitting that Hammam, even though he was only thirty-two years old, would be trained to take over the mantle. Fuad inherited the role from an older brother who had died, and that brother had become the *mukhtar* after the oldest brother in the family had died. Fuad also has a brother who is a *mukhtar* in Jordan, managing the branch of the family that fled there in 1948.

The *mukhtar* hears the plaintiff and the defendant in a dispute. Then, according to a highly elaborated and regulated system of procedures, he renders judgment. It is a system of trust, honor, and respect for authority. The people the *mukhtar* deals with are bound by cherished tradition to honor his judgment and comply with his decisions. There are approximately seventeen thousand members of Hammam's clan in the Khan Younis area of the Gaza Strip. His family, merely one of nineteen families in the clan, has approximately three thousand members. These family members are Fuad and Hammam's responsibility.

The clash at the soccer practice was appropriate for Hammam to handle because it was fairly but not extremely serious. If the incident had resulted in a severe injury—and thus an extended and expensive stay in the hospital—he would have needed to refer the case to his father. The more serious the problem, the older and more experienced the *mukhtar* needs to be. In the most severe cases, such as murder, the family *mukhtar* may not even handle the problem himself. Instead, a venerated *mukhtar* from a third family is brought in to resolve the dispute.

"Okay, tell me first which family was more at fault," Hammam asked the caller.

"It was the other family, *mukhtar*. Your family member, Sharif, was hurt more seriously."

Hammam drove north to the sports club, arriving quickly because it was the weekend, so the roads were less congested in Khan Younis than on weekdays. At the club he interviewed several witnesses to ascertain the true story before visiting Sharif in the hospital. Islamic culture demands strict honesty when someone reports a problem between families, and in Gaza people follow that duty. Fortunately, in this case the various witnesses were in complete agreement about what had happened.

Sharif was still fuming when Hammam arrived at the hospital. "I want my right *not* to forgive," proclaimed Sharif, still deeply aggrieved by the assault. "Please support me in this. I want revenge." For some situations, such as injuries or fatalities from car crashes, forgiveness is automatically required. Because they're considered the result of fate, no blame is assigned. But for most infractions, like this one, the *mukhtar* must decide between forgiveness and revenge.

"Have no worries," replied Hammam. "I will honor your request." He did remind Sharif, however, of the required three-day wait for Ali's family to decide how they wanted to proceed. Sharif nodded his acknowledgment and signed a short affidavit recording that he had chosen revenge instead of forgiveness. That revenge would be enacted according to the principle of "an eye for an eye": Sharif would strike Ali with a chain and hope he needed to get the same number of stitches—seventeen.

Now it was up to Ali's family. If they did not approach Hammam within the three-day *hudna* (truce), then it would be clear to everyone that Sharif was free to seek revenge. Ali's family discussed the situation. Finally, on the second day, his *mukhtar* visited Hammam.

"We would like to ask you to forgive our family," he said. "What do you require of us?"

Because of Sharif's affidavit claiming revenge, Hammam had the option to refuse the appeal for forgiveness from Ali's family straightaway. But because he'd been present at countless conflicts that Fuad had handled, Hammam had already learned to sense if a peaceful resolution would be possible. A common first step is to extend the *hudna* from three days to a week or more, an extension that often helps settle tempers and gives the offending family enough time to come up with reparative funds. Even when a family accepts forgiveness, it can still demand that their medical expenses be reimbursed. Emergency treatment for Sharif at the hospital was expensive.

"My family would like to have peace with your family," Hammam told Ali's *mukhtar*. "Therefore, I will extend the waiting period from three days to two weeks. But we would like to seal this pending forgiveness agreement with a sum of money to assure that our injured young man recovers successfully, that the stitches heal well, and that he returns to good health."

"Agreed," said the other *mukhtar*. "How much money do you require?"

Hammam had already contemplated the sum according to general guidelines that depend on the severity of the offense. But given the ever-worsening economic situation in Gaza, everyday people were strapped for money, and they all understood that this financial exigency required more forgiveness. Hammam decided on 2,000 Jordanian dinars (approximately $2,800), the currency often used for official matters in Gaza. After consulting with the hospital, he knew that it would be enough to cover Sharif's medical bills, plus a cushion for unexpected costs. He also chose that sum to communicate the seriousness of the grievance to Ali's family. He knew that it would take them time to gather that much money, so Hammam and the other *mukhtar* established a payment schedule in installments—two or three hundred dinars at a time.

Every bit as rigid as the cultural demands for complete honesty and transparency in these sacred interactions is the requirement for the *mukhtar* to keep strict accounts of these sums of money. It is done quite simply. Hammam would place the cash in a small envelope, write details of the case on the outside of the envelope, seal it, and put it at the back of a cabinet too high for any of the kids to discover it. Under no circumstances could he or anyone else use the money for another purpose. He would keep the money until the matter was resolved.

Hammam kept extending the *hudna* so that Ali's family could make a payment every week for as much as they could afford. After several weeks of payments, Sharif came to Hammam and declared that he had changed his mind; he was ready to forgive, and fully so. He didn't even want any money to offset his medical costs. That was good news to Hammam, but he still held off a bit before returning the money to the other *mukhtar*. He wanted to make sure the other family knew that the offense was serious. Just a little more time.

Sharif's case was not the only conflict that Hammam handled that day. His second call involved a mother who had broken her hip after being pushed to the ground while she was trying to stop a fight between her two youngest sons. The boys had failed to call an ambulance for her out of fear of enraging their older brothers for hurting their mother in the first place. Resolving this problem, like addressing Sharif's, involved multiple phone calls, private meetings, and creative strategies. The two brothers would end their strife and assiduously care for their mother's every need, or else they would be expelled from the family home.

Hammam also dealt with a man who often pestered him with recurring money problems. After arranging for the man to pay off the balance of his debt in monthly installments, Hammam authorized his release from jail.

This was a thrilling year for Hammam. He was honored that his father had appointed him to help with the nearly constant burden of resolving conflicts. He also felt at home in this role. He was good with people and liked nothing better than interacting with them and solving their problems.

Back in School Again

(2008, age thirty-three)

Now that their son, Fuad, was two years old, Shada and Hammam agreed that it was time for Hammam to begin graduate school. In October 2008 he began his master's degree program in educational leadership at Al-Azhar University. That day was profound.

First Hammam went to the large tree in the courtyard of the university and viscerally relived the agony he'd felt sitting in its shade after learning that he'd failed his senior year as an undergraduate. He paused to acknowledge how different he was now. Unlike during that awful moment ten years earlier when he'd realized that he had "committed a crime unto" himself, he now felt confident that he was a different man. He had become a good man whom his parents were proud of and who was proud of himself.

In his mind Hammam ticked off the evidence, the events that had allowed him to create this new, better self. He had repeated his senior year and passed with exemplary grades. He had excelled at his first job for the trading company. He was blessed to have married Shada. Together they had survived the destitute two years in Gaza City away from their families. Thanks to his father, Fuad, they had an apartment in the new family home. He had landed a rewarding teaching job at a nearby school. And now, best of all, he had fathered a son.

Yet life was arduous as he pursued this new degree. The blockade had become punishing. Everything seemed to be missing in Gaza, even the necessities. There was virtually no cooking gas or gasoline for cars, which were now running on oil. His class schedule ran from two in the afternoon to five or six in the evening. He had to leave his teaching early and race to find a taxi, but fares had doubled to ten shekels each way to the university. Once the lectures ended, he would race to find a taxi home.

Finally, in May 2010 Hammam proclaimed to a group of his professors, "I made it!" The day of his master's degree graduation was monumental to him. It was not just another example of his ability to work hard and succeed. It was also evidence of real personal growth. He marveled as he gazed across the stage at the professors, who were all wearing fancy academic garb—long, colored robes and tasseled hat. And so was he! Now he was no longer just a student, but a colleague of these wonderful men who had trained him.

At that moment he resolved to pursue a PhD degree as soon as he could afford the time and expense.

The family was growing. Mohammed, their second son, was born the year Hammam began the master's program. Their third son, Omar, was born the year he graduated.

However, while Hammam was pursuing his master's degree and his family was growing, his dreams and the hopes of many Palestinians were disrupted. On December 27, 2008, Israel launched what it called Operation Cast Lead, claiming it was in response to a recent increase in rockets launched into Israel from Gaza. Hamas claimed that these rocket attacks were in response to the IDF's ceasefire-breaking incursion into central Gaza.[38] The three-week assault began with the bombing of predetermined targets, including the power plant again. Then came an Israeli ground offensive into major towns and suburban communities in Gaza to destroy suspected rocket launch sites, followed by deep incursions into some towns and refugee camps to root out Hamas. A ceasefire occurred on January 18, 2019. During Operation Cast Lead, nearly 1,400 Palestinians were killed, more than half of whom were civilians, with more than 5,300 estimated to have been injured. In contrast, 13 Israelis were killed, including 4 civilians, and an estimated 500 were injured. Damage to Gaza's public and private infrastructure was widespread. Many educational and religious institutions and industrial facilities were severely damaged or destroyed. In addition, more than 3,500 homes were destroyed, causing more than 20,000 Gazan residents to be displaced.[39]

---

[38] Jim Zanotti, Carol Migdalovitz, Jeremy M. Sharp, Christopher M. Blanchard, and Rhoda Margesson, *Israel and Hamas: Conflict in Gaza (2008–2009)*, CRS Report No. RL40101 (Washington, DC: Congressional Research Service, 2009), 6–7, https://sgp.fas.org/crs/mideast/R40101.pdf.

[39] Israeli Information Center for Human Rights in the Occupied Territories (B'Tselem), B'Tselem's Investigation of Fatalities in Operation Cast Lead (Jerusalem: B'Tselem, 2009), https://www.btselem.org/download/20090909_cast_lead_fatalities_eng.pdf.

Fifty-One Days

(2012, age thirty-seven)

In late 2012 Israel launched what it called Operation Pillar of Defense. The Israeli military claimed that it was designed to deliver a painful blow to Palestinian resistance in Gaza. Hamas claimed that its barrage of more than 1,500 mostly makeshift rockets into Israel was in response to the assassination of two top Hamas leaders in downtown Gaza City. Ehud Barak, the prime minister of Israel at the time, said that his military dropped 1,000 more explosives than it ever had before, hitting 1,500 targets. The operation killed 167 Palestinians and injured 1,220. Hamas's rocket fire killed 6 Israelis and injured 240.[40] But these casualties were nothing compared to what would come two years later.

In 2014 the bunker-buster bomb smashed into the sandy street fifty meters east of Hammam's home, leaving a barren crater the size of a truck. The sound was deafening. The bomb made the earth shudder ferociously for hundreds of meters around, shattering windows and crumbling cinder-block homes. It propelled Habiba—Hammam and Shada's two-year-old daughter and youngest child—out of her small bed with a shriek: "Mama!" Hammam was closer; he grabbed Habiba, pressing her against his chest so that she could feel his heart beating. But all she could hear were her brothers' screams and sobs.

This nearby airstrike occurred midway through the fifty-one-day bombardment of Gaza that began on July 8, 2014, called Operation Protective Edge by the Israeli military. It was exponentially worse than the previous Israeli operations. By the end of the operation, the IDF had launched more than 6,000 airstrikes; killed more than 2,200 Gazans, most of them civilians; injured more than 11,000 Gazans; destroyed 18,000 homes, partially or completely; and displaced 500,000 people, representing 28 percent of Gaza's population. Approximately 73 Israelis (mostly soldiers) were killed, and more than 1,600 were injured. The most devastating feature

---

[40] Marcy Oster, "Soldier Dies of Injuries from Gaza Mortar," *Jewish Telegraphic Agency*, November 22, 2012.
https://web.archive.org/web/20181001142454/https://www.jta.org/2012/11/22/news-opinion/israel-middle-east/soldier-dies-of-injuries-from-gaza-mortar.

of Operation Protective Edge was that virtually the entire Gaza Strip was bombarded.[41]

In the summer of 2014, there were no safe places in Gaza, and this complicated Hammam's response to the phone call he received during the bombardment. For days people had been streaming down their streets, fleeing the heavy bombing in the eastern villages near the border fence.

The landline rang early in the morning. In broken Arabic the caller identified himself as the local commander of the IDF: "You have ten minutes to leave. We have targeted your house to be bombed." Click.

Hammam tore downstairs to consult with his father. They raced through all the central questions:

Should we leave?

If so, where would we go?

When could we come back?

Should we stay?

Which is risker: to stay or to go?

Should we split the family up, some going and some staying?

Or do we want to die together?

They decided to stay and protect themselves as best they could because there seemed to be no safe place to go. They figured that their chances of survival might be better than other people's chances, since their house was relatively new and built to higher standards. It might withstand the barrage of shells that the tanks on the other side of the eastern fence were firing every minute.

Hammam ran back upstairs, wondering where would be safest for the family. A metaphor leaped into his mind: *I am a chess player contemplating a move. I am a very good chess player.* His next move was to order everyone into the middle bedroom away from the outer walls, three kids on the bare tiled floor and two on the bed with Shada, everyone covering themselves with the thin sleeping mats. Then Hammam laid himself at the feet of the older boys, his torso against Mohammed's feet and his legs on top of Fuad's ankles.

Meanwhile, Fatima asked Hani's family to move in with her and Fuad in order to turn the family's first-floor apartment into a refuge. She and Fuad

---

[41] United Nations Office for the Coordination of Humanitarian Affairs (OCHA), "Key Figures on the 2014 Hostilities," June 23, 2015, https://www.ochaopt.org/content/key-figures-2014-hostilities.

pushed all the furniture out of the salon and covered the floor with as many sleeping mats as they could gather. She quickly gathered some food. But her shelter could hold only about fifty people crammed together. The rest poured down their street toward the city center. Some women were carrying their children, dazed and screaming, "Where are we?"

Fatima agonized.

What can I tell them? There is nothing in the city center for them. And the UNRWA shelters are already overcrowded with people grieving over loved ones who have been killed, distraught about injuries, home demolitions, horror. We are waiting for a miracle. We must keep this ray of hope alive in us.

This spate of shelling and bombing was a turning point for Hammam. The Strip had been bombed many times, but fifty-one consecutive, shattering days was worse than a nightmare. Hammam and his family had handled the previous war well. But this was too much. He needed to vent . . . into the threadbare pillow that struggled to soak up all his tears.

What is our crime? What crime have my children committed? I know the answer: You will say that we are Palestinian, and therefore we are terrorists! No, we are not! I hate war. I have always been for peace. I am against horror and terror and killing civilians. Shada has always been for peace. Fuad and Fatima only want peace. All my friends have yearned for peace. But where can I find it?

There is no peace. It is just a word.

Hammam knew he had to inspire the kids. The only thing he could think of was to promise them that he would take them anywhere they'd like once the onslaught ended. Of course, that "anywhere" had to be in Gaza, their little homeland, now horribly disfigured by the bombing.

Winter Coats and Phone Calls

(2015, age forty)

Hammam approached several boys one by one and asked them to come to his office. By now, a year after Operation Protective Edge, Hammam had risen to headmaster. Fortunately, his school had only one student shift per day, while most of the other schools had two or three shifts.

Hammam loved this job because he could tell that he was really helping these students. He thrived on mixing with some six hundred of them in the walled courtyard of the school before and after class and during breaks. The dirt courtyard was shaded by one large tree and surrounded by brilliantly colored art he encouraged his students to paint on the inner side of the concrete walls. He would talk and joke with them, and this ability to connect with students only improved his teaching. He saw them as his own children and felt a profound responsibility toward them.

Hammam then retreated to his relatively large, sparsely furnished office in the simple, concrete school building. He needed to ponder. A merchant had come to him the day before to donate cash. It would be up to Hammam to decide exactly how to use the money, as long as it was used to support the poor. Given the location of Hammam's school, the donor knew that it would have many impoverished students. Most of the students lived east of the school, near the one-hundred-meter buffer zone that the IDF enforced between a few villages and the fence that separated Gaza from Israel—a highly electrified fence covered in razor wire, with sentries and sniper turrets. Most of the students were poor, and Hammam kept stocks of notebooks, pens, rulers, T-shirts, and other supplies on hand to give out when anyone needed something.

He had thought all night about the best use of this money. He chose the specific fifteen students he'd asked to come to his office because he knew them to be among the neediest in the school. They lived in villages that had been pulverized during Operation Protective Edge, some subsisting in the rubble of their homes. Typically, such a student had a large family, perhaps ten members, and because neither parent had a job, the only clothing the kids got would be awkwardly fitting hand-me-downs from relatives or neighbors. Once the students had all assembled in his office, Hammam asked them if anyone had a jacket or coat for the winter. A few did, but most said no. Winter was approaching. He would use the donor's funds to buy them coats.

The first coats Hammam inspected were unsatisfactory—too cheaply made. He pressed the cloth between his fingers—it seemed too thin. He inspected the stitching—it seemed too loose. Imagining wearing the coat himself, he felt cold. Not good enough for his boys. He was determined to buy the same quality coat for his students that he bought for his own four children.

Fortunately, he soon found a more suitable product—thick, navy blue peacoats made in China and likely smuggled through the now purposefully flooded supply tunnels from Egypt that enabled Gazans to survive. Solid and dense to the touch, they felt well-made and had a lovely smell of newness. It was easy to imagine that they would hold back at least some of the cold. The funds would cover fifteen of these handsome coats. Hammam bought them and stacked them in the trunk of his old Hyundai sedan.

When Hammam showed the coats to the fifteen boys he had selected, he saw their eyes open wide and their mouths gape. They seemed dumbfounded with pleasure as they received their gifts. One of the more extroverted students was unable to keep his gratitude quiet and exploded: "You are the best teacher EVER!!"

Hammam always strove to make a difference and often worried that he couldn't do more. Although this busy day had been quite a satisfying one, it was far from over.

Hammam was among those fortunate enough to have a good job in Gaza, where just over half the men were employed in 2015. Among this privileged class, Hammam's slate of roles was not all that exceptional. Each role carried its own, often substantial, responsibility: oldest child, first son, brother of six, uncle of six, husband, father of four, doctoral candidate, headmaster, and part-time lecturer at two separate universities. And *mukhtar*.

Hammam's cell phone rang just as he was getting into his car after closing up the school at the end of the day. He was hungry for the meal that Shada had waiting for him. He answered the phone, and the caller began the ubiquitous, reciprocal exchange of greetings that manifests and enforces the politeness and social concerns of everyday Arab relationships. The string of preliminary greetings can proceed in an astonishing number of iterations. This caller kept it rather short because there was urgent business to conduct.

"Peace be unto you."

"And peace to you."

"How are you?"

"Doing well, praise God. And you?"

"Praise God, the same for me."

Then the caller, still unidentified by name, got to the point. The appellation he used in his next statement made clear the nature of this call—and why he was calling Hammam. "*Mukhtar,* I lent one of your relatives some money."

While being a *mukhtar*, like being headmaster, is all about service to others, it comes with a more broadly binding responsibility. He and his father are, literally, the ultimate authority in keeping the peace among the members of their large family and between their family and other families.

"Tell me what happened," replied Hammam, navigating the chaotic traffic with one hand as he drove home.

"Your relative broke one of my car's headlights," the caller continued. Two weeks had passed, the man had paid nothing, and the caller was desperate for money.

Such an appeal was so common, the problem so simple, that Hammam needed no time to contemplate. "Okay, please give me fifteen minutes, and I'll get back to you."

After hanging up with the plaintiff, Hammam immediately called the defendant's older brother, who wanted to know how much money was needed. Hammam told him it would be seventy Israeli shekels (approximately eighteen dollars), knowing himself what headlights cost.[42]

The brother replied, "Okay, stay on the line, please." He then called his younger brother on another phone, with Hammam able to hear the full conversation.

"The *mukhtar* tells me that you broke someone's headlight and that you haven't paid him for it."

His brother replied, "Yes, it's true."

"Why haven't you paid him?" continued the older brother.

"I've tried to raise the money, but I haven't been able to get it all, and I'm ashamed to go to him and only offer him part of the cost."

Shifting phones, the older brother said to Hammam, "*Mukhtar*, did you hear this?"

[42] Before 1948 the currency in Gaza was the Palestinian pound (also called the Israeli lira). The Israeli shekel (ILR) replaced the lira in 1980, and the ILR was replaced in 1986 with the New Israeli Shekel (NIS). Since then, the NIS has been the primary currency in Gaza and is used mostly for everyday transactions. The US dollar is often used for larger transactions, savings, and trade. In addition, the Jordanian dinar is sometimes used for savings, property transactions, and some legal transactions.

"Yes," replied Hammam. "I will get back to you." He ended that call and dialed the first caller, the plaintiff. After a shorter series of greetings, he said: "Okay, I have talked with the man and his family. It is not that he is refusing to pay, but rather that he has not been able to collect the full amount. He just needs more time. He has only been able to get forty-five shekels so far."

"He should have told me this," the plaintiff replied with some exasperation. "I am happy to forgive half of the cost of the headlight. Now that I know his situation, I will change my request of him to thirty-five shekels—not forty-five, not seventy. Please call him and tell him to meet me on El Bahar Street and give me only thirty-five shekels."

"Thank you very much," replied Hammam. "You are a good man. You are kind." The man effusively thanked the *mukhtar* for the compliment several times, and they ended the call.

Hammam dialed the younger brother directly this time. "The man has forgiven half of the price of the headlight. He only wants thirty-five shekels and will meet you on El Bahar Street this afternoon to collect the money. You made a mistake. You should have explained the situation and apologized."

Upon stating this decision, Hammam could hear the delight and relief in the young man's voice and needed no explanation that the burden of guilt and shame had been lifted by the kindness of the man who had been wronged. Forgiveness is an utterly crucial glue of cultural solidarity. Hammam also knew that, financially, saving the other half of the debt was a big deal for a poor young man. It was a day's wages for many. Or three round-trips to Gaza City by taxi for school, business, or shopping. Thirty-five shekels could go to paying off other debts. If he didn't have any other debts, that money would likely help his family eat: It could buy an entire chicken or twelve pounds of apples or eighty pounds of flour—easily enough to make at least a month's worth of the staple pita bread.

By now Hammam had arrived home. A rich blend of sweet and savory aromas filled the small kitchen. Shada was an excellent cook and an adventurous one at that. The two youngest children were also home: Omar, an ever-mischievous five-year-old boy, and Habiba, the darling of the family, still young enough to squeal with delight upon being captured during the hide-and-seek games she constantly instigated.

One bite into the meal, Hammam's cell phone rang again. Shada grimaced and then rolled her eyes with disdain when she learned the nature of the problem. Yet again, Hammam was being asked to resolve a monetary dispute. He was irked by the call as well, not because of the interruption, which was just part of his duty as a *mukhtar*, but because this guy kept getting in trouble, even though Hammam and Fuad had often helped him out with their personal funds.

Hammam always kept his cell phone on, even throughout the night. "I have to," he insisted. "I need to be available to solve problems."

In fact, some types of calls came only at night. Among other things, that timing provided the necessary cover for the most difficult problems—those involving women. One night a woman came to the house asking to see Hammam. He happened at the time to be visiting with his father in Fuad's second-floor flat. Both Hammam and Fuad heard the woman's request to see Hammam. Instinctively, Fuad's cultural antennae went off. It was unusual, to say the least, for a woman (presumably married) to show up at someone's home at night, especially if she wanted to speak with a married man. Fuad cautioned Hammam to be careful, but Hammam felt comfortable.

He went to the main iron gate. The woman's face was pale with fear and her eyes dark with worry. Hammam greeted her and escorted her to his third-floor apartment. He asked Shada to make tea and then to take her leave. "Try to be calm," he assured the woman. "Tell me what happened." She explained nervously that on her walk home from visiting a friend, a man pulled up beside her and offered her a ride. He said he was on his way home to pick up his wife. She took the bait. Shortly into the ride, the man pulled off onto a side street and started touching her.

She panicked but was relieved when the police suddenly arrived. It turned out that they had coincidentally been searching for this man, who was in trouble for other instances of harassing women. Thus the police didn't suspect the woman of any wrongdoing. They took her ID and told her to go home for the night and report to the police station in the morning. Instead, she went directly to see Hammam.

Hammam listened carefully to the story and told the woman that he would go to the police and handle the matter. This potentially serious problem required Hammam to consult with his father. Fuad's advice was that Hammam needed to keep this matter utterly private. Fuad would call the police chief and let him know that Hammam would be coming to the station to resolve this problem. When he arrived the next morning, a police officer assured Hammam that they were not charging the woman. "In that case," asked Hammam, "what would you like us to do?"

The officer said that they thought it was appropriate for her to come to the station to have a final talk before they closed the case. Hammam objected: "People would see her, and they would talk and insult her. Her whole family's reputation is at stake."

Hammam's solution required some creativity. He asked the police to come to his house the next day, and he would arrange for the woman to be visiting. This "coincidence" would give the police the chance to do their follow-up talk with the woman, without anyone suspecting that they had come to talk with her.

This coordination between the police and the *mukhtar* was not uncommon. In fact, during one recent month, Hammam had been at the precinct every single day to solve one type of problem or another. Once an officer quipped, "Hammam, we want to buy a desk for you to use here while you solve all the problems of your family!"

Hammam finished the day by driving a friend who had no car to Gaza City, an hour's journey there and back. They timed the trip so that Hammam could be back to pick up his two older sons from their schools. Miraculously, Hammam received no calls that night from anyone else he needed to help.

Enough

(2017, age forty-two)

From his bedroom Hammam overheard the kids discussing something in the living room. “We’re fed up!” they declared. They egged each other on: “Why should we be afraid to talk to Baba?” Omar seemed to be the angriest, so the group appointed him their leader.

Fists clenched against his short legs, Omar, just seven years old, went to find Hammam. “Baba, we need to have a family meeting!” he said sternly.

“Why, Omar?” asked Hammam.

“We have an important problem and want to solve it now!” insisted Omar.

More and more often, groups of family members had been coming to the house asking Hammam to solve their problems. Often, they’d stay for hours, crying and shouting. They sometimes came twice or three times a week.

Family meetings are the governing mechanism that Hammam’s family uses to make important decisions and solve problems. That is how Fuad and Fatima had raised Hammam and his six siblings. Problems are solved jointly. Any family member could call a meeting to discuss any concern.

“Baba, you sit there. Dudo (short for Fuad), there. Mama, there. Middo (short for Mohammed), there. Habiba, there.” Omar sat next to his father.

“So, tell me. What’s the problem?” asked Hammam. Omar became scared. “Dudo, you tell him,” he said. Dudo declined. “Middo, you tell him.” Nine-year-old Mohammed, highly respected in the family for his intelligence and poise, let it out:

“Baba, we want to talk with you about those two families who keep coming over. We want you to end their visits,” said Middo.

“But they are our relatives,” said Hammam.

“Okay, but we want to have our rights. We want to see you! We’re afraid when they are shouting. WE want to talk to you!” said Middo.

“All right, then. Let us hear from everyone.” said Hammam. “Speak for yourselves. Tell me your feelings and opinions openly and explain what you want.”

Middo continued: “When they come here, I’m afraid of their shouting. I worry that they’ll hit each other. Or when you shout at them, I worry that they’ll cause trouble for you.”

Dudo (eleven years old) said: "I don't like it that you're a *mukhtar*. You're dealing with other people's problems, but you don't deal with the problems of your sons."

Omar, veins popping out of his neck, added: "We have our rights. It's okay if people have a problem once a year. But these people have a problem once a day, it seems. Go to their house if you want to solve their problems."

After Omar's precocious oration, everyone smiled. "Shada, did you tell your sons to say this to me?" Hammam asked.

"No, definitely not." she replied. "These are their opinions."

"Habiba, what is your opinion?" Hammam asked his five-year-old daughter.

"Baba, I want to be able to sit next to you and talk with you without those other people around. I feel the same way my brothers do. I don't like it when those other people are here."

Hammam replied, "Okay, I have heard you, and you are united in your opinion. From now on, if anyone comes here to talk about their problems, I will go to their house."

The Biggest Shame

(2017, age forty-two)

Hammam had his cell phone on hand, but not just to field *mukhtar* calls. Today was the day that he would receive the text message from the bank confirming deposit of his salary for the next month. He knew the amount of his salary, of course, but the automatic deductions for telecommunications charges varied per month, so it was important to see just how much he had available to spend for the coming month.

What he read in today's text message stupefied him. His salary had been cut by 45 percent. No warning. No explanation.

Initially the shock paralyzed him, but then he was seized by a rush of emotions that were foreign to him. His heart began racing, his thoughts spun out of control, and his left knee began bouncing uncontrollably as he sat, wild eyed, reading the terse message over and over again. It was fear of a sort he had never known. Beyond the shudder of the surprise and the mystifying realization that it was his own president who had ordered the salary cut, he was feeling stabs of anxiety.

Despite the blockade, in force now for ten years, Hammam was managing reasonably on his full salary, and he knew he was much better off than many in Gaza. Unlike more than half of Gazans, he had a stable job with an adequate income. Life was, in this sense, good.

But how could he manage with just over half his salary?

The anxiety thrust him into a frantic calculation, one that he would repeat obsessively.

Okay, with the deductions, this leaves me with 1,500 shekels (roughly $500) for the month. Okay, here are my costs:

300 for utilities (phone, internet)

300 for transportation (for me and the kids to and from our schools)

200 for groceries (rice, oil, sugar, coffee, flour, bread, etc.)

250 for chicken (two whole chickens per week) and some occasional beef

250 for fruits and vegetables

Okay, that comes to a total of 1,300 shekels for the basics. That leaves me with 200 shekels spending money for the month. That comes to 6–7 shekels per day on average (less than $2).

There is no way we can manage on this. How dare I complain? We are much better off than most in Gaza. But how are we going to make it?

How can I continue paying installments to the dentist on the $500 bill we had for fixing all our teeth problems? What about clothes for the kids and Shada? Antibiotics for the kids cost me about 200 shekels a month. And what if someone gets really sick?

And what am I going to tell the kids? All of them got 97 percent or higher for the semester. They want a celebration. They deserve a celebration. What am I going to tell them?

Surely my full salary will be restored next month. There is no other way!

The year 2017 turned out to be terrible in Gaza. Salary reductions were just one element of the economic assault; the Palestinian Authority's plan was to coerce Hamas to join a unity government, as well as to collectively punish Gazans to somehow get them to overthrow Hamas, as if they had any energy or resources to do so. Financial benefits were suspended, and welfare payments were delayed or cancelled for seventy-six thousand families. Without any notice, twenty-six thousand employees were forced into retirement.[43]

Perhaps worst of all was the PA's decision to no longer pay Israel for its obligated portion of electricity for Gaza, a lack of payment that reduced the electricity supply to three hours per day or even less. The follow-up costs of this loss of energy were significant. Already, more than 95 percent of the water extracted from the Gaza aquifer was unfit for human consumption because of over salinization and nutrient contamination. Thus almost all Gazans were forced to purchase desalinated water, a severe financial burden for many families. The electricity cuts also reduced the water supply to more than a hundred water and sanitation facilities, resulting in the discharge of raw sewage into the sea and the risk of sewage overflow onto the streets.[44]

Hammam's salary, as well as the salaries of the approximately seventy thousand PA employees in Gaza, were not restored the next month or the next or the one after that. Hope became futile. Hammam felt that he could no longer manage in Gaza.

---

[43] Lamees Farraj and Tariq Dana, "The Politicization of Public Sector Employment and Salaries in the West Bank and Gaza," March 14, 2021, Al-Shabaka: The Palestinian Policy Network website, https://al-shabaka.org/briefs/the-politicization-of-public-sector-employment-and-salaries-in-the-west-bank-and-gaza/.

[44] United Nations Office for the Coordination of Humanitarian Affairs (OCHA), "Occupied Palestinian Territory: Humanitarian Needs Overview, November 2017," ReliefWeb website, December 20, 2017, https://reliefweb.int/report/occupied-palestinian-territory/occupied-palestinian-territory-humanitarian-needs-overview-2.

Family Meeting

(2018, age forty-three)

Life in Gaza only worsened in 2018. On March 30 some thirty thousand Gazans marched peacefully along the fence dividing Gaza from Israel. On that date in 1976, several Palestinian citizens of Israel in the Galilee were killed and hundreds were injured while protesting Israel's plan to confiscate Palestinian-owned land. That day—known as Land Day—has been marked every year since 1976. While only intended to last two months, the Great March of Return protests continued, every Friday, until December 2019. The IDF responded immediately with force, eventually killing more than three hundred people and injuring more than thirty-five thousand.[45]

At the time, Hammam messaged me via WhatsApp, "Life in Gaza has become unbearable. Everything is dark, without a horizon for the future of our children. We have almost lost all hope. Poverty is knocking on everyone's door and everyone is under one knife. We have nothing; I have not paid my internet or telephone bills for four months. Soon they will turn them off."

The only option Hammam could think of to secure a future for his children during what he saw as the worst year ever was a sacrilege to his utter devotion to Gaza: to uproot the family to Egypt.

He and Shada had many discussions. They devised two plans. Plan A was for the whole family to stay in Egypt for a few years to get themselves financially solid. Plan B was for Hammam to stay behind in Gaza while the rest of the family went to Egypt. Plan A was quickly scratched. The PA had gotten wise to such plans and ruled that it would no longer grant extended leaves.

So it had to be Plan B. Privately, Hammam knew that it would be excruciating to live without his family. Shada and the kids were the essence of his joy in life. But what was he supposed to do? It was his duty to provide the best life for the kids.

Time for a family meeting. He laid out Plan B.

---

[45] "Shattered Limbs, Shattered Lives," Médecins Sans Frontières (Doctors Without Borders) website, January 21, 2020, https://www.msf.org/great-march-return-depth.

Fuad (now twelve), was excited. "I vote yes. In Egypt maybe I could make some good friends and have a free life," he explained. "Here there's no place to go, and I'm often so scared."

Habiba (now five) exclaimed: "Yes, yes, I want to go! I vote yes too!" (For all Habiba knew, Egypt was a theme park.)

Shada added: "I too would like to go, but only temporarily. Gaza is our home. It's where our families are. It would be unthinkable to dislocate permanently." In every way, she suffered the smothering burdens of Gaza like Hammam did. She was desperate for a break. "It wouldn't need to be Egypt," she said. "Maybe Jordan, anywhere."

Omar (now eight) said: "Yes, it sounds fun to me. But what is your opinion, Baba? What do you want to do?"

Hammam's dispassionate response—"I will do whatever the family wants, *habibi*"—belied his mounting anxiety now that a family separation was being considered in real terms. He suppressed a mounting urge to cry.

He was now worrying about Shada. She was a brilliant counselor and partner, an astute manager of the household, a fantastic mother, a superb cook. She was his lover. But she didn't know how to manage the public sphere all that well. She didn't drive and had always relied on Hammam to do the shopping and plan family excursions. He worried that she would suffer without him.

He was equally worried about the kids. He had been watching a TV series on the traumas experienced by people who are displaced to other countries—about their struggles to integrate and the children's eventual adoption of the new culture's ways. What if he were to lose his kids in this way? That would destroy him.

Everyone was waiting for Middo (now ten) to speak. "I vote no," said the slightly built second son with the confident authority of an elder.

"Why?" asked Hammam.

Middo began with the practical, wondering how he would manage at school and with friends, since he did not speak "Egyptian." Hammam explained that it was the same language but that some words are pronounced differently, and he illustrated with examples. Middo was unpersuaded and moved on to his real concerns.

"This will cut us into two pieces," Middo asserted, "and it will be difficult for us."

"What do you mean by two pieces, Middo?" Hammam wanted to know. Even for Middo, this seemed like an exceptionally precocious insight.

"We are one body," explained Middo. "If you are here and we are there, the body will be cut in two. And I don't want that."

The room hushed as everyone absorbed this simple, astute point.

The family had been waiting for Middo to weigh in, not just because he hadn't spoken yet, but also because of his wisdom. They had learned over the years that he had an uncanny ability to dispense with the superfluous and see the real issues. His response turned the entire discussion around. New comments came quickly. Fuad withdrew his "yes" vote, and Shada did likewise.

While not mature enough to appreciate the practical complications of this "adventure," the younger two children, Habiba and Omar, had no trouble understanding—feeling—Middo's point. They wanted their Baba at all costs and also changed their vote to "no."

"The vote is 5–1 that the family not go to Egypt while I stay behind. That is the strong majority. Therefore, we will not discuss this plan again," summarized Hammam. At this moment, his emotional fever broke. He had been realizing how desperately he did not want this plan. He knew that his intentions to help his family were genuine, but he also knew he could not possibly go through with the plan. And he recalled his commitment to never leave his children without him. Relief spread through him like fresh air.

Somehow, he said to himself, we will continue forward to make life work in our cherished but ravaged Gaza.

Later that year, the PA raised their employees' salaries up to 75 percent of the original pay. And a friend persuaded Hammam to accept a loan. So financially they were in better shape.

Hammam took the moment to begin the last stage of his educational achievement. He enrolled at an Egyptian university to get a PhD in educational leadership, which had been his dream ever since he was a young man. He had no ambition to shift careers, since he was perfectly fulfilled with his headmastership. Still, it would be a great achievement. He was able to take the coursework remotely from Gaza. Then he would need to find a mentor to guide him through his dissertation.

Hammam finished his coursework in 2019, and after months of searching, he found a professor in Sudan who agreed to mentor him in person in Sudan while he wrote his dissertation. It took six months. Hammam's temporary separation from the family was acceptable because everyone knew its value.

Apart from his work during college that took him into Israel and the West Bank, Hammam had only ever been outside of Gaza to Egypt a few times. Thus going to Sudan was a huge undertaking. It was far away and unknown. He lived with six other students in a dorm room. The university was in worse shape than those in Gaza. But Hammam concerned himself only with his dissertation—and unexpectedly, his role as *mukhtar*.

Shortly after Hammam arrived in Sudan, the Palestinian embassy in Khartoum called. The ambassador was aware of his arrival and of his status as *mukhtar*, and he recruited Hammam to work on social problems in Sudan. Over the next months, Hammam gave many public seminars and workshops. One was on the Palestinian family and how working mothers can care for their children. Another was on the teacher-student relationship and another on bullying in schools. He was also appointed spokesman for all Palestinian students in Sudan.

Hammam survived emotionally on daily Snapchat messages with Shada and the kids until he completed his dissertation and returned to Gaza in September 2020. The hardest part of his experience in Sudan may actually have been when he first returned to Gaza. The coronavirus pandemic had been raging for several months, and Hammam was immediately quarantined in a facility within eyesight of his home.

In Gaza by that point during the pandemic, there had already been more than 2,500 cases of COVID and 17 deaths.[46] By 2022 those figures had risen to almost 82,000 cases and more than 400 deaths.[47]

---

[46] Samer Nazzal, "Coronavirus (COVID-19) in Palestine," December 4, 2022, https://web.archive.org/web/20201102212006/https:/corona.ps/details, archived November 2, 2020, from https://corona.ps/details, accessed April 4, 2020.

[47] "Risk of Disease Spread Soars in Gaza as Health Facilities, Water, and Sanitation Systems Disrupted," World Health Organization website, Eastern Mediterranean Region, November 8, 2023, https://www.emro.who.int/media/news/risk-of-disease-spread-soars-in-gaza-as-health-facilities-water-and-sanitation-systems-disrupted.html.

Trudging Forward

(2021, age forty-five)

Hammam and his family trudged forward during the pandemic. None of them got infected with the virus—fortunately, because with the deteriorated economic and medical situation in Gaza, they may not have been able to receive treatment.

The kids continued to get very high marks in school, despite renewed, incredibly intense, but relatively brief spates of bombardment and rocket fire in May 2021, August 2022, and March 2023, during which no one slept and the kids were in a constant state of anxiety and panic. Hammam and Shada were able to barely make ends meet on Hammam's reduced salary and the further loans he had reluctantly secured from friends.

> But there was one bright spot. On May 31, 2022, Hammam wrote to me:
>
> Praise be to God and thanks be to God under the auspices of His Excellency the President of the State of Palestine Mahmoud Abbas (Abu Mazen) and under the supervision of Dr. Ahmed Abu Houli in the outskirts of Al-Azhar University, I was honored today by the Department of Refugee Affairs of the Palestine Liberation Organization for my participation in the research competition for the best systematic scientific research on the issue of Palestinian refugees at the level of the homeland and the diaspora. My work on the difficulties that Palestinians face in providing e-learning to their children was rated among the top 30 research projects.

Khalil
The Defender of Human Rights

The Sandwich

(1976, age six)

Khalil folded his long legs under himself on the concrete floor, its coolness a luxury that offset the day's searing heat. After a plain supper of falafel, hummos, and fresh tomatoes, he and his siblings—two older brothers and three older sisters—had gathered in a semicircle to listen to their mother, Tamam (tah-MAHM).

The Abu Shammala single-story house was the last one at the west end of the Khan Younis refugee camp, a mile or so from Hammam's home. From the small, high window in the front room—which doubled as both the salon for greeting guests and Khalil's bedroom—people much taller than the six-year-old Khalil could gaze at the billowing golden sand dunes partially obscuring the electrified fence that protected Gush Katif, a sprawling block of sixteen Jewish settlements located inside the Gaza Strip between the camp and the sea.

The house was the typical cinder-block structure—weathered plaster on the outside, whiter plaster on the inside. Neatly arranged against one wall on the otherwise bare floor was a stack of light foam pads from Egypt—approximately two feet by two feet by two inches—each draped in worn, multicolored covers in every conceivable pattern. These beds would be laid out on the concrete floor when it was time to sleep.

Tamam was so tall that her children felt as if they had to look up almost toward the sky to see her face. The grown Khalil would get his height and lanky frame from her. Whenever she spoke, the kids listened attentively; she gave the impression of being an educated woman of letters, perhaps a teacher skilled in addressing a classroom of students.

Tamam ran the household and the children. She was born in Barbara, a village just north of today's border between the Gaza Strip and Israel. During the 1948 Nakba, her family—along with Khalil's father's family from nearby Beit Daras[48]—fled to Khan Younis and set up life there in the refugee camp that developed like a tumor on the bustling, historic city toward the

[48] Barbara, Barqa (Hussam's grandparents' village), and Beit Daras were among the 418 Palestinian villages destroyed by Israeli forces in 1948. See Walid Khalidi, ed., *All That Remains: The Palestinian Villages Occupied and Depopulated by Israel in 1948* (Washington, DC: Institute for Palestine Studies, 1992), 81, 82, 87.

southern end of the Strip. Khalil's parents were neighbors—and distant relatives, of course. Mohammed, Khalil's father, trained as a nurse but could only find work as a caretaker at what Gazans call the British Cemetery (officially the Deir el-Balah War Cemetery) a few miles away. Built in 1917, this graveyard is the burial site for hundreds of the British soldiers killed during Edmund Allenby's three-day assault on Gaza, which helped bring about the defeat of the Ottoman Empire during World War I.[49]

Several times a week, Tamam would gather all her children together. This wasn't home schooling—in fact, she was illiterate, having lived her whole life in extreme poverty. Education hadn't been an option. Instead, she taught her children lessons for the soul, expressed with such simplicity and conviction that she endowed her instruction with captivating authority. The curriculum itself was simple. Tamam lived assiduously by the main principles of Islam. What she most wanted from her children was for them to pray five times a day, fast during the month of Ramadan (beginning generally at age eight), stand against injustice, and always care for the poor.

It's not entirely clear why, but in a departure from the norm of mothers being most attached to their eldest son, Khalil was Tamam's favorite. He knew it, and so did his siblings, who often mentioned just how close Tamam and Khalil were throughout her life. *Hayk* (that's just the way it was). She would die in his arms in 2014 after succumbing to cancer. Her death would flatten Khalil.

That night's lesson focused on one of their close neighbors. Tamam liked to use real people to make her points. "Think of our neighbor Mohammed, children. He is a great example to us. You know he is a doctor, right? Well, I want to tell you that this didn't come easily to him. Did you know that when he was growing up, his family was even poorer than we are? They often had no electricity at all, but when that happened, Mohammed would just keep studying by candlelight until morning. His parents knew how smart he was, but they couldn't help him with the money he needed for all of his schooling. Other, kind people did that for him. Do you see the lesson? The poor can accomplish great things. Please, think of them always."

Khalil's family was itself quite poor. His father made only six hundred Israeli shekels (roughly two hundred dollars) a month, nowhere near enough

---

49 "Deir El Belah War Cemetery," Commonwealth War Graves, https://www.cwgc.org/visit-us/find-cemeteries-memorials/cemetery-details/71200/deir-el-belah-war-cemetery/.

for his family of eight. In contrast, those elsewhere in the camp who were fortunate enough to have a job in Israel earned that same amount per day. Khalil would watch his friends occasionally buy an ice cream. He had no money and refused to burden his parents to give him a shekel. Once Khalil was voted most valuable player in a children's soccer tournament in his area. The prize wasn't a jersey or new pair of shoes—it was a watermelon. But he knew that the organizers couldn't afford anything more.

Perhaps it was his reserve, or the fact that he listened before speaking, that drew Tamam to Khalil. Yet it was undoubtedly his behavior that pleased her the most. Once, for example, he came home excitedly after the first day of school to tell her about something that had happened. "Mama, I saw a girl in my class who looked terribly poor. I could tell because her school dress was dirty and torn. She had no shoes, just a pair of flip-flops that didn't fit her feet very well. I felt really sorry for her, Mama. And then I remembered what you always teach us about looking out for the disadvantaged. While all of us kids were walking home, I walked next to her and slipped half of my sandwich into her hand (that day it was a half pita loaf smeared with red pepper sauce). She seemed poorer than me and hungry. She deserved to have something to eat! I know I shouldn't have, but I looked quickly at her face. I think she was smiling."

Gratified, Tamam used Khalil's sandwich episode to inspire his siblings. "See your brother Khalil? What's in his pocket is not for him." After that episode, Khalil would often give that same girl the lira that his mom gave him every day to buy his sandwich.

Khalil knew that he was his mom's favorite, and he liked it. He also knew that people—family, friends, leaders, and teachers—saw him as important, experienced, and wise. But that's not how he felt inside. He saw himself as simple, inexperienced, and immature. And it turned out that these qualities—along with his naïveté—did little to equip him for the rigors of the *intifada* that was soon to come.

But the attributes that Khalil saw in himself were certainly not the ones that earned him the attention of the adults in his community. By the age of nine, he was attending mosque on a regular basis, wearing a white, ankle-length *gallabiyya*, which he washed and ironed on a daily basis. He went there not just for Friday communal prayer (*Jummah*) but at many other times as well, encouraging everyone he knew to go to the mosque to pray. Khalil's sole purpose in life was to do and to learn exactly what his mother asked.

The leaders of the mosque assigned Khalil progressively greater responsibilities. By the time he was thirteen, they had asked him to lead a Tuesday worship service after *Maghrib*, the fourth prayer of the day, performed at sunset. Then they asked him to help oversee the library. His responsibilities at the mosque led his friends to call him Sheikh Khalil. He revered the actual sheikhs, who eventually promoted him to youth leader. But their behavior devastated him emotionally when he witnessed them mercilessly beating a young boy for some minor sacrilege that in Khalil's mind barely deserved a verbal reprimand. He would never view Islam the same way again.

The Eruption

(1987, age seventeen)

In the spring of 1987, Khalil graduated from high school with a strong score of 72 percent on the *tawjihi*. Confrontations with the Israeli soldiers in Gaza had been increasing, especially at schools. Like mosques, schools were prime battlegrounds for the buildup of confrontations that led up to the *intifada*, and they remained so throughout the entire struggle.

Particularly at schools in refugee camps, the classrooms were bleak and overcrowded, with fifty-plus students crammed together, sitting three each at ancient and rickety wooden desks. The sheer number of students at each grade level often made it necessary to have three shifts per day, the first beginning as early as 6:30 am. In fact, on any given early morning except the weekend (Friday, which is the Muslim holy day, and Saturday), the packed camp streets seemed to sway with a sea of denim-clad students (girls wearing a simple dress over their jeans), all making their way to school toting similar, often oversized, secondhand backpacks.

One day shortly before the eruption of the *intifada*, some young men had been taunting Israeli soldiers with name calling, and a large squad of them stormed the school building. They kicked many teachers and students, injuring seventeen. Tensions were building, fostering the taut emotions that readied Khalil for the large confrontation to come.

It was the 6:00 a.m. radio broadcast on December 9, 1987, that alerted seventeen-year-old Khalil, along with all of Khan Younis—both the city and adjacent refugee camp—to the exploding *intifada*. It was the day after an Israeli had crashed his truck into a vehicle carrying Gazan workers, killing four of them and wounding ten.[50] As if a dam had burst, a mass of people gushed like a torrent down the main road toward the central mosque, a flow augmented by the endless tributaries of alleys and streets. The intensity of emotion stunned Khalil and swept him up into the current. The throng included all kinds of people: young children, high school and university

---

[50] "December 9, 1987: Intifada Begins on Gaza Strip," *HISTORY*, https://www.history.com/this-day-in-history/intifada-begins-on-gaza-strip; "December 8, 1987: The First Palestinian Uprising (Intifada)," *IMEMC News*, December 9, 2019, https://imemc.org/article/december-8-1987-the-first-palestinian-uprising-intifada/.

students, teachers and university professors, doctors, business owners, merchants, laborers, farmers, mothers, fathers, grandmothers, and grandfathers.

Khalil didn't know what their destination was, and the crush of bodies streaming next to him offered no clue. It was pure, unbridled energy. Something had taken over. The mass was one. It was going . . . wherever. Of course, he would be part of it. He was part of the one. Over his entire life Khalil had heard his elders talk about the Palestinian resistance that began in the 1920s. Every adult in the camp had either personally experienced one or more of the many storied episodes over the decades or had a close relative—a father or mother, an uncle or aunt, a grandfather or grandmother—who had. But Khalil hadn't been part of it himself.

"My emotions took over," Khalil recalled when I interviewed him for this book. "I just wanted to fight and help end our suffering. We wanted this occupation to end. I can't describe, believe me, I just can't describe what a wonderful feeling it was to share with my people—the struggle against the occupation."

The mass of people on the streets that day encountered an ominous squadron of Israeli soldiers, all toting machine guns. "There we were, just people throwing stones and sticks at machine guns. It was crazy. We just wanted to fight. We knew why, but we had no idea how." When the soldiers shot into the crowd with live fire, 4 Gazans were killed, and some 150 were wounded.

At least partly because of his respect for his parents and older brothers, Khalil had always prized the wisdom of age and experience, calling on it regularly to carefully analyze how events painted a larger picture. On the evening of the massive demonstration in Khan Younis, he went to sit with a highly respected elder in his camp to ask his opinion on the meaning of the day. "Do you think that this revolution will go on? Will it end well?" Still naïve about the intensity of the struggle that was now escalating so dramatically, Khalil couldn't imagine that it would continue much longer. But the elder's answer was "Khalil, this revolution will last for many years."

Khalil's theoretical connection to the struggle was concretized when the *intifada* broke out in 1987. But despite his presence on that first day of massive protests, he didn't engage in the almost daily contests that followed. He didn't like confrontation and stayed clear of soldiers, although he worried that his passivity would make his friends lose respect for him.

Like every Palestinian, Khalil was 1,000 percent committed to the struggle against the occupation. But because of his deliberative personality, he was not drawn to the mushrooming face-to-face, stone-throwing confrontations between young people and the IDF. He preferred using his brain to contribute. And beyond that, Khalil had excelled in school and dreamed of traveling abroad to go to college. He and his dad would talk over the options—Yemen? Libya? Egypt? It didn't matter where. He just wanted to get out of Gaza. Being active publicly might jeopardize that.

The ID Card

(1988, age eighteen)

Khalil broke his concentration on the marbles he'd just tossed and looked up over his left shoulder. Terror seized him. *My God! It's the Givati*, a notorious brigade of the Israeli military that had been dispatched to Gaza when the *intifada* erupted the month before.[51] He and his buddies had come outside the camp this cold, early January morning to avoid the clashes between the Israeli soldiers and local youth that were raging inside the camp. Khalil had seen the soldiers beating and kicking many people in the streets, in a frantic attempt to stop the throngs of kids, whose stone-throwing protests were only increasing as the weeks of the insurrection continued.

"Get over against that wall!" ordered the leader. "Keep your hands behind your heads and keep your mouths shut! Take out your IDs!"

Khalil and his pals were too scared to speak. They had all seen this drill play out. The soldiers, who were not much older than they were, would shout numerous questions in broken Arabic or unintelligible Hebrew:

"Who are you?"

"What are you doing here?"

"Did you throw stones?"

"Why did you throw them?" (even though they said they hadn't)

"Which of your friends have been throwing stones?"

Khalil knew that if their answers didn't suit the soldiers, they could beat the boys with their wooden clubs—the clubs Israeli Defense Minister Yitzhak Rabin had recently authorized his soldiers to use to break Palestinians' bones."[52] Not knowing what the soldiers would do, Khalil's heart was pounding so hard he thought it would explode out of his chest. *How severe would they be today*? he wondered.

---

[51] "The Givati Brigade: Protecting Israel's Southern Border," FIDF (Friends of the Israeli Defense Forces) website, https://www.fidf.org/how-we-help/adopt-unit/adopt-brigade/givati/.

[52] Reuters, "Colonel Says Rabin Ordered Breaking of Palestinians' Bones," *Los Angeles Times*, June 22, 1990, https://www.latimes.com/archives/la-xpm-1990-06-22-mn-431-story.html; "Israel Declines to Study Rabin Tie to Beatings," *New York Times*, July 12, 1990, https://www.nytimes.com/1990/07/12/world/israel-declines-to-study-rabin-tie-to-beatings.html.

But then, another shock. A band of mothers suddenly appeared around the corner. Each woman was holding up the hem of her long, dark *burka* with one hand and raising her other hand in a fist, punching the air above her scarved head, screaming even louder than the soldiers: "Leave them alone! They've done nothing wrong! They're just kids, for God's sake! How dare you! Go away! Now!" Khalil's muscles relaxed a bit at this sight. *They'll protect us*, he comforted himself.

Suddenly, a young girl trailing the mothers awkwardly flung a small piece of crushed cinder block toward the soldiers. It hit one soldier in the back, but the fragment was so small and the velocity so slow that he may not have even felt it. *This is going to get really bad*, thought Khalil. However, the Givati squad started to retreat, apparently not wanting to get embroiled with this mom army. But far from being relieved by their withdrawal, Khalil felt a renewed panic. As they left the lead soldier yanked the boys' ID cards out of their hands.

In those days, the Israeli Security Agency (ISA) issued an ID card to every Palestinian sixteen years of age and older. Anyone found without it would be grilled and detained (possibly indefinitely) or imprisoned. When Khalil had received his ID two years ago, he'd said to himself, *I will never—NEVER—let this ID out of my sight!*

Now it was gone, and he was illegal.

Back at home the entire family agonized all afternoon. They played out the various scenarios of Khalil getting caught and being separated from them. How could they retrieve his ID? Was it possible that the army would return it? Would the military authorities summon Khalil to pick it up? The uncertainty about what would happen made him panic.

Late that evening the ominous pounding of soldiers' wooden truncheons on the heavy, rusted metal front door made the house shudder. Khalil's father opened the door, and in barged the same Givati soldiers who had taken away the IDs that morning. Khalil recognized every one of them, but they didn't seem to remember him. They grabbed Khalil and his older brother Jabbar and marched them out the door and around the corner to the main street of the camp. They would have also taken Khaled, the oldest brother, if he'd been home.

"Clean up this mess!" the commander shouted at Khalil and Jabbar after they had joined a much larger group of men of all ages who'd been rounded up that night. They began removing the day's thrown stones and dragging away the smoldering tires that protesters had lit during the day to disorient the soldiers. Some of the men began painting over the graffiti of patriotic slogans that demonstrators had written on walls in flowing Arabic, using brushes and buckets of whitewash that many families kept on hand just for this task.

Throughout the hours of work, Khalil's mind was on high alert. *What if they demand my ID*? he asked himself a hundred times.

Then, inevitably, came the command: "Get into one line facing us and get your IDs out."

Khalil's chest seized up, his knees began trembling, and his thoughts started to spin. Midway down the line, standing next to Jabbar, he repeatedly asked his brother in a panic, "What should I do?"

Jabbar quickly got fed up and said, "Just calm down, Khalil. There's nothing you can do now. Just tell them the truth. You'll just have to take whatever they dish out."

Khalil almost peed in his blue jeans when the commander got to him. "I am very sorry, sir, but I don't have my ID," he said, quivering.

"Why the hell not?" the commander shot back.

"The soldiers took it from me this morning, sir."

"Sure they did," the soldier scoffed. "Go to that wall where the jeeps are. Keep your hands behind your head, look straight ahead, and keep your fucking mouth shut!"

Toward the end of the line, the commander encountered Muslih, Khalil's ID-deprived marbles buddy. Within seconds, Muslih was standing next to him by the wall. They were both shivering not only from the wind blasting in from the sea, but also from the sheer panic they shared when they caught each other's eyes. Khalil's mind raced over the multitude of detention stories he had heard from relatives and friends. The commander dismissed the rest of the cleaning crew. Khalil turned his head and risked a last glimpse of his brother. Jabbar gave him the clenched fist: *Be strong!*

Without a word, soldiers as young as Khalil and Muslih flipped them around, blindfolded them, and cuffed their hands behind their backs. Khalil had always imagined that those white plastic zip ties would hurt, but he had no idea. He wanted to scream when they cinched them so tight that he felt as if the rigid plastic would slice through his wrist bones. His knees screamed with agony when they shoved him into the jeep, his kneecaps crammed into the corrugated iron channels of the vehicle's floor. Khalil could hear the soldiers jump in and sit on the benches that lined both sides of the jeep, cackling like drunkards on the ride to the security headquarters.

At the Israeli military compound just a mile or so from Khalil's camp, soldiers yanked the two friends out of the jeep, ripped off their blindfolds, and marched them into the center courtyard to what looked like a pen. The night was dark, but the moonlight allowed Khalil to make out that the dimensions of the pen were about two by two by three meters. It had a dirt floor, with sides made from flimsy sheets of tin and a roof made from sheets of corrugated asbestos. The soldiers slashed the painful zip ties and silently pushed Khalil into the pen through the tin door, attached with heavy wire hinges. Khalil felt like a piece of garbage being pushed into a dumpster packed with fifteen other boys.

"Muslih, are you there? Are you okay?" His friend—a few years older than Khalil and sort of his mentor—responded immediately from what seemed like a few bodies away.

"Yes, I'm here."

"What's happening to us? What are they going to do with us?" whispered Khalil.

"I don't know," Muslih replied. "Just try to stay calm and be strong. We'll make it through this."

Khalil didn't know most of the other boys. Because they were all streetwise enough already to watch what they said—they'd heard about spies and collaborators—their conversation was stilted. He could trust Muslih, however, so they could talk to each other. Years later, when Khalil looked back at that terrifying ordeal, he shuddered to imagine how he would have survived without Muslih's companionship.

After Khalil had shivered through a sleepless night, his dread came into clearer focus: It was the fear that the military officers would interrogate him and that he might succumb. He'd heard that even if you hadn't done anything, what the interrogators wanted was a confession, which they'd use in a military court and which would likely land you in prison. If that turned out to be the case for Khalil, his parents would suffer greatly, not knowing where he was and what was going to happen to him. If he went to prison, he'd ache for them. And the ordeal would interrupt his precious studies.

The procedures revealed themselves that first day. Soldiers ushered them out of the pen single file to pee under a nearby tree. They shit in a little channel dug under one of the sides of the pen and when finished pushed the excrement out with a wooden paddle. Three times a day, soldiers delivered meals of bread, cheese, and eggs in an old wooden box.

The exhaustion that set in over the next days was crippling, and the monotony deadening. But miraculously, Khalil went into a rescue mode that he didn't know his brain possessed. It began one morning when he felt like a mental fever had broken, rendering him clearheaded: *I did nothing wrong! I didn't have my ID because the damn soldiers took it from me! That's it! And now I'm being kept in a pen like an animal? This is crazy. No human deserves to be treated this way, especially an innocent one.*

This was injustice, he realized, the very condition his mother had exhorted him to decry.

Khalil also found some peace by looping memories of his interactions with the two key women in his life: his mother and his "girlfriend," Hanan, a girl at school that he had a big crush on. He replayed as many of his mother's lessons as he could recall, always smiling when the loop landed on the sandwich episode. And then he would think about Hanan.

Walking to class on the first day of school the previous year, Khalil froze when he saw a certain girl across the way. *She is SO beautiful*, he thought. *I love her*. Such a thing—this love at first sight—was something he'd never felt before, and he just had to see her again.

From that day on, Khalil walked the same path every day to catch a glimpse of her. He saw her several times. Then one day his heart leaped. He saw her again, and she snuck a peek back at him. And then the following week, the unimaginable happened. Hanan had wrapped a note inside a tissue, tossed it off to the side of the path, peeked at Khalil, and then pointed at the note. Khalil's heart exploded! *What*? *She wrote something to me*? he thought. *What did she write*? *Did she say she loves me like I love her*?

Khalil waited an agonizing ten minutes for the mass of kids to clear out, and then he rushed to retrieve the note. Fingers afire, he tore open the folded paper. In lovely script, she'd penned: *I love you. It makes me so happy to see you every day.*

Oh, my God! he thought. *Is this really happening*? He was delirious with joy.

The lead soldier interrupted Khalil's reverie: "Get ready! We're taking you all to Ansar II,"[53] he bellowed, referring to the same prison that Hammam's father was in earlier. Was this Day 4? Day 5? Khalil had lost track.

---

[53] Ansar II was originally an army base outside Gaza City that the Israeli military converted into a prison. Hammam's father, Fuad, was imprisoned there for five years. Palestinians gave it the nickname "Ansar II," in reference to the infamous prisoner of war camp that Israel erected near the village of Ansar in southern Lebanon after Israel's invasion of

"Fuck . . . Ansar II?" murmured many of the boys through clenched teeth, having often heard brutal stories about this prison in Gaza City. Soldiers cinched on the vile plastic shackles and marched the exhausted group onto a bus.

The ride from Khan Younis to Gaza City should take thirty minutes, max. But the driver took his sweet time, allowing his fellow soldiers to have some fun. "Fuck the PLO! Fuck Abu Ammar (Yasser Arafat)!" they chanted.[54] Their command that the boys join in the chant disgusted Khalil, and he nearly vomited when the soldiers jammed a rifle butt into a boy's forehead to illustrate the consequences of noncompliance.

In those days Ansar II was a collection of canvas tents clustered in a large, walled-off area not too far from the beach. It was cold enough already, but the winds from the sea made it even colder. The soldiers yanked Khalil and the others off the bus. When he caught a glimpse of some young boys who each had a plaster cast on a forearm, the sight produced another spasm of fear-induced nausea in him. He stuck close to Muslih.

A soldier blindfolded them, and they stood outside for the entire night and the next day. Eventually, his legs ached so severely that Khalil needed to shift positions. But the moment he started to squat, a wooden club smashed his right leg: "Stand up straight and don't move again!" barked the soldier.

Frozen and psychologically drained, he and Muslih had little to say to each other anymore. But both of them acknowledged with dread that here, finally, the interrogation would occur.

Lebanon in 1982. See Anita Vitullo Khoury, "Uprising in Gaza," Middle East Report 152 (May/June 1988), https://merip.org/1988/05/uprising-in-gaza/.

[54] The Palestine Liberation Organization (PLO) is an umbrella organization for various Palestinian political groups. It was formed in Egypt in 1964 with the goal of establishing self-determination for Palestine. Yasser Arafat (Abu Ammar) had founded the political and military organization Fatah in 1959 and was appointed chair of the PLO in 1969. He would go on to be elected president of the Palestine National Authority (PNA, or PA) in 1996. The PA was organized as part of the Oslo Declaration of Principles that brought an end to the first *intifada* in 1993. See *Encyclopedia Britannica Online*, s.v. "Yasser Arafat," accessed December 14, 2024, https://www.britannica.com/biography/Yasser-Arafat. Israel accepted the PLO as the representative of the Palestinians, the PLO renounced terrorism and recognized Israel's right to exist in peace, and both agreed that the PA would be established and assume governing responsibilities in the West Bank and Gaza Strip over a five-year period." See "The Oslo Accords and the Arab-Israeli Peace Process," US Department of State, Office of the Historian, website, https://history.state.gov/milestones/1993-2000/oslo.

Over the course of that night and the next day, they heard soldiers come and pull one after another of their group away. At some point Khalil started convulsing in fear from the shrieking he heard. *Whatever they're doing in there, can I stay strong and refuse to give a false confession just to stop the pain? Will I see my family and Hanan soon? Will I still be able to continue my studies*? He forced himself to remember that he wouldn't be able to experience any of those things if he caved in to the interrogator's demands.

Feeling dazed as the sun went down that second day, Khalil realized how quiet it had become, as if he and Muslih were there alone now. His mind tried to puzzle it out: *What had happened to the others after their interrogations? Did they go to court? To a different prison? To the hospital? Had they been freed?*

Sometime later, two silent soldiers came and dragged them both into the administration building. *Are they going to interrogate us together*? Every one of his muscles tightened.

Once they were inside the building, the soldiers yanked their blindfolds off. Blinking, Khalil could eventually make out the contours of the room. It didn't look like any torture chamber he'd ever imagined. The image cleared, and he saw that they were in an office, standing in front of a large desk. The chief intelligence officer was leaning back in his chair, staring at them.

"Why are you two here?" he asked. "There are no charges against you. Give me your ID cards."

Khalil was dumbstruck. Seriously? he thought. Did he really just say that? What kind of cruel injustice is this?

Muslih mumbled the story: "We have no IDs because soldiers confiscated them, and then they arrested us for not having them."

"That's it?" said the commander. He took down their names, birthdates, and residences. Then, with a flick of his wrist, he said, "Leave."

Just like that.

Young soldiers snipped off their plastic cuffs, brought them their clothes, and pushed them out the door. Khalil and Muslih just stood there outside the prison, too exhausted and incensed to be happy.

Khalil had spent most of his life in the southern part of Gaza and wasn't familiar with transportation back to Khan Younis. Fortunately, Muslih was. Standing on the street, he extended his finger downward and to the right, signaling that they wanted to go south. Eventually, a dilapidated, orange seven-seater Mercedes slid to a stop in front of them. The front passenger window was open; Muslih leaned in and said, "Khan Younis." Without a word, the driver gestured them in and accelerated as soon as they'd entered and taken the last two remaining seats in the back of the vehicle. Muslih whispered to the person next to him that they'd just gotten out of detention and had no money. "No problem," the fellow passenger said.

He reached into his pocket, took out a ten-shekel coin, and tapped the shoulder of the passenger in front of him, who immediately extended his open hand back to receive the payment. "For two," whispered Muslih. That passenger in turn tapped the shoulder of the driver. "For two," he whispered. The driver reached his hand back, took and glanced at the coin, tossed it on the dashboard, fished around the spread of coins there, found a five-shekel coin, and reached his hand back. The passenger behind him took the coin and passed it back to Muslih. All of this happened in twenty seconds.

Meanwhile, Khalil had fallen asleep, his head against the sooty window. As the car slid to a stop outside Khan Younis, Muslih woke him, and the two hopped out, the car speeding ahead as their feet landed on the sandy road.

Although Khalil and Muslih had been freed from the bizarre detention, they weren't really free. They still didn't have their IDs and had to navigate the seven hundred meters or so of the camp to reach their homes. Being caught again without the precious cards could mean prison. After taking some deep breaths, they made a feverish sprint through the large camp. When they reached the intersection where their paths home diverged, they gave each other just a quick, wordless hug.

Khalil saw a light through the tall window of his house. He thought he recognized his mother's silhouette and tapped on the thick iron door. The rusty bolt slammed open to reveal Tamam, with Khalil's father and siblings behind her, rushing toward the door. They couldn't have known he would come home that night, but his mom had kept vigil every night.

Khalil fell into a wordless embrace with his mother that squeezed out bottomless sobs from both of them. "Why don't you have a coat on, Mama?" Khalil finally asked. "It's freezing."

"I couldn't allow myself to be warm knowing that you were cold," she replied. He then hugged his dad and each of his siblings. The air was dense. Everyone knew this wasn't the time for talk. His mother hurried to prepare some food as everyone else stood, heads bowed, eyes red with tears.

In the seconds it took Khalil to fall asleep on his mat, he thought about how much he hoped he'd be able to see Hanan soon. She hadn't graduated yet, and so the next morning he went to the spot where he might see her walking to school. And there she was. They waved, their eyes sparkling at each other. Like everyone in the camp, Hanan knew soldiers had apprehended Khalil. But she could not have appreciated that she was now looking, not at a recent high school graduate, but at a man transformed by a ludicrous ordeal.

Detention had changed Khalil. It had taught him firsthand how serious was the need to be free from domination. Even more fundamental to his developing character, he had come to know a new dimension of the injustice that his mother had taught him to decry.

That evening Khalil asked his father and brothers to teach him about the various Palestinian political factions. He decided that he would choose a group to join. He was now an activist. "The soldiers made me one," he told them.

After getting four photos taken the next day at his brother Khaled's photography shop, Khalil went to the Israeli civil affairs building outside the camp and applied for a new ID. They gave him a temporary one, and he picked up his official ID a week later.

Chocolate

(1990, age twenty)

For nearly two years after his detention, Khalil devoted himself to applying to universities outside Gaza, just as he and his father had planned. Khalil applied to universities in Libya, Yemen, Egypt, Jordan, and the West Bank. Although he received several acceptances, the IDF rejected his applications to leave Gaza to attend any of those schools—unless he agreed to be a collaborator by spying for them in Gaza. They used all sorts of blackmail to pressure him during these years.

At the same time that he was applying to study abroad, Khalil also tried to find work so that he could help his struggling family. He was fortunate to find a job among the roughly one hundred thousand Gazans who were permitted to do daily work in Israel at that time. Workers would get up at four in the morning, make their way by group taxi to the Erez crossing, undergo lengthy security checks by the Israeli military, take an IDF bus to various parts of southern Israel, and then be bussed back to Erez in the early evening. Most of these Gazans did construction or agricultural work, but Khalil's job was at a chocolate factory.

That five-month period was important for Khalil. It was the first time he'd earned money, and he was proud to finally be able to help his family in a significant way, earning triple his father's salary. It was also the first time in all his twenty years that he had stepped a foot outside of the Strip. Delighted to escape the smothering entrapment of Gaza, he felt an inkling of what freedom might be like.

It was also the first time Khalil had ever interacted with anyone who was not either a Gazan or an Israeli soldier. He thoroughly enjoyed talking with his coworkers during breaks; they all were friendly. He grew particularly close to Eliyahu, an Ethiopian Jew about the same age as Khalil who served in the military in addition to working at the chocolate factory. "I grew to love him," Khalil recalled.

He actually saw Eliyahu once in Gaza. While walking one day near one of the many checkpoints the military had set up throughout Gaza, Khalil spotted his friend. Khalil waved excitedly, but Eliyahu didn't see him. "What do you want?" asked the squad leader sternly.

"I just want to say hello to my friend," replied Khalil.

"Your friend?" asked the leader incredulously.

"Yes," replied Khalil with excitement. "We work in the same factory."

Khalil knew that what he was doing was extremely risky: He might be labeled a collaborator, and he knew from prison how collaborators were treated. But he wanted to greet his friend. The squad leader, realizing how rare this moment was, acceded to Khalil's request and let Khalil approach.

For his part, Eliyahu was also acutely aware that this uncommon moment was risky—that he too might suffer scorn from his comrades. But he too wanted to greet his friend. Cautiously, he extended his arm and shook Khalil's hand. Perhaps to save face in front of the other soldiers, Eliyahu said to Khalil loudly, "Please tell your friends not to throw stones. I want end my shift here and get back to the factory."

The Academy of the Palestinians

(1990, age twenty)

Deciding to become an activist did not mean that Khalil would join the front lines of the stone throwers. He preferred to mostly work behind the scenes, planning and organizing demonstrations. Yet on May 20, 1990, one of the few times Khalil ventured out to demonstrate publicly, Israeli soldiers grabbed him for throwing stones. With an existing record of detention for the confiscated ID, Khalil was immediately sentenced to three months in prison.

He was sent to the new Ktzi'ot Prison deep in the Negev desert, some two hours from Gaza. Constructed to handle prisoners from the *intifada*, it would soon become the largest Israeli detention facility. Palestinians referred to it as Ansar III. Each section of the prison contained two or more tents and was surrounded by ridges of sand and gravel blocking visibility between sections. Each tent was approximately 50 square meters and held twenty to thirty prisoners.

Prisoners from the West Bank and Gaza were bused to Ansar III. Khalil was a bit nervous, not because he feared mistreatment in prison—he had demonstrated that he could handle extreme treatment during his detention—but because he was unfamiliar with how Ansar III worked. When he got off the bus after a scorching journey through the desert, he was thus delighted to be greeted by a group of prisoners welcoming this new busload.

They gave a brief overview of the prison and then asked each newcomer which political faction he belonged to or wished to join. A representative from Khalil's faction took him to their tent, where a warm welcome awaited him. "What's your name?" "Where are you from? "How are things with you?" and "How was the journey?" were common opening questions from the throng of prisoners. The tent leaders had brought biscuits and coffee from the central kitchen. They sat together for an hour singing patriotic songs, and then the leaders gave Khalil a quick orientation about the physical layout and social structure of the prison, such as the locations of the other factions' tents, the status of any ongoing conflicts between groups, and the best ways to interact with other groups. Khalil felt welcome and happy, comforted by the presence of the older prisoners, thinking that they would take care of him if there was any problem. The fact that revered leaders of his faction celebrated him personally made him feel important.

The daily schedule was highly regulated. Prisoners were awakened at 6:00 a.m. by an announcement from the prison loudspeaker. They washed their hands and faces and then had one hour to read from the few available books. At 7:00 a.m. a breakfast of *fuul* (cooked fava beans), coffee, and tea was brought to the tents by members of the food committee—prisoners who cooked and delivered meals.

After breakfast the prison guards conducted the first of three daily roll calls. Guards ordered all the prisoners to exit their tents to be counted in the open space. After the morning roll call, a doctor visited the prisoners to see who needed medications for headaches or other simple ailments.

Then lessons would begin, taught by senior prisoners, many of whom were professors, doctors, or lawyers. They conducted three levels of lessons, depending on how much a prisoner knew about his political faction. After the lessons were over, prisoners had some free time to sit and casually talk with one another. A few years later, each tent at Ansar III would have a radio and a TV, but during this first year of the prison's operation, there were none.

Lunch, always consisting only of vegetable soup and rice, was at 1:00 p.m. Like breakfast, it was served in the tent because of the day's searing heat. Afterward, there was time for napping or socializing. The second set of lessons began around 4:00 p.m. and lasted until around 8:00 p.m. Dinner, served outside in a common space, was always a replica of breakfast but with the addition of falafel sometimes. The weather was typically warm and breezy at night.

Generally, the food was quite poor, "not suitable for anyone to eat," Khalil recalled years later. Each prisoner received only three ounces of meat per week.

The third set of lessons, mostly discussion about the day's learning, began after dinner and lasted until the third roll call at 11:00 p.m. After roll call, prisoners were allowed to walk around their section of the prison and chat. At midnight the loudspeaker announced: "Good night. Return to your tents and sleep."

Early during his time at Ansar III, Khalil wrote a brief letter to his parents that was delivered to them by a prisoner from Khan Younis who had just been released. Khalil urgently needed to let them know where he had been sent. Detainees were taken away after their trial, and their parents weren't informed where.

> My dear Father and Mother,
>
> I want to inform you that I am in the Negev at Ansar III. I was sentenced to three months of administrative detention. Please don't worry about me. It is my duty to struggle for our homeland. I am okay. I am not being tortured. Please send me some underwear.

A prisoner's family was allowed to send clothes such as underwear and blue and white sweatsuits, which were delivered by one of the attorneys who regularly visited the prison camp.

"Khalil, please come here," beckoned the leader of his faction, who was in charge of the faction within the prison and was also its spokesperson for all outside communications, such as press interviews. Khalil, just two weeks into his sentence, went to the corner of the tent and sat before the leader. "It is my time to return to Gaza. Our steering committee has selected you to replace me."

"This is a very great honor, sir. But I am very young," replied Khalil.

"Yes, you are young," the leader replied, "but we've noticed that you're serious and dedicated and that you talk quietly and easily with the others. Have no fear, we will prepare you for your duties." Khalil's leadership skills would in fact be tested just two weeks later.

Sometimes leaders of the various factions would determine that a prisoner needed to be punished. Usually this was because they had discovered that the prisoner had been a collaborator for the Israeli military, either before going into detention or while in the prison itself. The protocol was to close up the tent and beat the accused.

One morning while milling about the outdoor common space during a break, Khalil saw Hassan, an older prisoner, closing the flaps of their tent. Inside the still partially open tent, Hatim, a young man around Khalil's age and somewhat of a troublemaker, was crying and screaming repeatedly, "I am not a collaborator!"

Before his imprisonment, Israeli soldiers had fired live rounds in Hatim's legs during a demonstration that turned violent. The resulting surgeries left his legs uneven in length, and he had a noticeable limp. Also, he was socially maladjusted, doing and saying things that irritated the other prisoners. But Khalil's instincts told him that Hatim was not a collaborator.

Rushing to the tent, Khalil ordered Hassan to stop lowering the flaps of the tent. Hassan shot back, "He's a collaborator! He deserves to be punished!"

"What is your evidence of this?" asked Khalil, but Hassan met this challenge with silence. "He is just an injured, troubled boy, Hassan," continued Khalil. "We should be caring for him. And let's not let the prisoners from other factions see us behaving as if we're in a jungle." For Khalil, this was a clear instance of the injustice his mother had been teaching him to fight his whole life.

Hassan and those who supported him refused to follow Khalil's order. Khalil went to stand directly in front of Hassan, towering over him, and in his deep voice said firmly but calmly, "Hassan, you know that I am in charge now. You must raise the flaps immediately." After Hassan stood still for a few moments, this reminder of Khalil's authority convinced him to comply.

Khalil went over to Hatim, took him out of the tent, and tried to comfort him.

When Khalil was released from prison at the end of his three-month sentence, he returned to Gaza a stronger person. During his eighteen-day detention two years earlier, he had discovered his inner fortitude in surviving painful and degrading circumstances. At Ansar III Khalil developed leadership skills and learned a tremendous amount about history, political theory, and activism. This intellectual and political growth in prison was so common that soon, when young men were arrested, they would say to their captors, "Good, please take me to the Academy of the Palestinians."

Cairo

(1996, age twenty-six)

The semester had already started at the Islamic University of Gaza while Khalil was in prison at Ansar III. Because he didn't want to miss the semester, he had asked his oldest brother, Khaled, to apply for him. Fortunately, there were only a few students applying for English literature that semester, so the university agreed to accept Khalil without an interview. As soon as he was released from prison, Khalil began his studies. The Israeli military had recently closed both the Islamic University and Gaza's other main university, Al-Azhar University, as well as its several colleges, so lessons were held at various mosques and in professors' homes.

Khalil loved and excelled at his studies over the years. He also quickly became the leader of his faction at the university—and eventually, at all Gaza's universities and colleges. He had emerged from prison confident in his ability to lead and unwavering in his commitment to challenging injustice.

If the naïveté Khalil had always felt had been transformed through his *intifada* experiences—his initial detention and subsequent imprisonment—his years as a student political leader while earning his bachelor's degree in English literature catapulted him into a self-assured young man of twenty-six. Among many activities, Khalil was responsible for coordinating with the administrations of all the other universities and colleges in Gaza, representing his faction at all official political meetings, and speaking with the media. At last, the authority everyone attributed to him might be warranted. Yet he was still inexperienced in many ways.

During his senior year at the university, Khalil was selected to receive a scholarship to attend a conference in Germany. The faxed invitation instructed him that he would need a visa to enter Germany. Except for his stint working at the chocolate factory in southern Israel just outside Gaza, Khalil had never been outside the Strip, and he was excited. Some people advised him that it would be best to get the visa from the German embassy in Cairo. He had a cousin there, and his parents had made the long journey a number of times. But that was the extent of his familiarity with traveling outside Gaza. Khalil made the journey alone, armed only with his cousin's telephone number and address. He would call once he got there.

His brothers escorted him in a taxi to the Rafah terminal and wished him well. The first stage of the process was to submit his passport to the Palestinian Authority (PA) officials. Since the PA had become the official governing body of Palestine in 1994, all Palestinians were issued a PA passport. No visa was required to enter Egypt. He knew that Israeli officials were monitoring everything by camera. Presumably, the PA officials shared passport information with the Israelis, who could order them not to allow Khalil to exit. Fortunately, the Israelis did not intervene. His papers were stamped, and then he and other people trying to enter Egypt were ushered to a small bus that drove them the one hundred meters to the Egyptian side of the crossing. They waited an hour or so before being let into the terminal. There Khalil submitted his papers as before—documents recording his name, age, address, ID number, and the organization requesting permission for him to cross.

Again, they waited for hours, all the while wondering if they would be allowed to complete the crossing or be sent back to Gaza. After three or four hours, his group of hopeful passengers were called up to the dingy window, their papers were stamped, and they were escorted to a bus waiting to drive them the eight hours to Cairo across the Sinai Desert and over the Suez Canal. It was a brutally hot day.

Although he was tired from the long entry process, Khalil forced himself to keep his eyes open as the bus started its journey through the Sinai Desert. The expanse gave him his first view of the world outside Gaza, making him aware of just how small his land really was. During the journey the bus stopped at five checkpoints, where Egyptian soldiers entered the bus and checked everyone's documents.

When the bus finally reached Cairo, Khalil found a pay phone and called his cousin to announce his arrival and receive instructions on how to get to his apartment. It was in downtown Cairo and turned out to be walkable from where Khalil was calling, but finding his way there was easier said than done.

Growing up in the crowded Khan Younis camp hadn't prepared Khalil for the overwhelming frenzy of Cairo. He was an expert in navigating his refugee camp, then housing forty-three thousand people. But Cairo had more than a hundred times as many people. His first challenge was to cross the boulevards. These thoroughfares were wider than four camp blocks, with more cars careening along them than Khalil had imagined existed in the entire world. He waited a full thirty minutes before he saw a gap in traffic that he figured was large enough for him to risk sprinting across the boulevard with his long legs. Later his cousin scoffed at his naiveté: "You did what? Are you kidding me?! The cars will never stop unless you start crossing!"

The next day his cousin told Khalil how to get to the German embassy, where he took his place in a line of hundreds waiting to get their visas. Impatient after hours of waiting in the hot sun, Khalil flagged an official passing by and asked about the process. "You're from Gaza?" said the official in surprise, "Sorry, we only give visas to Egyptians. You'll have no luck here. Go home."

Oh well, thought Khalil fatalistically, at least it was nice to get out of Gaza for a while.

Sahar

(1996, age twenty-six)

"For our interview today, can we please meet at the YWCA?" Khalil asked me. "I'm doing a training there, and we can find a space to talk." There was nothing unusual about his request; we had held our interviews in various places: at coffee shops, while walking, in the salon of his home, and so on. But it turned out that Khalil's choice for the location of today's meeting was strategic.

"Brian, please, can I talk to you about something personal?" asked Khalil midway during our interview, sounding unusually shy.

"Of course," I responded. "What is it?"

Ever since Khalil had talked about Hanan, his "girlfriend" in high school, he hadn't spoken much about women during our interviews. But now he was ready. He explained that recently a friend and fellow student at the university had told him about a young woman named Sahar (SAH-har). Back in those days, she was one of the few women who wanted to work professionally in human rights. Saleh, Khalil's friend, described her as extremely dedicated and urged Khalil to allow her to join the student group that Khalil led. Intrigued, Khalil asked Saleh to arrange a meeting between him and Sahar at the YWCA, where she was working at the time.

The meeting—actually the interview—went well. They talked for an entire hour about human rights problems in Gaza perpetrated by Israel and the PA—and more specifically about Sahar's knowledge of their political faction and her interest in representing women students as a member of Khalil's student group. Khalil found Sahar to be confident and professional, and she was certainly courageous for breaking the traditional female role of staying in the background. Shortly after their meeting, Khalil invited her to join the student group to represent young women.

The more time Khalil spent with Sahar, the more he fell for her. "Would you talk to her for me to find out what she feels about me?" he asked me. Khalil had both a professional and personal concern. If his assistants in the student group saw him talking privately with Sahar, they might criticize him for having let her join the group without going through the normal process. And for all he knew, she loved someone else, and hearing that directly from her would hurt Khalil. He'd rather hear it from me and then try to move on.

When I talked to Sahar, I began by explaining my research and my association with Khalil. I had never played matchmaker before, and eventually I decided to just lay it out straight. "Actually, Sahar, Khalil wanted me to tell you that he cares a lot about you. He can't tell whether you feel the same way about him. Would you be open to talking with him about personal matters?" She beamed in response, and I could tell that she also cared for him. She gave me permission to relay her feelings.

When I told Khalil later that afternoon, he broke into a smile. "Really?" he asked. "She loves me like I love her?"

"It seems so."

They started spending a lot of time together—walking, sitting and talking, going to coffee shops and restaurants. Falling in love quickly, they soon discussed their engagement. However, Khalil wouldn't graduate for another two months and had no money to speak of and no job; he was still dependent on his parents. But both young people were equally eager to move as fast as possible toward marriage.

Khalil called a family meeting and told everyone about Sahar and how much they wanted to get married. Speaking directly to his parents, he said, "I really love this girl and want us to become engaged as soon as possible. I know that neither you nor I have any money. But I've already confessed my love to her. I would feel like a coward if we couldn't proceed. She's told me that she had received other engagement requests."

"Let's talk to Khaled," said Khalil's father, Mohammed. Khalil's oldest brother wasn't at the family meeting because he was at a wedding in town. Khalil went to find Khaled, and after the ceremony, they walked home together. Khalil told his brother all about Sahar and how much they both wanted to become engaged as soon as possible.

"Please, could you possibly help us, brother?" Khalil asked eagerly. Khaled didn't need to think about it. He, like the rest of the family—especially Tamam, their mother—was thrilled that Khalil had finally found someone he loved. "Of course I will, Khalil! That's what we do in this family. We help each other."

The next day Khalil and his father went to see Sahar's parents to formally propose the engagement. Her parents accepted readily, and together they began discussions about the engagement ceremony. A week later Khalil's mother went with one of her daughters and continued planning the ceremony with Sahar's mother.

Dream Job

(1998–2014, age twenty-seven, and on to forty-four)

Two months into his engagement to Sahar, Khalil was invited to apply to be director of Al-Dameer, one of Gaza's human rights organizations. He had never had a professional job before, and he badly needed one. Sahar had been paying as much as she could from her salary to buy furniture; Khaled was helping with the wedding expenses. Khalil knew that it was time to get his career started, and this was a dream opportunity. He also knew that he was quite young for such a high-level position, but he had already learned repeatedly in his life that his youth was no barrier to being appointed to responsible positions, from his various duties at the mosque as a boy to his leadership role in prison.

Khalil had one nonnegotiable condition: that he be allowed to develop the organization completely independent of any political influences. Over the last nine years, Khalil had already learned plenty about the failures of political leadership—shortcomings he had witnessed during his detention, imprisonment, activism, and current work as a student leader. He made it clear that he was interested in defending the human rights of everyone, that he would harbor no favoritism, and that he would "speak truth to power," no matter who those powers were. The committee liked this clear-eyed stance and hired Khalil in March 1998.

Khalil and Sahar got married on July 9, 1998. Neither family could afford to pay for the typical extravagant wedding, but it was beautiful nonetheless, full of excitement and harmony. In October 1999 their daughter Nour was born, followed by their son, Mohammed, in November 2000, and finally their daughter Nesma in November 2002.

Once he was hired, Khalil immediately dove into his new job, often working twelve to fifteen hours a day to revitalize and reshape the organization. His two immediate priorities as the new director were (1) to raise funds for the ailing organization, which at the time had a budget of only $10,000 and (2) to work with other human rights organizations to develop a clear, motivating mission statement centered around defending the civil and political rights of all people. To achieve these goals, Khalil had to learn how to create a budget, hire a staff, and cultivate donors. Although these business tasks were time consuming, he found them fairly easy and succeeded at all of them.

In the close-knit society of Gaza and the even tighter sphere of human rights efforts in Gaza, people started noticing his activities, and Khalil took great pleasure in the fact that he was increasingly seen as an important leader in the Strip. He was constantly organizing, giving press conferences and media interviews, organizing youth training sessions, and repairing relationships and fostering new ones with local and international NGOs, among many other tasks. Eventually, Khalil was elected leader of the umbrella organization overseeing all human right activities in Gaza. The previously naïve traveler transformed into a seasoned visitor to numerous world capitals to represent Gaza's human rights community. Unlike when he was forbidden to leave Gaza to study, Khalil now had status as a human rights leader, and Israel didn't want to make trouble with human rights organizations.

Describing his work over the eighteen years that he held this position, Khalil said: "It became a part of my body, my blood, and relationships with people." Naturally, much of his work was documenting and publicizing the continuous human rights abuses of the Israeli military's occupation, between and during the successive bombardments of the Strip. A letter Khalil wrote to UN Secretary General Kofi Anan indicates how bad conditions had already become by 2006, with the blockade imposed on Gaza after Hamas's election victory in the Palestinian Legislative Council and subsequent power struggle with the PA. Khalil knew that he would likely receive no response, but his duty was to expose these issues.

> The Honorable Kofi Anan
> Secretary-General of the United Nations
>
> Dear Mr. Anan:
>
> We would like to inform you about the situation in the Occupied Palestinian Territories, particularly in the Gaza Strip. The situation is very difficult because of the continuous Israeli violations of Palestinian civilians. Since June 24, 2006, the Israeli Defense Force has imposed a siege around the Gaza Strip, such that none of the citizens can leave, either to Egypt through the Rafah Terminal or to Israel and the West Bank through the Erez Crossing.
>
> The military operations of the Israeli Defense Force during this period can be considered war crimes according to international

law, particularly the destruction of the main power plant that supplies the majority of the Gaza Strip. This has left a population of 750,000 civilians with only four hours of electricity per day. This has caused panic among the citizens, and it has severely disrupted normal, daily life. The hospitals have many cases that cannot be treated without electricity. Some patients, like those with cardiac problems and some of the disabled, need a continuous supply of electricity to operate their oxygen and life support equipment.

Israeli jets destroyed both of the bridges that connect the northern and southern parts of the Gaza Strip. This has made it very difficult for citizens to reach their places of work and for patients to reach the hospitals. The Israeli planes also strafed the football field of the Islamic University where 13,000 students were in attendance.

Day and night Israeli fighter jets intentionally create sonic bombs that shatter windows and cause great fear among the citizens. Especially among the children, there are many cases of psychological disturbance. It is not possible to tally all of these cases; there are so many. Our children even ask us what the international community is doing in response to these war crimes that Israel is committing against them and their people.

What is the use of having international law and the Fourth Geneva Convention if they cannot protect the women, the children, the elderly, the sick, or the natural surroundings and infrastructure within the Palestinian Territories?

We are petitioning you, sir, to raise your voice in defense of international law to put a stop to the crimes being committed against the Palestinian Territories and their people by the Israeli Defense Force.

We in the Palestinian Human Rights Organizations responded within minutes of the kidnapping of the Israeli soldier in Gaza and we demanded that the kidnappers respect international law

> and the human rights of the soldier.[55] We also argued for the necessity of cooperating with all the international efforts to put an end to this crisis and to return the soldier safely to his government.
>
> We petition you, sir, to intervene immediately in order to prevent a human disaster among the Palestinian civilians, all of whom will pay its heavy price.
>
> Sincerely yours,
>
> Khalil Abu Shammala
> Executive Manager

Later that same year, on a human rights website, Khalil published a more personal comment on the dire situation:

> Nesma, my three-year-old daughter, feels a lot of fear when she hears planes flying in the skies of Gaza. Whenever she hears the sound of the planes, her body shakes and she starts crying because she has become used to hearing a sonic bomb after the noise of the planes. Nowadays, the Gaza Strip is facing a real act of war, where the Israeli forces are using psychological torture against the Palestinian civilians by using sonic bombs.
>
> We, the older people, are suffering psychologically as we are not afraid for ourselves but we don't know how to calm down our children, or how to explain these sonic bombs to them. "Are they fireworks or a balloon blast?" they ask.
>
> We can no longer hide the truth from them because they figured it out themselves when the four-month-old baby Iman Hijo was killed, when the Ghalia family was killed on the beach of Beit Lahiya and when six-year-old Muhammed Jamal Rouqah was killed by an Israeli strike while he was going to tell his friends that his father came back from Dubai and bought him toys and gifts.

---

[55] For more on this Israeli soldier, Gilad Shalit, see "Hammam: The Social Man," page 53. See also Tareq Baconi, *Hamas Contained: The Rise and Pacification of Palestinian Resistance*, Stanford Studies in Middle Eastern and Islamic Societies and Cultures (Stanford, CA: Stanford University Press, 2018), 116.

Nesma, my three-year-old child, spoke some words I didn't want to hear as a father, never wanting my children to face such a situation. She now speaks of "shelling, airplane, tank, missile, firing, resistance and occupation."

I would have liked for Nesma, her brother Mohammed and her sister Nour to live a quiet life, enjoying their time like all other children around the world and to live all their life stages sure of a better, wonderful, active future. I would have liked them to achieve all their dreams without any fear of a glimpse that could steal the life of any one of them while they are on the street, or riding in a car, or even while walking on the beach.

All the children of Gaza live in fear during the day. Even in this very hot summer the children of Gaza cannot go to summer camps to spend their summer days because the parents are afraid for their children due to the shelling.

Gaza children are enquiring, "What self-defense is Israel speaking about while they are using this massive military machinery against them? What self-defense causes the destruction of important vital structures that then prevents the patients from having their right to proper medical care with no obstructions and cuts the electricity power from a population of 750,000 citizens in the Gaza Strip?"

The children are enquiring about the position of the international community that doesn't raise any voice to protect them. They are astonished by this silence that gives Israel the green light to commit more crimes.

The children of Gaza are not sure now that international law and international conventions are capable of protecting them.

Will Nesma, the three-year-old child, suffer? Who will guarantee her to live without suffering psychologically through her lifetime?

> What will the Israelis say to Nesma? What will the international community say to Nesma while she is living in nervous shock for the rest of her life?[56]

But Khalil also decried the abuses of two different Palestinian governments. Before Hamas was elected in 2006, when the Palestinian Authority was still in charge, the PA arrested Khalil three times for his publicly criticizing its growing corruption. For example, he was one of twenty to thirty signatories on a press release that criticized the PA for having physically beaten one of its legislative council members in the West Bank. After Khalil had spent one day in jail, several prominent community leaders appealed to Arafat and secured Khalil's release. Arafat knew and respected his family and assured Khalil that his punishments would not be severe, asking him simply to watch what he said.

After the election of the new Hamas government, Khalil wasted no time in criticizing them as well. Already in 2006, he wrote a letter to the editor of a Palestinian newspaper that said, in part:

> It's not acceptable for us to suffer the ambiguities between party decisions and government officials' points of view. It's not reasonable to read on the front page of a newspaper a statement from one of the government representatives, only to find a contradiction on the third page of the same newspaper by another representative of the government.[57]

In 2012 the attorney general of Hamas summoned Khalil for interrogation, accusing him of inciting public opinion, creating sedition among the citizens, and threatening the security of the energy authority. Hamas claimed that Khalil had said that the Hamas-run energy authority was responsible for the energy crisis in Gaza. For unknown reasons, Hamas didn't follow through on the arrest.

Khalil was fearless about criticizing abuse and corruption on all sides. In 2014 he was openly critical of PA president Mahmoud Abbas, citing multiple domestic and international failures in making life better for Palestinians. And

---

[56] Khalil Abu Shammala, "Director of Al-Dameer Association for Human Rights," Arab Commission for Human Rights website, https://achr-lb.com/newen77.htm.

[57] Khalil Abu Shammala, "Flashes," *Al-Watan Voice*, June 3, 2006, https://pulpit.alwatanvoice.com/articles/2006/06/03/46601.html.

the following year, Khalil came to the defense of a high-ranking Hamas leader with a large international portfolio who had been accused by his fellow Hamas leaders of being a collaborator with Israel. This accusation deeply upset Khalil, not only because the man was a friend from back in their university days, but more so because Khalil saw no effort on Hamas's part to follow due process. They just made scandalous accusations with no evidence. And no one else was supporting the accused man or taking any interest in how his wife and family were doing.

Khalil made the dangerous decision to air this matter in public by writing a letter in the man's defense and publishing it as widely as possible in local newspapers and on websites. When challenged shortly afterward by another Hamas leader as to why he wrote the letter, Khalil responded by email:

> This is the loyalty of the friendship . . . and . . . I feel that you have jumped past all the legal procedures; you should decide whether you are an authority or a military group. If you claim that you are a government, then you have police, procedures, courts and you treat him as any ordinary person.

Hamas would have more to say to Khalil.

Tamam

(2010, age forty)

The others didn't seem to notice it, but Khalil certainly did. And the observation made his gut tense up. He knew at some level, still vague, that a catastrophe was coming his way like a slowly developing tsunami. As it turned out, it would be the most painful period of his life.

Her words were slightly slurred.

"What is it, Mother? Is there something wrong?"

"Don't worry, my son. It is nothing. Your father is a professional nurse. We think maybe I have an infection in my throat, or some such thing. *Khalas*, everything is okay. Don't worry."

Khalil's gut said otherwise.

His mother's given name is Tamam, meaning "fine" in English. And she had fulfilled her name in every sense by making Khalil feel fine—loved and understood—throughout his entire life. To that very day, when he needed comfort, he would lay his head in her lap and feel . . . fine . . . safe.

It had turned out to be a hectic day for Khalil. Now that Nour, Mohammed, and Nesma were out of school for summer vacation, he had asked his parents to join them for a week in his Gaza City apartment. He had driven down to Khan Younis to pick them up and then brought them back with him to the city. After dropping off his parents at the apartment, Khalil excused himself; he needed to monitor a developing crisis.

That day a Turkish-flagged ship, the *Mavi Marmara*—part of a larger aid flotilla of six ships—was motoring resolutely toward Gaza in defiance of the long-standing Israeli naval blockade of the Strip. Khalil needed to dispatch his staff to prepare for the possibility of an incident. As it turned out, the day ended catastrophically—with the death of nine Turkish activists at the hands of Israeli forces in international waters.[58]

When Khalil returned home that evening, he noticed the early signs of his mother's sickness. When he surreptitiously went to the wastebasket to

[58] In 2014 a tenth Turkish activist died from the injuries he sustained during that attack, after having been in a coma for more than four years. See "Turkish Man Dies of Wounds Sustained During Israel's Attack on Solidarity Ship," *IMEMC News*, May 24, 2014, https://imemc.org/article/67911/.

inspect the tissues she had coughed into, he knew that the tsunami was cresting—that everything was in fact *not* okay, *not* fine.

Khalil went into leader mode. He split himself into two individuals: the already mourning son and the pragmatic, take-charge caretaker. The next day, without telling anyone that he had seen dark blood on the tissues, Khalil took his mother to the Red Crescent Society clinic in Gaza City, where he knew they had a CT scanner.

Because of his high standing in the community, the doctors permitted him to view the images of his mother's chest as they began to appear on the monitor. Khalil saw out of the corner of his eye the two pathologists exchanging concerned looks. They seemed to be calculating how to break the news to him. "Don't try to hide anything from me," Khalil insisted. "I see them," he said, and with a trembling index finger he pointed emphatically to the illuminated masses on the monitor: "one . . . two . . . three . . . four."

Some instinct told Khalil that this wasn't the whole story. "I'm sure this isn't the main site of the cancer. Let us face the full problem head on." he told the doctors, asking them to also scan his mother's brain. The doctors complied soberly, and no words were necessary when the image revealed four further tumors. The doctors concluded that these tumors were the primary site of the cancer. They diagnosed it as stage 4, assessing that she had four months to live without any treatment. At that time, no cancer treatment was available in Gaza. She would need to go to Cairo, but the doctors warned that it was likely too late to make much of a difference.

The tsunami had hit. Khalil could not have found words to characterize the devastation he felt. She was essential to his life. And she was leaving.

Khalil kept control of his emotions until he could find some privacy back home. He went to his bedroom, slumped his long frame on the bed, let his face fall into his big hands, and burst into a fit of sobbing. He wept tears of rage that screamed at the injustice of life. Sure, death is part of life, but to lose someone so beautiful, so essential, so strong . . . nothing could assuage the rawness of that agony.

Khalil took his mother to Cairo to receive radiation therapy for the brain tumors, and they spent two weeks there. He finally decided to stop the treatment when the latest scan revealed no change in the size of the brain tumors and cancerous lesions covering almost her entire chest. This was the end. It would be better for her, easier for her, if they didn't prolong her pain. Khalil would bring her home to die in dignity. So they made their way back to Gaza in the sizzling desert heat that was no match for the fire searing Khalil's heart.

Tamam and her husband Mohammed spent much of the final weeks of her life at Khalil and Sahar's Gaza City apartment. She loved Sahar dearly, more so if possible than her own daughters. Like her unique bond with Khalil, her closeness with Sahar exceeded her love for her other daughters-in-law. She was also extremely close to Khalil and Sahar's children: Nour, Mohammed, and Nesma.

By now, of course, Tamam had guessed the seriousness of her condition.[59] She could tell from everyone's looks and tone. "Do you think that I'll ever return to the kitchen?" Tamam asked Khalil softly one night. She was lying on the sofa with her head resting in his lap, looking up into his eyes. *Such a question, it just tears your heart out*, he thought.

All he could offer was "Allah can do everything, dear Mother. Just trust in him."

Once her husband asked her, "Do you fear death, my darling?"

"No, no," she replied with a voice feebler than her unwavering strength of character. "I'm not afraid. I know that I will die, and that you will die as well. *Ahlan wa sahlan*. "Let death come as it will."

Such a strong woman, thought Khalil.

One week before her death, Tamam asked to go to their simple family home in the Khan Younis refugee camp. Khalil and his brothers, Jabbar and Khaled, and one of his sisters, Hiyam, arranged a plan. They didn't want her to sleep alone. Each would take turns sleeping in the second bed in the little bedroom. Their father was in an adjacent room, in near constant tears.

But when it was his turn, Khalil wouldn't take the second bed; he lay beside her.

"Do you know what, Khalil?" she asked one night.

"What is it, my Mother?"

"I always look forward to your turn. Your brothers are not as soft and kind as you."

One week later doctors advised Khalil to give Tamam the morphine they had provided. But he didn't . . . not yet. Then his mother's breathing became heavy. With the family around him, he laid her head gently in his lap.

"What would you like, dear Mother?"

---

[59] In many Asian and Middle Eastern cultures, a cancer diagnosis is withheld from the patient.

She returned his sober gaze and said, “I want to rest now.”

He gave her the morphine tablets.

At 6:00 a.m. the next morning, Hiyam—it was her turn—woke him and said their mother’s breathing had turned to gasping. Khalil called the ambulance and went with her to the hospital. The doctors confirmed what he already knew: This was in fact the end. He called his brothers:

“Your mother is dying. Please prepare the funeral.”

As for him, he had first discovered her disease, and he would be with her to the end.

Tamam took her last breath at 4:00 p.m. At last, she was free from pain . . . But oh, my God, the sorrow.

The Takedown

(2015, age forty-five)

Over the next five years, Khalil suffered profoundly from the agony of losing his mother, but he couldn't let it interfere with his work. In fact, he accelerated his efforts—conducting even more human rights training workshops for students and adults, giving even more press conferences decrying both Israeli and Hamas abuses.

Then one morning the headline in one of Gaza's newspapers floored Khalil. The article claimed that he was behind a current NGO scandal. *Absurd!* he thought. *I had nothing whatsoever to do with that!*

Accusations had been made in the press about the mismanagement and malfeasance of a major European NGO. Khalil sat on its board of directors, as he did on numerous boards, but his role was only perfunctory. He wasn't supervising its work and had no clue that its local director was embezzling funds.

As ridiculous as this accusation against him was, Khalil couldn't laugh it off. Gazans vigorously consume—and create—conspiracy theories. A fear began welling deep inside him. Khalil immediately went to his colleagues in Gaza, both those at his own organization and other people in the Gazan human rights community. "Should I resign from that board? he asked them. Their advice confused him. Some said certainly not: He would lose his reputation, and he should defend his innocence. But as logical as that advice seemed, it felt hollow . . . somehow distanced and empty . . . as if they were defending a principle, not him personally. Had he lost some of their loyalty?

And it wasn't just Khalil's colleagues, but his friends and even some family members as well. He could tell. They were just somehow more distant and didn't appear interested in empathizing with him. Khalil was aggrieved at the thought that he was losing his standing. He had thrived off of respect and adulation his entire life—from his childhood, when his height, deep voice, and dignified reserve had attracted a following, to his leadership during the *intifada* and in prison, to his tireless work as one of Gaza's most prominent human rights activists. The whole matter consumed him. He perseverated: *Why have I been targeted? Where was the trust? The loyalty?*

He began spinning, careening.

And then the call came.

"It's for you, Khalil. It's the [Hamas] security service," said his assistant. Khalil had no reason not to take the call or not to agree to the requested meeting. He was always willing to meet with anyone. One of the requesting officers was actually a college classmate, so how bad could this be?

The small restaurant the officers chose for the meeting seemed unusually vacant as Khalil entered. He spotted them in a distant corner. The silence in the room and the officers' stern demeanor screamed trouble and danger to him. After fewer pleasantries than the culture demands, the officers unleashed a litany of charges. They pounded him relentlessly, without a whiff of interest in his protestations. Their "evidence" was purely circumstantial, and some of it pathetically contrived at that.

They accused him of embezzling from his own organization. A cutting insult. He lived in a rented two-bedroom apartment and could barely afford the fees for his kids' schooling. They accused him of spying for the PA security services. Ridiculous, given that Khalil had never withheld his blatant criticism of the PA's corruption. They accused him of spying for Egypt. Silly. Like many NGOs, he worked with the Egyptian officials in trying to secure exit permits for Gazans—students, people seeking medical treatment, and so on—through the Rafah crossing.

"We'll be seeing you again," said the lead officer ominously as they dismissed him. They didn't arrest him, but he knew they probably would. Khalil couldn't fight the growing realization that they were taking him down. No longer was Hamas going to put up with his criticisms of its mismanagement and unjust treatment of individuals. You don't challenge authority forever—or at least not this one.

Hamas officers would end up interrogating Khalil several times, but that first ordeal was devastating. It sent him into a tailspin, unleashing emotions he didn't recognize, making him feel out of control, even out of body. He couldn't stop himself from worrying. A terrified mind was taking over, a self he didn't know, and it panicked him.

In the end Khalil wrote the board of Al-Dameer a single-sentence resignation citing personal reasons. But the damage was already done. He was too numb to feel the depth of the agony of resigning from the place that had been his life's work, where he had discovered that he could truly be himself, condemning injustice, whatever its source. But it was clear that resigning was his only option.

And home was his only refuge, where Sahar and the kids, unfailing in their loyalty, kept plying him with exhortations of confidence and love. But they were becoming increasingly concerned. They didn't recognize this man, and they too were beset with anxiety. At times Khalil would just stare at the ceiling for hours. Other times he would laugh unpredictably, make faces, or experience what seemed like hallucinations.

At one point Sahar lost it. She grabbed his cell phone, threw it to the floor, and stomped it to pieces. She could no longer tolerate the incessant calls from reporters and Khalil's persistent calls pleading his case to anyone who would listen. When he started becoming paranoid, even accusing family members of wanting to destroy him, Sahar reached out to Khalil's brother Khaled, who had stepped up as the family's chief advisor after their mother died. Their father was now too old and infirm for that role.

There were precious few psychiatrists in Gaza then, and even fewer psychiatric medications. The psychiatrist Khaled finally found immediately prescribed an antipsychotic medication for Khalil, who at that point was so psychologically frail that he had no energy to resist and fight the shame: A Gazan *man* being seen by a *psychiatrist* and taking *medications for mental health*? The medication knocked Khalil out. He would sleep through the night and then most of the day. He felt like a zombie. The medication seemed to be only making matters worse, and the family became gravely concerned. A replacement medication made him feel, in his own words, like "a piece of wood."

After several family conferences, everyone decided that Khalil needed to get out of Gaza.

Exile

(2015, age forty-five)

Fortunately, Khalil's Israeli permit to leave Gaza for the West Bank was still valid. He first went to Ramallah in the West Bank, after passing through the lengthy Israeli security controls at the Erez crossing in Gaza and then taking a ninety-minute taxi ride. In Ramallah he stayed with Ahmed, a friend. Ahmed gave him his own key, but Khalil hardly ever left the apartment. He was still waylaid by the medicine, having lost all grounding and sense of self-direction.

After two weeks in Ramallah, Khalil felt the need to be with family, so he went to Amman, Jordan, to stay with his sister Haneen and her six kids. He took a bus from Ramallah, a two-hour journey that included lengthy Israeli and Jordanian security processing at the Allenby Bridge across the Jordan River.

"Please don't ask me any questions," Khalil implored Haneen as she opened the door, with all the children excitedly behind her. "I just need to be away from everything. I want to forget." She had never seen her little brother so gaunt and disheveled. Shortly after arriving in Jordan, Khalil stopped taking the medication; in Jordan it was just too expensive. The family gave him space to recuperate. The kids did their best, but eventually they encouraged him to play a variety of card games with them, and that turned out to be a therapeutic distraction from perseverating on his troubles.

The scandal did not leave him alone, however. Local newspapers and media websites were publishing all sorts of nonsense: that he had "escaped" Gaza to avoid his guilt; that he was in Brussels, but also in Dubai and Cairo. Soon enough, the phone calls started coming, despite his new private number.

The first call was from a journalist who wanted to talk about the embezzlement accusations. "How did you get this number?" asked Khalil. The caller dismissed Khalil's concern with something like, "Oh, you know, that's our job as journalists." Khalil figured that a "trusted" friend may have given out his number. The caller cited the varying estimates floating around the media: Khalil was said to have stolen $400,000 or $600,000 or even $1 million from his organization.

"That's ridiculous," said Khalil with great exasperation. "Our entire budget was $1.7 million, and I stole a million of that? The organization would have collapsed. And by the way, where is this million I am supposed to have stolen? My family of five lives in a two-bedroom rented apartment!"

And then a mysterious call from an unknown number came, claiming to be a journalist from Barcelona. "We want to interview you concerning the attacks on human rights defenders in Gaza," he said.

Khalil responded, "I resigned from my organization and therefore have no authority to speak on behalf of the human rights community. I no longer give statements to the media." He hung up politely.

A week later an email arrived. The journalist, referencing the previous phone call, said he understood that Khalil would not speak about his own situation, but the journalist wanted to talk about other human rights leaders in Gaza who were being criticized by Hamas. And he wanted to talk about Khalil's personal life. The journalist brought up the embezzlement accusation again, promising that he'd keep their conversation off the record—surely Khalil would want to comment before he published his story.

Khalil had no reason to trust this stranger, and once again he politely declined by email. The journalist got the message this time and didn't approach Khalil again.

Two things saved Khalil's sanity during his nearly half a year in Jordan. The first was that as soon as he arrived there, he set up a Snapchat account and talked with Sahar and the kids constantly—five, six, seven times a day. On one of these calls, Nour, his sixteen-year-old older daughter, reassured him: "Don't worry, Baba. Don't believe all these things people say about you. We know you are good. Please be strong. You'll be fine. We love you so much. Please come home and be with us." Sahar also exhorted him to be strong, to forget about all the nonsense. They had a future to plan now.

Second was the unfailing adoration of Mohammed, his nephew with Down syndrome. He worshipped Khalil and was always at his side. Even now, Mohammed will call occasionally, asking, "Uncle, where are you?"

Some three months into Khalil's stay in Jordan, an international human rights organization based in Amman got word that Khailil was there and asked him to consult with them as they built their organization. Khalil eagerly agreed, but after three months the group was still not ready to proceed, and Khalil decided that he could not wait any longer before returning to Gaza. He was feeling stronger mentally, and he missed his family terribly. He also missed Gaza. It was home, and he didn't want to live anywhere else.

A New Life

(2016–2022, ages forty-six to fifty-two)

Khalil sat alone, having a smoke, in the salon of their two-bedroom apartment on the sixth floor of one of the many high towers in the Tel el-Hawa neighborhood in southeast Gaza City. Sahar was at work; the kids were at school. He'd been home from Jordan for five months now and had just come back to the apartment from an unexpected visit to see his brother.

"Is there anything wrong?" Khaled asked.

"No, no," replied Khalil, "I'm just a bit lonely and wanted to talk."

Khalil had returned to Gaza unceremoniously. Only a few friends and family met him at the crossing. Hamas appeared to be satisfied that they had sufficiently diminished him, and so they left him alone. In the months since Khalil had returned from Jordan, his loneliness had been self-imposed in the sense that he had walled himself off from his "friends," those who had not supported him during his takedown, although he had supported and defended them throughout his whole career.

Shortly before noon, Khalil could hear footsteps climbing the concrete stairs. It would be Nour, he knew, who was returning home after studying for the *tawjihi* with her classmates. She was seventeen. Entering, she saw Khalil on the sofa and exclaimed, "Hi, Baba. How is your day going?" Khalil waved and gave her a big smile.

"I'm okay, dear. How was your morning studying?" Upon seeing and hearing Nour, his firstborn, Khalil felt a flood of love. His recent crisis had taught him just how essential his family was to him; in fact, he had survived the crisis for them. Although his future was unclear, he was certain that the well-being of his family would be his only priority.

Shortly after Nour came home, more footsteps approached the door. This would be Mohammed coming home from school, sixteen and now nearly as tall as Khalil, whom he beamed at upon entering the apartment. Following shortly behind was Nesma, now fourteen. "Hi, Baba. How was your day?" After about an hour, Sahar arrived for her lunch break. After checking in quickly with Khalil, she joined Nour in the kitchen to help her finish the lunch preparations. It would be lentils today. Throughout the meal, Khalil surveilled his family and felt utterly at home with the people he knew loved him completely.

After lunch Sahar returned to work. A nap enticed Mohammed down the hallway. Nour returned to her studies, and Nesma sneaked some time on her iPad. Khalil returned to his "office" on the sofa and checked his phone. Still no text message. He'd been waiting for days to hear when his severance pay would be released, and he needed the money badly.

It was clear to everyone when Khalil resigned before leaving Gaza—now nearly a year ago—that he would receive a respectable severance after eighteen years of dedicated service. When he returned from Jordan, his organization—feeling that it needed to cover its bases in the face of the media's accusations that Khalil had embezzled—insisted on hiring an independent auditing firm to do a full accounting of the budget and Khalil's financial decision making. It had already been more than two months since the firm submitted its report.

After another month of waiting, Khalil did finally receive his full severance. But far more important to him than the money was the signed statement accompanying the severance that absolved Khalil of any financial wrongdoing. His heaviest burden had been lifted at last. No one came up with a speck of evidence that he had spied for either Egypt or Israel. But the embezzlement allegation had survived. To have it dismissed now was a moment of closure: The crisis had ended.

Khalil used up the severance by paying off several loans he'd received from friends during the crisis, but mostly by paying Nour's undergraduate tuition, which was Khalil's highest priority. The ensuing financial burden was heavy.

"Baba, please don't be angry with me. I don't want to embarrass you, but do you have any money?" asked Nesma shyly one day. "I promised my friends I'd go with them to a restaurant over the weekend. But if you don't have any money, please forgive me for bothering you."

Khalil asked when the dinner was going to be and then said, "Of course, sweetie. I will have some money for you by tomorrow." He didn't have a single shekel, so he went to his brother Khaled and asked for his help.

"Khaled, I can't deprive my kids of what they need. This is my responsibility." He hadn't forgotten the poverty they were raised in, the many times his father didn't have any money for them, but he wanted a better life for his kids. Naturally, Khaled provided for Nesma.

The next day, Mohammed asked for some money to go out for coffee with his friends. Back to Khaled.

The next month one of Khalil's sisters called late at night, "Dear brother, please, I need $500." She didn't specify what she needed the money for, but he could tell it was important from the urgency in her voice. At that time, Khalil did have $1,000 dollars in the bank from some consulting he'd done. He immediately drove to the bank and gave his sister what she needed.

And then Khaled, his most reliable source of financial help, ran into some difficulty with his business and asked Khalil, of all people, for $5,000, knowing that his brother had some consulting income coming in. But no way did Khalil have that kind of money. Nevertheless, the family imperative is that you don't say no to a member who needs help. "Sure, brother, I'll get it for you," he assured Khaled. He spent the next day borrowing money from his friends.

And then there were his two nephews who were ready to marry. Neither of them had enough money and naturally turned to family. Khalil couldn't help out much, but he did what he could.

Even though many people had asked Khalil to reenter the formal human rights community, he was not ready to do that, because he was still feeling bruised and bitter. So he began exploring various other livelihoods, none of which strayed far from addressing issues of injustice. One day he saw an opening for a fellowship at an esteemed NGO based in London. He fit the requirements well, and so he applied. But then he received this email:

> Dear Khalil,
>
> Greetings. I'm writing to you without mentioning my name because of my position at my place of work. I hope that you understand. I want [to] tell you that I have heard that there was some bad faith in the selection process for the fellowship you applied for. Specifically, some letters were sent to the committee defaming you. The result was that your name was removed from the competition. I know of your good work in human rights and the benefit it has brought to so many people, and I feel it my duty to acknowledge this and express my thanks to you, as all people should. I hope that this email may help you.

Apparently, that position was too close to his former field of work, and some influential people in that field didn't want him to reenter it. The crisis wasn't over after all.

Khalil gradually reconstructed some of his friendships and made many new ones. Over time, he started to feel comfortable again in his cherished homeland. As for work, he decided to spread out and use his considerable skills. He began consulting with some local NGOs, writing for various publications, starting a business venture with friends, joining and developing a media company, and more. Over the next several years, these different professional endeavors provided Khalil with an adequate income, which he used for only one priority: helping his children maximize their education.

Nour and Nesma achieved astounding scores on the *tawjihi*. In 2017 Nour scored a 95.3 percent, and in 2019 Nesma scored a 95 percent. Mohammad wasn't so diligent in his senior year and scored a respectable 65 percent in 2018. He took university more seriously and became a top student in his class.

Nour went on to graduate from Al-Azhar University in 2021 with a degree in law and was then hired by the Palestinian Centre for Human Rights in Gaza. Her work focused on documenting crimes and building case files for the UN's International Court of Justice. She set her sights on doing graduate work outside Gaza, with the goal of becoming a diplomat.

In 2022 Mohammed graduated from the same university with a bachelor's degree in translation and was hired by the prominent Jawwal telecommunications company in Gaza. He is also very active in civil society organizations, as well as in theater and traditional dance. His goal is to get a graduate degree in IT at a university outside Gaza.

In 2020 Nesma began her studies at Al-Azhar in computer engineering. She was supposed to have gotten her bachelor's degree at the end of 2023, and Google had committed to hiring her as a web developer after she graduated.

Hussam
The Educator

The Poster on the Wall

(1986, age thirteen)

Thirteen-year-old Hussam lay supine on the polished tile floor, his scrawny body "cushioned" by a couple of centimeters of cheap foam crumbling inside the faded bed mat. He fixated on the tattered curtains wafting in and out of the square opening in the unplastered cinder block wall.

Hussam's active mind raced, waking him every time he dozed. Never had he yearned so hard for a dawn. This was the most important day of his life: He would stop being a kid, just playing around. He would be a man.

The moonlight provided just enough illumination to bring into view the frames of his three younger brothers (two others were yet to be born), each crumpled in different configurations on their own pads in this, the third bedroom of their single-story refugee-camp home. Hussam took seriously, and greatly enjoyed, his significant duties as the leader of this group. The eldest son in Gazan culture bears much of the weight of caring for, protecting, and training the younger siblings—even older sisters, of whom Hussam had three. Tonight Hussam was especially proud of the example he would set for his siblings tomorrow, because they too needed to know what he had learned.

Four months earlier

"Stay back, Hussam," whispered his frail grandmother in her gravelly voice, as all the other grandchildren rose from the cool, tiled-floored corridor of the family home. She had finished another storytelling session of her tales from the old days. With her twisted, leathered hands misshapen by decades of toiling in the soil but now steady in her lap, his grandmother, somewhere in her eighties, rhapsodized about the delights of life in their ancient Philistine village of Barqa, just thirty-seven kilometers up the road from al-Nuseirat, where they now lived. She told the stories so beautifully that they always mesmerized Hussam.

He could imagine himself playing in the orchards and fields pregnant with fruits (white guavas, mangos, dates, oranges, clementines, mandarins, strawberries, avocados, and endless sorts of melons) and vegetables (potatoes, onions, carrots, tomatoes, beans, peas, eggplant, okra, and more) that large extended families grew on irregular parcels of land just a few kilometers in from the glorious Mediterranean. He also saw himself playing not just with his myriad cousins but with the Jewish kids from the neighboring village as well.

Hussam adored his grandmother's tales, which were repeated frequently and almost identically by his uncles, aunts, and the elders of the camp. He felt relaxed and free when he heard these stories, almost as if a fresh breeze flowed right through his whole body. In his younger years, he had thought that for sure the family would move back to Barqa. *Why not?* he had reasoned. It was just up the road. That would be a great life, he mused—so much different from his life right now.

His fantasies ended, however, when his *jidditi's* (grandmother's) hands began to shake as she moved on to the painful tales. He did not want to have been there in 1948 when the Jewish forces started dropping bombs, each so earsplitting as to deaden the mind and make the ground shudder like concentrated earthquakes. He did not want to have been clutching his mother's skirt during the panicked search for a safe place as the tanks and bulldozers rumbled into the village.

And he knew he would have been just as disappointed, even disgusted, that the Egyptian and Jordanian forces—there to beef up Barqa's paltry defenses—just up and left. *Why would they do that?* he thought. *What, they decided we weren't worth fighting for?* Just a couple of times, he even allowed himself to fault the Barqians themselves. *Why didn't they fight harder? Why didn't they stay and protect their land? I would have!* he would think with his childish mind, which couldn't grasp that the Barqians really had no choice but to save themselves.

His grandparents and their children, along with 250,000 others from all over southern Palestine, made their way south to Gaza, the only direction open to them. After days of trudging—the fortunate ones wearing some form of shoes in various stages of cracking—pulling or pushing ancient donkey carts loaded with the belongings they had managed to grab in the chaos, they ended up in al-Nuseirat refugee camp, adjacent to the town of the same name a few miles south of Gaza City. They had relatives there. The population of the camp and the surrounding municipality was approximately 50,000 at this time.

Hussam kneeled into his grandmother as she rested her curved spine against the powdery concrete wall of the narrow corridor. "Hussam," she said, "you are smart and determined. I see passion in your eyes when you hear these stories of our people, and I see that you feel their truth. But that is not enough. To be a leader, you must know the truth for yourself."

Hussam smiled at the high compliment. It electrified him inside, coming at just the right time. He had been restless for months now. He was growing older—already thirteen—and the cultural imperative was unambiguous: He was to become a "man." That meant engaging actively to help his people.

Hussam had loved his childhood. He delighted in playing hide and seek, marbles, and all sorts of card games in the camp's warren of narrow alleyways. Mostly, though, he loved the makeshift soccer matches that broke out in the dirt streets, with goal standards fashioned out of . . . whatever and balls assembled from increasingly clever blends of scrap cardboard and plastic. His body played the sport nimbly. Perhaps he had inherited the skill from his father, Fares (FAH-rehs), who had been a professional player and was now the head of the soccer league in the whole Gaza Strip. Even if he had not inherited his father's skill, he still would have favored soccer: His father did, and he idolized his father.

But now duty called. He wasted no time, spending the rest of the day outlining his new task. He wrote out a set of questions:

> Is this our land or Jewish land?
>
> If it is theirs, how should we live with them?
>
> If it is our land, how should we behave?
>
> If it is our land, what should we do to get it back?
>
> What can I do to help with the cause?

Now energized by the clarity of his mission, Hussam set out with his characteristic compulsive overdrive. First he needed to read everything he could find. With no computers or internet (it was the 1980s), he haunted libraries every day right after school let out, researching the history of the land and its people. He went not only to the little school libraries in the al-Nuseirat refugee camp, but also to the big public library in Gaza City. His father gave him the two shekels round-trip taxi fare to get there.

Over the weeks, Hussam read one book after another, stuffing as many as he could into his backpack to take home for the allowed week. Soon the librarians recognized him and would let him hunt through the dusty stacks on his own. After he had read all the relevant books he had found—he read only Arabic in those days—he moved on to magazines and newspapers. His curiosity was feverish. He returned to the Quran and read it again—but this time for what it said about Palestine.

After four months of reading, Hussam felt saturated. He had found little contradictory information, but there was so much to absorb. Everything seemed to be jumbled in his head, and it discouraged him. Then one day after school, when he had dragged himself to the library to read still more, he came across a periodical that featured a series of articles titled "Palestine across the Ages." When he finished the series, his tension melted into a satisfying closure. This was it! "Palestine across the Ages" had done it for him. Hussam loved the fact that the series tied all the information together: historical, geographic, political, and religious. It included quotations from the Quran and even the Jewish Bible. The author, a Palestinian historian, presented the material with just the organization that Hussam prized. Most importantly, the author documented his points. This made it credible. Here was evidence that met Hussam's standards. He needed to read no more.

His verdict after all of this study was that the land belonged to his people—that they had the right to call it theirs, to live on it, cultivate it, and govern it. In his heart Hussam had always felt the truth of his grandmother's tales and the accounts of his parents' lives under Israeli occupation. Now his mind was also convinced.

How could he share this precious information? It didn't take Hussam long to realize that school was the best place to begin his teaching. None of what he had learned was in the curriculum. Since its inception in 1967, the Israeli occupation had forbidden schools to teach Palestinian history. Textbooks omitted the word *Palestine* and all its derivates. No map demarcated Palestine. He was certain all students and teachers would be thrilled to learn this history. In school and the Israeli media, it was as if an entire people—everyone he knew—was continually being erased. Only at home or in the mosque or on the streets could children like him learn who they really were.

In those days it was customary in middle schools and high schools for students to prepare posters summarizing lesson content and hang them on the wall at the back of the classroom. It was a way for students to distinguish themselves and get extra credit. Hussam had not done a poster lately. One afternoon the idea hit him: His next poster—eventually, a series of five posters—would detail what he had learned through his research. They would not be just any posters elaborating on class material, but would instead venture into forbidden history and politics. He felt energized thinking that he could help fill this void, that he could help his people by passing on what he had learned. He would be taking action, the kind of action worthy of a man.

As soon as class let out on Sunday, Hussam scurried to the various shops in the camp's central market to gather material: the poster board, two thin strips of wood to tack on the top and bottom of the back of the board to keep it flat, a piece of string to hang it on the wall, and sheets of regular paper to write on and then attach to the board. He was savvy enough to know that compelling content was not enough. To attract students' attention, the poster had to be visually striking—so he chose paper with brightly colored borders. He also knew that he didn't dare use a combination of the four colors of the Palestinian flag: red, green, black, and white. An Israeli military law forbade any use of that color combination, whether in clothing, artwork, craftwork, ads, or elsewhere. He thumbed through the various paper samples, finally landing on blue, green, and yellow.

Hussam hurried home with his materials to the small, barely furnished room at the back of the ground floor of his family's house, where he could work uninterrupted during the late evenings. Every night that week, Hussam worked hard to put the whole thing together—logically, factually, and chronologically—making sure the result was persuasive.

He needed nine sheets of paper to lay it all out. Three rows of three sheets—perfect. Hussam's design used the right two columns on each sheet to record part of the history of Palestine as he had learned it in the "Palestine across the Ages" articles. He devoted the far-left column to other matters. One was a fact sheet titled "Did You Know That . . . " On this first poster, he completed that question with details about the body: the amount of blood the heart pumps and the total length of the blood vessels that transport it throughout the body. He was sure that his classmates would find this interesting. Another sheet contained a joke he had recently learned.

Hussam wrote all of this text in his best Arabic script, his right hand making rhythmic movements to the left as if he were creating a piece of art. Gazans prize penmanship so much that parents enroll their children in summer school to work on refining it. Because Hussam wanted to excel at everything, he had worked hard on his handwriting, despite his annoyance that perfecting it during the summer often took him away from playing in the streets.

He took Friday and Saturday—the weekend—to refine and rewrite anything that needed further edits or did not meet his lofty standard of penmanship. Sunday would be the day to act. He felt a surge of pride when he finished the poster late Saturday night. He stretched back in his chair. There it was before him: well-ordered, attractive, and vital.

At last, when he scurried to the window for the umpteenth time, Hussam saw the first light of day. His anxious wait was over. He set his plan in motion according to a schedule he had devised with characteristic exactitude. He showered in the water the sun had yet to heat up. It dripped from a tube attached to one of the black plastic fifty-liter tanks that peppered every rooftop. Although he wasn't the least bit hungry, he forced himself to eat two crispy falafel balls that were still dripping with warm oil, and he dragged a piece of soft, fresh pita through some garlicky hummos and gulped down a cup of syrupy tea. His mother would permit no less.

Hussam slung on his backpack crammed with books and homework. His left hand gripping the poster, he shot out into the back alleys of al-Nuseirat camp to head to school. He loved these alleys, so narrow a sizeable man could stick out his arms and touch the buildings on both sides, even narrower when fragrant laundry hung from sagging plastic lines on both sides of the alley. He would breathe the aroma in deeply and sometimes brush up against the freshly washed sheets. The alleys were also safer than the streets—impossible for soldiers in jeeps or tanks to navigate.

Hussam burst into the empty classroom, dull with the whitened chalkboard and colorless stone floor. He squeezed through the desks to get to the back wall. There wasn't much light—just one small window toward the top of the wall—but he knew that the poster's splash of color would catch everyone's eye. As his fifty classmates streamed into the room, he adjusted the string to make the poster hang perfectly level on the nail right in the center of the wall. They saw the poster, gathered around it, and read the text.

Just then Mr. Hussein, the math teacher, entered. The students stopped chattering as they rushed to their seats, sitting two each at the twenty-five marred, wooden desks with wobbly, rusty, metal legs. Hussam was so eager for Mr. Hussein to notice his poster that his legs were twitching with excitement.

The teacher set his papers down on his small, wooden desk in front of the chalkboard. Then Mr. Hussein looked up, greeted the class, and glanced quickly at the back wall. His gaze rested on the colorful poster hanging there, and then he threaded his way to the back wall and read the poster. The room was silent.

Hussam, looking around, marveled to himself: He is reading the entire poster! I knew he would love it!

"Who made this poster?" Mr. Hussein asked as he returned to his desk. Hussam's hand shot to the ceiling, and with muffled excitement proclaimed, "I did, sir."

Without pausing, Mr. Hussein said: "Well done, Hussam! Now let's get to work, young men."

Hussam felt proud and contented. He understood that the fantasy he had allowed himself to indulge for a second—that his teacher would delay the geometry lesson and share Hussam's lessons with the entire class—was expecting too much. Still, it meant the world to him that Mr. Hussein, a respected elder, had taken the time to read his poster—and that he approved of it.

There was no break before Arabic class began. Just as Mr. Hussein was leaving, Mr. Wael, the head Arabic teacher, shuffled in. He noticed Hussam's poster and went to the back wall to take a closer look. Hussam filled his lungs with a deep breath, standing tall with a proud smile, waiting for round two of validation for his outstanding work.

"Who did this?" Mr. Wael yelled, startling Hussam out of his reverie.

Mr. Wael seemed so upset that Hussam had a moment of hesitation about confessing. But he asked himself, *Should I pretend I did not do it? No. It was good and right.* His confidence and pride won out.

"I did, sir."

"Come here!" the teacher commanded. Hussam obeyed and nervously approached the front desk. Face to face, their eyes met. Mr. Wael's eyes were distressed, Hussam's wide open with alarm.

"What have you done, Hussam? You cannot do such a thing!" he exclaimed, almost frantically.

"But why not, sir?" Hussam pleaded in genuine surprise. "This is important information that we should all know. It's about our Palestine."

"Of course, it is excellent information," the teacher replied dismissively. "But you have no right to do this. You have put me in grave danger. Don't you know the soldiers could send me to prison for allowing such a thing in my classroom? Take it down now!"

Reeling, Hussam staggered to the back wall, his hard-soled shoes making the only noise that broke the room's haunting silence. He lifted the poster off the nail, rolled it up carefully, and reluctantly slid it under the bench next to the door where students stored their backpacks. When the bell rang for the morning break, Hussam plodded over to the tree in the courtyard.

"Wow, Hussam! What you did was great!" raved his classmates. "How did you learn all this stuff? It is so amazing to learn about our people, our history! Will you do more, please? And don't let Mr. Wael bother you. He was very wrong to treat you like that. He was unpatriotic. Maybe he has problems. Don't worry. You did great!"

Hussam smiled at this praise, pleased that his classmates approved of the poster. But when he had planned this moment so carefully, he had not expected to end up feeling troubled in addition to proud. He felt neither shame nor regret. Students and teachers valued the information he provided. But Mr. Wael? *Maybe his personality was shy. Maybe he was under stress. Maybe the Israeli military had arrested him before. Maybe he had a unique philosophy about when and how to resist.*

Scaling the Wall

(1988, age fifteen)

Catching his breath, Hussam noticed the Israeli squadron leader staring at him from the other side of the ten-meter-wide dirt road. The road was now littered with chunks of cinder block, and the air was thick with the rank, oily smoke from a burning tractor tire, mixed with the acrid residue of tear gas. The sergeant's eyes burned into Hussam's like lasers. He called over his five soldiers and pointed in the direction of his stare: "There he is, grab him!" Fifteen-year-old Hussam had been leading today's clash, and the captain knew it.

The four-hour battle had been the common seesaw version: The boys—clad in jeans, white T-shirts, and checkered red bandanas covering their faces—hurled fist-sized pieces of broken cinder block at a squad of Israeli soldiers who had made an incursion into the camp. The soldiers—clad in olive-green uniforms—would retreat a bit to avoid the cinder-block barrage, and then they'd fire cannisters of tear gas to force the boys to retreat a bit, and back and forth it would alternate with neither side ultimately winning much ground.

Hussam whipped around and tore down an alley behind him into the heart of the camp. Glancing over his shoulder, he confirmed that the squad was after him—and oddly, not far behind. *How did they cover so much ground so quickly?* This was his territory, and unlike the soldiers, he knew it completely. He had never had any problem losing soldiers before, both because he ran so quickly and because unlike his pursuers, he was not carrying a sidearm, semiautomatic rifle, baton, knife, or helmet and was not wearing heavy black boots.

As always, Hussam turned every corner in his attempt to shake the soldiers, but his frantic backward glances revealed that, in fact, they were gaining ground. *Why aren't I losing them, like always*? His lungs started to burn. When he tried to speed up, he started careening around corners, and his skinny legs—which now felt like putty hardening into lead—slid out from under him a few times, sending him sprawling in the sandy dirt.

Hussam had always been nimble at dancing over the rivulets of raw sewage in the alleys, as he made his turns—but now, after rounding just one corner, he stepped midstream into the sewage and landed face first in the muck. Retching and frantically smearing the filth from his eyes, his mind felt numb as he struggled to process what had just happened: *What's wrong with me? I have never done such a foolish, clumsy thing before!*

Hussam reached a critical juncture: Turning left would soon take him to a dead end, a stone wall built to block the alley; turning right would land him in the main part of the camp, offering him endless chances to lose the soldiers. Yet Hussam turned left! He knew even as he was turning that it was the wrong direction, but he seemed to have lost control of his body. He sprinted the fifty meters toward the wall, the soldiers at his heels, their insults in Hebrew and broken Arabic stabbing into his frantic brain.

There was no toehold in the wall, but no worries: Hussam had scaled it many times before because it was a shortcut to his best friend's home. As he leaped to grab the top of the wall, his feet betrayed him, and he landed face first, the rubble cutting into his forehead. The soldiers were now just meters behind him. The next leap landed his fingers on the edge of the wall.

Just as his shaking arms lifted his waist to the edge of the wall and he got a whiff of escape, his mind exploded with terror as he felt a gloved hand grip his right ankle.

"We've got you, you fucking Arab pig!"

As the soldier began yanking his spent body off the wall and toward his certain doom, Hussam shot up in bed. He was drenched in so much sweat that he felt as if he hadn't dried off after a dip in the sea, his heart pumping so hard it seemed ready to burst right out of his chest.

The nightmare . . . again.

The *intifada* had broken out in 1987, just a year after Hussam had made his mark through his series of posters. He joined and quickly became the leader of the Pioneers, a youth group in his camp, after vetting them carefully. He would only be involved with serious kids who didn't act impulsively but instead thought things through and planned their actions. He would not join a group like that band of hooligans who frequently came to his school, stirring up the students to demonstrate when there was no logical reason at that moment to protest.

The Pioneers often met secretly underneath the massive *Jummaiz* tree in the large orange grove just outside the camp. An Israeli military law forbade group meetings. These sycamore fig trees, cultivated in Egypt and the Gaza area for millennia, can grow up to twenty meters high, have an immense canopy, and bear fruit several times per year. It was a perfect place to ensconce themselves.

They planned and executed public demonstrations on a variety of key memorial days, especially Nakba Day (catastrophe), May 15, commemorating the 1948 displacement of more than seven hundred thousand Palestinians as Jewish forces began the establishment of the State of Israel, and Land Day, March 30, marking the 1976 killing by the Israeli military of six unarmed Palestinian citizens of Israel who were protesting the confiscation of Arab land.[60] The Pioneers also demonstrated to commemorate Israel's many assassinations of Palestinian leaders and to protest actions by Israeli forces in Jerusalem and the West Bank.

The Pioneers also planned for the numerous encounters they knew they'd have with Israeli soldiers: the almost daily raids the soldiers would make at Palestinian schools and the filthy, humiliating language they'd use as they patrolled the camp streets, ranting at Palestinian men, women, and children. But the Pioneers also orchestrated more strategic encounters. One of their favorites was taunting squads of soldiers into entering the camp by screaming at them that they were cowards. Soldiers would often take the bait and begin chasing the kids deeper into the camp until eventually the dirt roads became too narrow for the IDF vehicles to proceed. In the places where the soldiers were forced to stop, the kids had pounded nails into the dirt to puncture the jeeps' tires. Groups of youth were waiting and would then rain down stones upon the squad, while the soldiers called frantically for backup or fled on foot.

[60] Mohammed Haddad, "Land Day: What Happened in Palestine in 1976?" *Al Jazeera*, March 30, 2024, https://www.aljazeera.com/news/2024/3/30/land-day-what-happened-in-palestine-in-1976.

Escape

(February 1989, age sixteen)

A bit wiser now after months of experience and likely with the aid of a coerced informer, the soldiers moved down the main drag of the camp, headlights out, with only the slight crunch of their tires on the sandy road. Finally, they reached the home of Hussam's friend Bassam, where ten boys had gathered in the large front room for a planning session. Caught up in their deliberations amid partially empty glasses of tea and coffee, the braver of them smoking cigarettes, the boys were oblivious to the soldiers' approach until the iron battering ram pounded the home's metal door.

"*Allahu Akbar*! The soldiers are here! The soldiers are here! *Allahu Akbar*!" The boys closest to the door used the traditional shout "God is Great" to alert the others to a crisis. They all raced out the back door of the house and jumped over the back wall into the narrow, one-meter-wide alley separating Bassam's home from a neighbor's house. Most escaped by going down the alley to the right.

For whatever reason, after jumping the wall into the alley, Hussam and one friend, Maher, chose to go to the left into the neighbor's yard, but the gate to the alley beyond it was locked. Frantically, Maher chose to enter the neighbor's house and hide. Before Hussam could make his decision, the squad of soldiers appeared on top of the wall, looking down on him. He felt he had no choice then but to surrender and told the soldiers so. Spotting a wooden ladder in the yard, he grabbed it to climb up to them. Once the soldiers moved away to make room for him on the wall, Hussam leapt immediately forward into Bassam's yard and over another wall into the street. He raced across the main drag. Then he used a half wall to leap up to the rooftop of a house. Careful not to twist his ankle by catching his foot in the grooves of the corrugated asbestos roof panels, he jumped the small distance to the next roof and then another and another.

Now well into the residential area, he dropped down into the courtyard of a house. The startled grandmother knew exactly what to do. She darted inside, grabbed the change of clothes that many families kept on hand for a moment like this, tossed them at Hussam as he entered the house, and motioned to a room where he could change. Soldiers were becoming adept at memorizing the garb of young people so that they could catch them elsewhere in the camp.

Luckily, the packet contained jeans and a T-shirt that were different colors from what he was wearing, and Hussam threw them on in a matter of seconds. It was understood that he would come the next day to pick up his own clothes. He whispered his peace greeting, "*Asalamu aleki, hajjeh*," so as not to awaken others, using the term of endearment for a woman old enough to have taken the pilgrimage (*haj*) to Mecca required of the most faithful Muslims. Then he gently slid the bolt of the door open and slunk into the alley to the *hajjeh*'s whisper, "Peace be with you, my boy."

Even though it was pitch dark and he was disguised, Hussam kept close to the walls of the houses as he moved down the various alleys. Although his heart had calmed down a bit, he was still extremely frightened—surely the soldiers were after him. In fact, he was so scared that he didn't have sufficient mental space to credit himself with having executed a truly clever and daring escape.

Knowing that his home was just around the corner, Hussam started to relax, only to be accosted by a scene that filled him with dread. A big commotion was taking place right outside his home and along much of the alley. His parents, uncles, aunts, and brother Mohammed were going door to door pleading with their neighbors to know if anyone had seen Hussam. Word of the raid on Bassam's home had already spread throughout the camp.

Bassam's father had called Fares, Hussam's father, to drop the heavy news of the raid, saying: "I'm so sorry, Fares, but Hussam is missing." Fares's entire body tensed, and his mind felt as if it had been flooded with liquid anxiety. There was nothing worse than not knowing your son's location.

"There he is!" yelled an uncle as Hussam emerged into the dim light cast by the open doorways. Rasmeya (rahss-MEH-yah), his mother, led the sprint toward him, engulfing him in her arms and covering every centimeter of his face and head with kisses. "*Alhamdulillah*! Thanks be to God! You are safe, my son," she sobbed in relief. "*Alhamdulillah! Alhamdulillah!*"

Fares arrived in a sweat, threw his arms around both his son and his wife, and kissed Hussam endlessly on both cheeks. "You are safe, my son! *Alhamdullilah*," he unburdened himself over and over and over again.

As his parents escorted Hussam to their house through the crowd of well-wishers, all exclaiming the same refrain, he felt no pleasure. Fares and Rasmeya—having instructed the other children not to pester him—let Hussam relax and nibble at the plate of pepper-speckled scrambled eggs and tomato wedges that his brother Alaa had rushed to prepare once he heard the euphoria in the street.

"*Alhamdulillah*," said Hussam softly, expressing thanks for the food, as he rose to wash his hands. It is customary for people in Arab cultures to end a meal by washing their hands. "If it's okay, I'd like to go to bed now." Fares and Rasmeya exchanged a concerned glance. After Hussam left the room, Rasmeya went to the boys' bedroom, which was now empty of all Hussam's brothers, who remained huddled and whispering with their sisters in the salon. She knocked gently and entered to find Hussam sitting cross-legged on his bed mat, head hanging low.

"Tell me, my son, what grieves you?" she said softly as she nestled against him on the mat. Hussam didn't like to cry but he couldn't keep his eyes from welling up with tears.

"I feel so bad, Mama. I had no idea that my escape would cause you and the family so much suffering. I was selfish, just thinking of myself. I wanted to show how brave and clever I could be in getting out of that situation. Please forgive me."

Rasmeya realized that this was a moment when she could teach Hussam something she had been holding inside for a long time now. But that could wait until tomorrow. "Don't worry, Hussam. All we care about is that you are well and safe. Nothing else matters. Put it out of your mind. Go to sleep, dear son." Hussam's mind quieted down a bit as he felt his cherished mother's love and wisdom. When he lay down, he immediately fell asleep.

"Please join me in the living room, Hussam," said Rasmeya the next morning as the family was finishing breakfast. "Yes, Mama, I'll just wash my hands quickly." When Hussam sat down next to his mother in the living room, Fares entered the room and sat a bit farther from Hussam on the same sofa. He didn't want to disturb the connection between Rasmeya and her eldest son. Rasmeya began to speak:

"Hussam, first we want to tell you that we are so proud of you for doing everything you do. You are excelling in school, you have kept your promise to your father that you would not let your activities interfere with your school work, and you help us so much with the other children. And you know that we also support your activities challenging the occupation. That is our duty—all of us. But Hussam, it's not good for you to be reckless. What if the soldiers had been quick enough to shoot you in the back as you fled from them? You know that happens all the time. Just think of your cousin Jihad—shot just last week, and now he's in a wheelchair for the rest of his life. Being active against the occupation is good, but you must be smart about it. Getting shot does you no good. You have your entire life ahead of you to make your mark."

The Warning

(May 1989, age sixteen)

Everyone in the family was sitting on the floor of the salon, relaxing after finishing Rasmeya's specialty: grilled chicken and roasted pumpkin atop a mountain of fresh *maftoul* (couscous). Making *maftoul* from scratch is a painstaking process that took her most of the day. The mound of food, artfully arranged on thin, stainless steel trays, looked so beautiful and enticing that foreign visitors often photographed it. Surrounding the trays were small dishes of broth, plain yogurt, and a salad of crisp chopped cucumbers, tomatoes, parsley, and lemon juice. Sitting around the trays, each person would spoon one or more of these condiments onto the food directly in front of them, eat the mixture from the tray, and then repeat this process until they were full.[61] It took two large trays to feed Hussam's family, including his parents, and each tray was encircled by as many family members as could squeeze in. After they'd finished the meal, the air was still lusciously fragrant with the aroma of the chicken and the garlic, thyme, and sumac that Rasmeya used to coat the chicken before she grilled it.

"Hussam, I would like to speak with you, please," said Fares as he stood up from the floor and went to wash his hands in the sink in an alcove of the hallway.

"Right away, Baba," replied Hussam, wondering what was up. Normally, it was his mother who sat him down for talks to correct him or set down rules, like when she'd told him not to be reckless after his narrow escape from Israeli soldiers a few months earlier. Hussam scanned his memory but turned up nothing that he might have done wrong. He started to worry a bit.

"Son, the *intifada* has been going on for some months now, and my instincts tell me that it will continue for a lot longer," began Fares as the two sat side by side on one of the sofas. "Because it seems that you want to be very active in the struggle, there are some things you need to know." Hussam had no idea what was coming.

---

[61] In Palestine most large meals are eaten in this way. Depending on the type of food or the custom of the family, people eat these meals either with their hand or with a large spoon. Gazans eat while they are sitting on the floor or seated at any available table large enough to accommodate the trays.

"Regarding political resistance to the occupation, you are free to do as you see fit. You are a man now. It is your right and duty as a citizen. But I have two demands of you."

Hussam looked his father directly in the eye, sensing something serious. But he also allowed a quick smile, because against the weight of the topic, he felt empowered. After all, his father was talking to him man-to-man!

"Of course, Father. What would you have me do?"

"First, like your mother and I have said before, you must not let your political activity interfere with your studies. Above all else, your education will equip you to serve your people, your cause, our cause. Our struggle will likely go on for a long time in the future, so you need to strengthen yourself with the knowledge and skills that education will provide. You must continue to come home every day after any activity and prepare for your classes."

"Of course, Father. I will continue to do it gladly. I love school."

"Second, do not implicate or hurt anyone." Hussam was not sure what his father meant.

"What I am talking about, son, is that if you remain active in the struggle you will certainly be detained or arrested, perhaps even taken to prison. During the harsh interrogations, the soldiers will do anything to get information out of you about others. You *may not*, under any circumstances, reveal the names of any other person. Doing so would be a betrayal of the cause and bring great shame upon you and the family."

Continuing to look his father directly in the eye, but now no longer smiling, Hussam said with a certainty born of pure allegiance, "Father, I promise I will never do that."

But Fares kept the pressure on: "If you violate this latter condition, I will forbid you from ever returning to my home."

The air in the room suddenly felt heavy as Hussam continued to look into his father's eyes. His mind and heart whirling, he held back tears in response to the harsh threat of rejection. His father had never, ever, threatened him before in any way. The thought of it crushed him. But at the same time, he couldn't imagine his father ever banishing him; it just didn't fit with how much he knew Fares loved him.

What was perfectly clear to him, however, was that this was a profoundly important matter. His father seemed to be telling him that being an activist involved more than just the careful planning and execution of actions—and all the thrill, satisfaction, and fear that such planning and execution entailed.

He seemed to be saying that harsh experiences were coming his way—that being a man meant being responsible not only for himself but also for others. Before letting Hussam go, Fares summarized his lecture in four rules:

> Rule 1: Do not give them any information.
>
> Rule 2: In particular, do not implicate other people. This would hurt the person and shame you.
>
> Rule 3: Do not confess any of your own behaviors.
>
> Rule 4: Endure. The torture will eventually stop.

Detention

(October 1989, age sixteen)

Fares's lesson came none too soon. Barely a month later, now two years into the *intifada*, the family was shocked out of their sleep by the dreaded *Bam! Bam! Bam! Bam! Bam!* There was no mistaking who was at the door. The soldiers with their hardwood batons were the only ones who came at two in the morning—the only ones who banged so fiercely on the door.

Fares's stomach tightened, and his jaw clenched. *Here we go again*, he thought. He didn't want to be hauled off to detention yet again. Because he was an outspoken critic of the occupation, the IDF often detained him for a day or so to keep him under surveillance. They would also detain him the day before any Palestinian anniversary that would bring protests. *Don't they get it: This intimidation doesn't work!* He flipped on the single naked bulb lighting the entrance, opened the heavy front door, and solemnly addressed the captain of the soldiers:

"What is it that you want this time, Captain?" asked Fares.

But this time the captain's reply was unexpected. "Do you have sons?" he asked Fares dispassionately.

Oh geez, thought Fares, here we go again with the games.

"Yes, Captain, I have six sons, as you can see before you," Fares retorted as he waved his arm dramatically toward all six of them. As they often did, the children were sleeping together on mats in the ground floor salon, where there was a TV. "You've seen them before on your many past visits, of course."

"Tell me their names."

Fares let out a long, resigned breath and went through the motions, pointing out each son as he ticked off their names, beginning with the farthest away: "Well, there's Ashraf, then Mohammed, then Alaa, then Omar . . .

"Where is Hussam?" the officer interrupted.

"Right here, in fact" said Fares, gesturing not far from his feet.

Ignoring Fares's protest, the officer switched his stare to Hussam. "Get ready. We want to take you . . . for just five minutes or so."

Now sixteen, Hussam had acquired a lot of experience out on the streets. He knew risk. But he had never been captured before. And even though he had seen this drill during the many times Fares had been pulled from home and brought to detention—and had heard about it in countless tales told by relatives and neighbors—he suddenly realized that he had no idea what was going to happen to him.

Somber as he stepped around the other kids on his way to the bedroom to get dressed, Hussam worried about how long he would be gone. He knew of course that the "five-minute" announcement was nonsense, but how long would they keep him? Would it just be for a few hours? Or overnight, as they had kept Fares so many times? Pulling on his jeans and T-shirt, he wondered when he would next sleep in that room.

Would it be the eighteen-day detention that so many people reported? He took it to the extreme, contemplating the worst-case scenario of ending up in prison for months, even years. This demoralized him. *How can I possibly live so long away from my parents? How are my brothers and sisters going to grow up without my care? And my God, my education! Will I ever be able to catch up on my schooling?*

As he stepped back through the long faces in the hallway, everyone was silent except for the whimpering of the youngest kids. At the open door, Rasmeya hugged him and Fares squeezed his shoulder, both assuring him, "Don't worry, son, everything will be okay. We love you. We'll be here waiting for you. Be strong."

Just a few meters outside the doorway, the captain wrapped a cotton blindfold around Hussam's head, pulled his arms behind his back, placed white plastic zip tie handcuffs around his wrists, and cinched them into the skin. Hussam didn't resist; there would have been no point. Two soldiers gripped his armpits, pushed him toward the waiting jeep, and then threw him onto its bed. He collided with two other boys who were already there, and he assumed that they must also be part of the roundup.

During the fifteen-minute drive south to the military complex in Khan Younis, everyone was silent, with the soldiers riding in the bed of the jeep using the captives as footrests during the ride. Soldiers took the three boys roughly by the arms as they exited the jeep. Still silent, the soldiers marched them forward and then yanked the boys' blindfolds off their heads. They were standing outside one of several large canvas tents that filled a courtyard. A soldier unlocked the door, slashed the white zip ties, and pushed the boys into one of the tents. Inside the tent, many young people were lying on soiled bed mats set on top of simple wooden bed frames. The beds were wide enough to sleep two. Hussam counted twelve beds and calculated: two people per bed times twelve beds equals twenty-four people. He counted fifty boys.

For the first eleven days, the routine was horribly monotonous. They did nothing other than force down the stale bread—sometimes rotting eggs—and gulp down the water that a guard would bring them at 6:00 a.m. and 6:00 p.m. on the dot. Then at 8:00 p.m. they'd walk single file to the squatter toilet in the shed at the corner of the courtyard, where the stench was stomach churning and a horde of huge flies whirred maniacally. The boys would talk, of course, and try to humor themselves with jokes and games. But they said little about any political activity. They all understood that one or more of them could have been planted as coerced informants—collaborators.

For no discernible reason, on Day 12 things changed. In the early morning after the boys had eaten, soldiers began taking Hussam and a few of the others out of the tent and placed each of them individually next to the buildings encircling the courtyard. On that day and those that followed, the boys were ordered to assume a sitting position there, but without anything to sit on. And they were forced to stay there, sometimes for the entire day, their bare feet often directly on the sharp stones that were spread about a meter wide from the wall of the buildings.

From his forced sitting position in the courtyard, Hussam could hear shrieks coming from an interrogation room inside a building. But one day when he was placed directly below the window of an interrogation room, he heard every word and sound. The officers spoke Arabic.

"Stand up straight! Confess that you threw stones two weeks ago!"

Pause. The sound of a thump (*maybe the baton on flesh: upper arms? lower back?*). The boy grunted.

"Confess, punk!" *Thump! Thump!* A louder grunt.

"Okay, okay, okay, please stop hitting me. Yes, I threw stones." *Thump!*

"You dare throw stones at our sacred soldiers!" *Thump! Thump! Thump!* A long scream.

"Tell us the names of the others who were with you!" *Thump! Grunt.*

"No, please, sir," the boy begged. "I can't . . . *Thump!* . . . Please, sir, I can't give names. *Whack! Whack! Whack!* (*maybe on bone now: knees? head?*) Sharper screams.

"God almighty, please stop hitting me, sir! Okay, okay, Bilal S. was with me."

"Who else?" Whack! . . . Scream! . . . Whack! . . . Scream!

"Omar A. was also there." *Whack!*

"Please, sir, I can't take this anymore!" A dull thump (*maybe a knee to the groin?*) . . . a gut-wrenching shriek.

"NAMES, goddammit!" *Whack! Whack! Whack!* Louder shrieks.

And on and on it went, through as many as twenty names—most of them probably fake, thought Hussam, because he recognized only a few of them. Finally, the captive spurted out (*bloodied mouth, most likely*?): "I can't take it anymore. I'll sign whatever you want, I'll confess to anything. Just give me the paper. I'll sign it. I beg you, please just let me go."

At one point a terrifying rumor began circulating around those waiting to be interrogated. "We've heard that they'll jam the stylus of a pen right into your dick!" Beyond the utter shame he would suffer if they exposed his privates, the thought of the pain that such defilement would bring made Hussam feel as if his slim body had been electrocuted.

A few days later, his whole body quivered when Hussam was ushered into a room for his own interrogation. With the benefit of the preview, he knew what was coming, but that made it even worse. He had never been beaten before. Wondering if he'd be able to avoid pissing himself, he cringed as the dour interrogator entered the bare, white-walled room where Hussam had been ordered to stand, handcuffed and flanked by two junior officers, the ones who would beat him.

On the walk to the interrogation room, Hussam had burned into his mind a stern and insistent mantra from his father's lessons: "Confess to nothing! Give no one away!" Thank God he had such good mind control, because everything he was expecting to happen came blasting at him. He had guessed right. They began with the soft tissues of the upper arms, thighs, calves, and lower back, relentlessly pounding him with their batons after his every denial: "No, I didn't participate in throwing stones." "No, I don't know anyone who did." "No, I'm not involved in fighting you." They also choked him blue and whacked his knees with their wooden sticks. He'd guessed right again: The dull thump he'd heard was a soldier's knee directly to the groin. The searing, convulsing pain was the worst agony he had ever experienced.

Through his own grunts, screams, shrieks, and tears, Hussam's relentless, wholesale denial seemed to throw the interrogator off.

"Who are your friends?"

"I don't have friends."

"How come you don't have friends?

"My studies are the most important thing to me. I only go out to buy things for my family."

Then the predictable shift to Fares.

"Well, what about your father?"

"My father is a teacher and a good football player. He has nothing to do with this."

"Who are his friends?"

"I don't know."

"Do you see anything, any people coming, plotting things?"

"No, I haven't seen anything."

"Do you . . . ? "Do you . . .? "Do you . . . ?

"No." "No." "No."

Then back over the same territory again and again.

"Do you know any people who are involved in this uprising?"

"No, I don't know any such people."

He could tell he was winning the battle when the bribes and threats began.

"You know, we can arrest your father if you don't tell us what we want."

"Do as you must."

"You know, we can release you if you tell us who they are."

"I don't know any such people."

"We can keep you in prison forever."

"Well, I have nothing to say. That's up to you. I haven't done anything."

After a couple of hours, two soldiers dragged Hussam back to his tent, his legs pounded blue; he was unable to stand, let alone to walk. Although the two boys who had taken him from the soldiers tried their hardest to be gentle, Hussam screamed in pain as they set him down on one of the beds in the tent. Every centimeter of his body was on fire.

Although no one could have detected it through his battered face, Hussam smiled to himself and wept: "I did it. I did my duty. I confessed to nothing and gave no one away. They are not invincible! I beat them!"

They let him go on Day 18.

Prison

(December 1991, age eighteen)

Two months later, on December 29, 1989, Hussam was convicted—"without a confession!"—by a military court for having thrown stones. Rather than just hearing a rumor, this time soldiers had actually observed him and testified against him. The court fined him 1,000 shekels (about $400) and sentenced him to nine months at the Ansar III prison, deep in the Negev desert, where Khalil had been the previous year.

Hussam wasn't frightened by this sentence. He was fresh off the horror of his detention, and he figured it couldn't be any worse in prison. Moreover, he would gain new knowledge at the Academy of the Palestinians.

Hussam had two concerns: (1) being separated from his parents and eight siblings and (2) having his education interrupted. The prison sentence would last for his entire eleventh-grade school year, on top of the many previous disruptions caused by frequent curfews and school closures.

Most of the prisoners at the massive tent prison were much older than Hussam. Many were doctors, lawyers, and professors who were serving yearslong sentences for having been public in their support of the resistance against the occupation. Hussam enjoyed the many courses thoroughly and felt like he was deepening his understanding of the occupation. Otherwise, he did not talk about his activities or ideas. He was hypervigilant about being overheard by a collaborator who could get him convicted of a much longer sentence.

When Hussam was released from Ansar III, his peers showered him with adulation. They said that he seemed different—much more like a man than the boy he had been when he was convicted.

Naturally, Hussam focused on one objective after prison: getting back on track with his studies. He made up his eleventh-grade year, completed his senior year, and despite all the interruptions, he was still able to achieve a 62.5 on the *tawjihi*.

The *intifada* was still raging during these two years. Although he continued to advise the Pioneers, Hussam stayed as far away from Israeli soldiers as he could. They had confiscated his ID when he was released from prison. Since Hussam now had a prison record, if Israeli soldiers caught him without his ID, he would be sent back to prison immediately, for who knew how long.

A Dream Fulfilled

(1991–1994, ages eighteen to twenty-one)

Hussam got his undergraduate degree in English at Al-Azhar University in Gaza City shortly after the *intifada* had ended as a result of the Oslo Declaration of Principles (sometimes referred to as the Oslo Accords), the back-channel negotiations between Yasser Arafat (then in exile in Tunisia) and Israeli leaders. Facilitated by US President Bill Clinton, it was celebrated on the White House lawn with handshakes between Arafat, the chair of the Palestine Liberation Organization (PLO); Shimon Peres, the prime minister of Israel; and Itzhak Rabin, the Israeli defense minister.

For Hussam and those Palestinians who were not members of Arafat's Fatah party, the Oslo Declaration was both a betrayal and an insult. It was a betrayal because Arafat did not consult with his people on this plan. Nor did he consult with the leaders of the other Palestinian factions. Arafat and his advisors alone—none of whom had been in Palestine for decades, none of whom fought the *intifada*—made the agreement. And a look to the map that was the basis of the agreement revealed how it kept Palestinians isolated and disconnected, the furthest thing from the independent state that Hussam had fought to achieve over the past six years of the *intifada*.

The agreement provided no free passage from Gaza to Jerusalem or the West Bank; Israeli forces and settlers would remain in Gaza; and the West Bank looked like a patchwork quilt, with Israel retaining full control of 60 percent of the territory—the areas that had the best soil and direct access to the West Bank aquifer. There was hardly any continuity among the hundreds of towns and villages, and none with Jerusalem. The West Bank was all carved up with Jewish-only roads connecting Jewish settlements.[62]

Hussam was unable to fathom how this agreement could possibly bring about real peace. He reasoned that peace could be real only if Palestinians had full autonomy, including the right to travel freely from one country to another. Real peace would mean that Palestinians were no longer treated as subhuman.

---

[62] Rashid Khalidi, *The Hundred Years' War on Palestine: A History of Settler Colonialism and Resistance, 1917–2017* (New York: Metropolitan Books, 2020), chap. 5; Avi Shlaim, *Iron Wall: Israel and the Arab World*, updated ed. (London: Penguin Books, 2014), chap. 13.

This was a troubling, depressing period for Hussam. Of course, he was thrilled to have completed his primary dream of graduating from university. But beyond his frustration with the Oslo agreement, none of the maturity he had gained during the *intifada*—through activities, detention, and prison—had prepared him for the reality of politics. Most importantly, he didn't know anything about cronyism or corruption.

Despite being top in his graduating class, he was passed over for multiple scholarships abroad for graduate work. Only those students who were members of Arafat's Fatah party received such awards. But worse was the publication of articles that revealed the social and moral failings of some top leaders of his own political faction. These revelations ended Hussam's naïveté. He felt shell-shocked and profoundly betrayed. After all he'd sacrificed out of respect for these leaders! Their behavior was unthinkable. In the end, convinced that he couldn't trust any politician, Hussam resigned from his faction.

Soon he found his first job. It was perfect for him: an instructor at a new technical college in a town just south of Nuseirat.

And then . . . he met Mai.

This Should Not Happen!

(1995, age twenty-two)

A young boy opened the door when Hussam knocked. He was late to the party at the house of Fares's distant cousin to celebrate the return of a relative who had been in the Gulf for many years. They exchanged peace greetings, and Hussam introduced himself. The boy pointed to the stairwell. "Please go up to the third floor, and you'll find everyone there."

Dressed in his customary dark-brown sports coat, powder-blue dress shirt, no tie, black pants, and polished black shoes, Hussam started to climb the stairs. Head bowed and brow furrowed, he was lost in thought as he ruminated over the stressful problem at work that had caused him to be late. As he turned the corner to go up the stairs to the second floor, he was startled out of his ponderings. Coming down that same flight of stairs was a young woman. Hussam froze for a second as he thought, *Oh, dear. This should not happen!* There was no way to exit the staircase at that point, so both of them continued, shifting their bodies sideways to pass each other. Hussam gave the young woman his instinctive peace greeting—and although he knew he shouldn't look directly at her face, he did it anyway. They both felt extremely awkward.

The awkwardness was multifaceted. When at all possible, in Palestinian culture one avoids this sort of close encounter between an unmarried man and an unmarried woman. They should not be alone together, and their eyes should not meet. Mai (MY) felt particularly uncomfortable because she was only eighteen, four years younger than Hussam. She had not yet joined the party upstairs on the third floor and had just left her bedroom on the second floor to grab something from the kitchen on the main floor. The fact that she was in her house clothes, not wearing a *hijab*, increased her shame. *This should not happen!* she said to herself.

Mai had been raised by extremely conservative parents, particularly her father. They were not necessarily more religiously orthodox than others, but they revered the rigid customs of their culture, especially when it came to relations between the sexes. Naturally, Mai had internalized those values, and thus her shame at that moment on the staircase reflected both her disappointment in herself and her sorrow that she had gotten into a situation her father would strongly disapprove of. When Hussam looked at her, she snapped her head down, whispered her return peace greeting, and rushed down the rest of the stairs.

But there was much more to the awkwardness that they both felt. Their respective parents had arranged for them to be married. And they knew it.

For Hussam the conversation had occurred right before he graduated. "Hussam," said Fares, "your mother and I would like to speak to you. Please come outside with us." The house was crowded with the whole family, and Rasmeya and Fares wanted this discussion to be private.

"Hussam," asked Rasmeya, "do you know Mai Abushawish?"

"I have never met her, but yes, I have heard a lot about her. In fact, many of our English teachers have been mentioning to me recently that she is a great young woman, top in her class."

Hussam did not need to query why his mother was asking. He was at the culturally ideal time to marry. For the past year or even longer, his aunts and uncles—and his mother—had been regularly asking about his marriage plans. He had no doubt that his mother and father were actively looking around for a suitable bride. The fact that his teachers were promoting Mai to him just confirmed that the process was well underway.

"Well, if you like," Rasmeya continued, "your father and I could propose your hand in marriage to her."

"Thank you, Mama," replied Hussam, "but I do not feel ready for marriage right now. I'm still in college. I don't have a job or any savings. I just couldn't afford a marriage at this time."

"We understand," Rasmeya continued. "We're only thinking of an engagement now. You could wait to get married until you finish your degree and find a job. To be honest with you, Mai's father has been to see us, suggesting strongly that you and Mai should marry. It seems that she has been receiving proposals lately, and her father is convinced that you are the best fit of all of them. This is unusual, as you know, for a bride's father to approach the groom's father, but he is very passionate about this. And your father and I agree that she would be a great wife for you."

Hussam saw the logic. If they are a good match, it would be best to formalize it now.

"Okay, Mama, I agree."

Fares was some meters away, smoking a cigarette. Traditionally, he would be the one to have this discussion with Hussam, but he trusted Rasmeya more than himself on personal matters. After Rasmeya told her husband that Hussam had agreed to proceed, Fares went over to him. “Son, are you certain about your decision?”

“Yes, Father, I’m certain.”

Mai knew that the young man she had passed on the staircase was Hussam. After one of Hussam’s sisters had pointed him out, she had seen him a few times across the courtyard that separated the male and female students at the university. She found him handsome and knew his reputation for loyalty and dedication, but she particularly admired Hussam for his leadership and activity in the *intifada*.

Hussam, however, had never laid eyes on Mai. Yet somehow, instinctively, he knew that she was the young woman he had passed on the staircase. And to be honest, he felt extremely lucky to have seen her, especially without her *hijab*. In a fully traditional arranged marriage, the couple often do not see each other until the day of the actual marriage. Beyond feeling fortunate that he had been able to get a glimpse of his future wife, Hussam also felt blessed that she was so beautiful. Mai’s hair was the darkest brown, straight, and long. Her brown complexion was satin and flawless, her features pleasing and strong. And in her black eyes, Hussam sensed maturity and sensitivity. He instantly knew that he would love her.

Efficiency

(1995, age twenty-two)

The festivities were well under way for the wedding of Samar, Hussam's oldest sister. Family and friends had gathered at Hussam's home, awaiting the final ritual before the actual ceremony. Soon his sister's husband-to-be would arrive and escort her to the wedding parties where the marriage would be formalized.

Fares was delighted with this marriage of his oldest daughter, his first child. But he was also conspiring. He stood in a corner of the salon chatting intently with Yousef, Mai's father. They both nodded in agreement: Since the families were already gathered, it would be efficient, though not traditional, to announce the engagement of Hussam and Mai—which neither of them knew anything about.

Hussam was in another corner of the room chatting with one of his cousins. Mai was doing likewise, but more in the center of the room. Fares waved his hand at Hussam to get his attention, as if to say, "Hussam, please come here." Yousef made the same gesture at Mai. Careful not to look at each other, Mai and Hussam cautiously walked over to their respective fathers, speechless, brows furrowed with the tension of not knowing what was about to happen at this unusual meeting.

Yousef spoke first in his quiet but authoritative voice. "Mai, this is Hussam. I know him well, and I believe you also know of him. He is a good man, and I think that of all your suitors, he is the best fit for you. He has proposed for your hand in marriage. What do you think?"

Mai was stunned. You could see it in her bulging eyes.

What is this? I have been told nothing about this. This is so embarrassing for me. Sure, I like Hussam, and I haven't been opposed to all the talk that the two of us are right for each other. But I had expected any marriage proposal to be handled in the traditional way.

Hussam was also quite surprised, expecting that this proposal would be handled privately, and he felt really bad for Mai, since she had been taken totally off guard.

The fathers appeared unbothered by this straying from tradition. The efficiency of it all was more appealing to them. They gave Mai a few moments to compose herself.

Privately, her answer was yes, she would agree to marry him. But culture forbade her from saying that directly. Rather, she looked up at her father and asked, "What do you think, Baba?"

"Well, Mai, Hussam is a good man, and I like him. But this is up to you."

"Well, if you think he's a good man, then I think he's a good man too."

Deal done. That was the culturally appropriate way to say, "Yes, I want to marry him."

Since it was Fares's home, he took the lead in making the announcement. The women made the high-pitched trilling sound of the *zaghrouta* common at celebrations, and the men yelled their congratulatory "*Mabruk!*" (congratulations!) with all the exuberance of being delightfully surprised. But everyone had known for weeks that this marriage was being arranged, and they had anticipated this happy announcement the moment they saw both fathers talking with Hussam and Mai.

Good News

(1999, age twenty-six)

Arriving home from work one day in 1999 during the brutal July heat, Hussam saw a solitary envelope addressed to him lying on the table in the salon. It was odd somehow, this envelope, longer than envelopes he had seen before, and an unusual cream color. When he picked it up, it felt heavy, and the paper wasn't smooth like other envelopes. He stroked its texture with his thumb a few times, thinking that whatever was inside the envelope must be valuable. Hussam's back straightened reflexively as he read the words "Brigham Young University," and he inhaled quickly as he realized the gravity of this moment—no doubt, the letter would be a notification regarding his application to a master's degree program at BYU.

At the time I was a professor at BYU and had encouraged Hussam to apply because the Mormon standards at the university were quite compatible with Muslim standards—not consuming alcohol, refraining from sex before marriage, and so on. I knew that there were Palestinian students at BYU, but none from Gaza yet. I promised Hussam that if he were to be accepted, I would happily serve as his sponsor.

Hussam had now been working for four years as an instructor of English at the Palestine Technical College in Deir el-Balah, a small town just south of Nuseirat. He loved his work and adored his students. But over those years, he had begun to feel antsy. He worried about stagnating. He was excelling at what he did, but that's why it was time to progress, to learn more. And to be honest, the tough life in Gaza was wearing on him. He wanted a break from it.

Over the previous year or two, Hussam had applied to many universities around the world that offered graduate training in educational leadership, which seemed like a perfect fit for his professional interests. The cost of submitting so many applications—as much as fifty dollars each—was a hardship, but he was determined and made the finances work. It frustrated him that he had heard nothing back from any of those universities, not even to acknowledge receiving his application. By now he had begun to worry that the notion of traveling abroad for graduate study was nothing more than a fantasy among the thousands of fantasies that arose from every household in Gaza, only to remain suspended in midair until they inevitably evaporated into nothing. He had begun to let go of his dream and to accept, once again, the reality that he would never leave Gaza.

"I got an answer! I got an answer!" he screamed to anyone who might be home. It turned out that not all the siblings were there, but both his parents were. This was every bit as huge a moment for Fares and Rasmeya as it was for Hussam. A son, their eldest, might have a chance to experience the world and to bring great honor to the family through a graduate degree. They hurried to the salon.

Hussam picked up the small paring knife that he had grabbed from the kitchen and slid it ever so carefully under the flap on the back of the envelope, wanting to do as little damage as possible to the precious paper. Slowly he pulled out the contents. He thought, *Remember, this is going to be a rejection. Don't be disappointed. You'll move on from this*. Both hands shook as he locked his eyes on the opening sentence. His breath stopped, his brow furrowed, and his eyes did not blink. Fares and Rasmeya were beside themselves with anticipation. But Hussam was in his own world, staring at that first sentence, reading it over and over again with the gravest of expressions on his face. Eventually, his eyes welled up as he absorbed its meaning. Then he shut his eyes to try to hold back the tears and laid his head back on the top of the sofa. Finally, he sucked in a long breath as he let the letter fall into his lap.

After a few seconds, Hussam sat up straight, opened his teary eyes, looked at Fares and Rasmeya, and . . . exploded: "THEY ACCEPTED ME!!!!!"

The salon instantly fell still but with a silence that was buzzing with energy—with shock, delight, and a sense of momentousness. Fares sat frozen and speechless. Rasmeya could only say "*Alhamdullilah*! Thanks be to God!" a million times. They leaped up from their chairs to flank Hussam on the sofa, hearts overflowing as the three of them embraced. *My God, our son is going to travel to America! He is going to see a world outside of Gaza! He is going for his master's degree! Alhamdulillah! Alhamdullilah*!

The silence was interrupted by a timid knock at the door. Mohammed went to answer it, knowing it was Mai because as soon as he had heard Hussam's outburst about the acceptance, he had dispatched Alaa, the next oldest brother, to run the eight hundred or so meters to Mai's home and ask her to come over. And of course, Alaa had spilled the news to Mai, as well as everyone else who was outside in the alleys. "Hussam is going for his masters!"

Everyone stood up as Mai entered. She offered her peace greetings, and they all returned them in unison. As always, Mai was reserved, her face composed, but there was a glimmer in her dark eyes. Fares and Rasmeya excused themselves from the salon. Although technically the engaged couple were not allowed to spend time together unsupervised, they trusted Hussam and Mai. This was clearly a moment to be shared in private.

Mai wasn't permitted to hug Hussam, but she grabbed both of his arms firmly and looked directly into his eyes. Her voice shaking with excitement, she said: "My love, I am so very happy for you! I am so proud of you! You've worked so hard to achieve this." They would talk later about how his acceptance to graduate school in the United States would affect their relationship, deciding eventually that because the program was only a year, there was no reason to marry quickly so that Mai could accompany him. They both understood that Hussam needed to concentrate fully on his studies.

Although the acceptance letter brought excitement to the family, it also brought considerable pressure. It had taken such a long time for the letter to reach Gaza that the specified arrival date in Provo, Utah, was not far away! He needed to secure a visa immediately and buy the airline tickets, luggage, and clothes. And the farewells—so many farewells.

Palestinians were not allowed to use Tel Aviv's Ben Gurion Airport, an hour's drive northeast from Gaza, and it was extremely difficult to get permission from the Israeli military to make the ninety-minute drive east through Israel and the West Bank to cross the bridge into Jordan and fly out of Amman. As a result, Fares—who oversaw the travel arrangements, which he funded by withdrawing some of his retirement savings—had only one option for Hussam's journey: drive south for eight hours through the Egyptian Sinai desert to Cairo, take a flight to New York City, then take another flight to Salt Lake City, UT. Some Palestinian students at BYU—who had written to Hussam when they'd learned of his acceptance—would meet him at the airport and drive him the fifty minutes south to Provo.

A New World

(1999, age twenty-six)

After Hussam arrived at the airport in Cairo and was ascending the aluminum staircase to board his plane to New York, he couldn't open his eyes wide enough to accommodate the sheer size of the Boeing 767. It looked a hundred times bigger than his house. He had never been on an airplane before, and for that matter, he had never seen one—other than the screaming F-16 fighter jets that regularly strafed the skies over Gaza or the thundering B-1s that dropped tons of bombs on the Strip.

Once he had gotten settled in the narrow, not-so-comfortable window seat in row 51, Hussam finally allowed himself to feel excited. He was embarking on a huge adventure, and although what would come was a complete mystery, he was not lacking in courage. This was the next step in his journey of manhood, and he was up for whatever it entailed. At the same time, his mind was not at peace. Hussam realized that he had actually never done anything alone before—ever. There were always lots of people at home, school, and work, and even during all of his protest activities, he always had his fellow Pioneers, supporters, mentors, and prison mates. But no one was with him now. He started missing his family and Mai—and he even wondered whether he should go back home.

Hussam took some comfort in the fact that a good portion of the people on the plane seemed to be Egyptians. Although they weren't Palestinians, they were at least Arabs and most of them probably Muslim as well. He figured that if he had a problem on the flight, plenty of people who spoke his language could help him. Their presence lifted his mood a bit as he chuckled to himself at their goofy Egyptian dialect.

When the plane began its takeoff, Hussam got really swept up by the experience. He smiled when the plane started thrusting into the air and was utterly mesmerized by how something so immensely heavy could climb so quickly. By now his entire face was pressed against the plexiglass window. His eyes stretched open as wide as they'd ever done before, and he nearly giggled when the massive sprawl of Cairo, city of eight million people, began to slowly disappear. It was like a gigantic magic trick.

Hussam was extremely grateful to Fares for having bought him a window seat. For much of the eleven-hour, sleepless flight, he simply gazed out the window—which also served as a convenient escape of sorts from his seatmate, who pushed Hussam's elbow off the common armrest and even began ordering alcohol. At this, Hussam's entire body tensed up. Alcohol was *haram*, forbidden! Hussam wrestled with this challenge: *Okay, maybe he's not Muslim. Maybe he's a Christian Egyptian, and alcohol is not forbidden for him. But doing this forbidden thing so close to me makes me very uncomfortable.*

It was raining, so Hussam was not able to see any of New Jersey or New York from the air as the plane landed. Anyway, he was exhausted and not up for any more overwhelming encounters with newness, as awesome as they had been. The immigration and customs line extended forever, and though it fascinated Hussam to hear so many different languages and to see so many different-looking people with bewildering clothing, he was feeling terribly alone. It didn't help that the immigration officer actually said nothing to him as he inspected Hussam's documents and slammed down the stamp.

Exiting the immigration hall, Hussam was blasted with the noise and bustle of what seemed like thousands of people, all craning their necks like a bunch of chickens to see who was exiting. Bleary-eyed and flagging with exhaustion, Hussam simply stopped in his tracks until he spied me waving and smiling at him. Hussam instantly felt energized—as if his body had been jolted back to life.

Hussam hurried past the barricade to join me. As we kissed each other on either cheek, Hussam exuberantly effused: "Peace be unto you, Dr. Barber. How is your health? How is your family? How are you? Thank you so much for meeting me! How are you? It's great to see you!"

Hussam and I had a few hours to spend together in New York before his flight to Utah that evening. He was excited about the visit to the UN Security Council that I had arranged. Even the idea made him feel a bit at home, since he had studied at UNRWA schools through high school, and his father had been a teacher at an UNRWA school as far back as Hussam could remember. And though his family hadn't needed it yet, the UN provided basic food and medical treatment to hundreds of thousands of Gazan refugees, including many members of his clan.

As we waited in a short line outside the UN building, a man came up unexpectedly to Hussam, stretched out his hand, and greeted him cheerfully. Hussam smiled instantaneously at the direct and personal approach, feeling particularly relieved because he had sensed no friendliness in New York so far. The sidewalks were crowded, but when people passed each other, they never greeted each other, never even looked at each other.

Hussam yanked his hand back and his body instantly stiffened when the man said, “I’m from Israel. Where are you from?” The veins in Hussam’s face doubled in size, his forehead grew sweaty, his fists clenched, and his eyes took on a wild look. He stepped a foot back and stared at the ground. *How can I shake hands with an Israeli?* he thought.

“He’s from the Gaza Strip,” I offered.

“Oh, fantastic!” said the man, “I like Palestinians. I sincerely hope that someday you will have your own state and be represented here at the UN.”

Hussam’s head snapped up, his eyes widened in amazement, and all he could say was “Really?”

He needed a few seconds to try and make some sense of this totally unexpected encounter. He began to feel very badly. Reaching out and grabbing the man’s hand with both of his own, Hussam said, “Sir, and Dr. Barber, I am so, so sorry for my reaction. Please forgive me. I was rude. You see, you are the first Israeli I’ve ever met, other than the soldiers who say ugly things to us and beat and kill us.”

Hussam was happy to leave New York later that evening and eager to move on. Hopefully, Utah would not make him feel so upset. Although he would not have admitted it, he was hurting when he said his goodbyes to me at JFK Airport. He was leaving behind his one connection to home, and although he knew he’d see me again soon at BYU, he just didn’t want to let go of me now. The past few days had been intense and emotional; he felt overwhelmed.

Utah

(1999, age twenty-six)

The drive from the Salt Lake City airport to Provo with the Palestinian students had been pleasant. Hussam gaped at the size of the mountains encircling Salt Lake City. The sun was setting, so the reds and oranges and darkening blue of the sky made him feel at home. One of the joys of living in the Gaza Strip was to view the wildly beautiful sunsets over the Mediterranean every night. Hussam often went to the roof of his home to get a full view of the sea. It had been a taxing and dramatic journey to leave home, but now he was among friends, among those who knew what his life was like, among those he could trust.

Hussam politely turned down the Palestinian students' offer of dinner. They all went up to the room, his new buddies wrestling to carry Hussam's single piece of tightly packed luggage, lopsided because of all of the uneven stuffing Hussam and his mother had done. The room was small, with pretty blue wall-to-wall carpeting. *Strange*. He noticed that the walls had divots that looked a lot like the divots in the cinder-block walls of his home, except that they were thickly painted. The single bed was wider than his bed mat at home, and it sat very high. There was a black refrigerator almost half the size of the one his whole family shared. *All for me?*

Despite these amenities, Hussam's stay at BYU did not begin well.

"Doctor, could you please tell me why exactly I am here," Hussam said to the white-haired doctor at the health clinic where he reported for a medical exam during his first week on campus.

"Oh," the doctor replied, surprised by the question, "this is just a standard medical checkup that we're required to do with all our international students once they arrive." Hussam relaxed a bit at this assurance, but he still gripped the edge of the examining table tightly, embarrassed to be shirtless. Sure, the doctor was a man, but he was a stranger who didn't seem particularly warm. Hussam shivered as the doctor probed him with the cold stethoscope, but the procedure was familiar to him.

"All seems well, Mr. Abushawish. All we need to do now is take a blood sample, and then we'll be done."

Hussam's body seized up. He spun his head up and to the left to stare directly at the doctor: "But, why, sir? Why do I need a blood test? What are you worried about?"

"Oh, don't worry. We just need to do a test for tuberculosis," replied the doctor, sensing Hussam's alarm. Although the doctor was trying to calm Hussam, he only made matters worse when he used the T-word. Hussam was aware of tuberculosis and knew people who had contracted it in Gaza. His research into it had scared him. Although it wasn't lethal, the disease was highly transmissible by air, and he remembered worrying that if he ever got tuberculosis, it would be terrible because he would likely pass it on to his family and Mai. This is why he was extremely relieved to see that among the several vaccinations he got before leaving Gaza was one for tuberculosis.

"Well," said Hussam to the doctor, "there is no need to check for that. As you can see, I got a vaccination for tuberculosis and other diseases before leaving Gaza."

"I understand," replied the doctor, "but we are required to test anyway."

The verdict came a couple of days later, at a follow-up appointment to discuss the test results. "Mr. Abushawish, I'm afraid that you've tested positive for tuberculosis," said the doctor, as he turned toward Hussam. Hussam's breath froze, his muscles became rigid, and a hurricane was raging inside his brain. He felt panic, as he had so often experienced when facing deadly peril during the *intifada*. But this episode was even worse. During the *intifada* he had figured out how to cope, contextualize the moment, and fight the panic with his passion for liberation. But now he had no clue how to fight an invisible enemy like a disease that could ruin his entire life.

Flailing, Hussam begged, "What does this mean, doctor?"

"If the test is accurate, I am afraid that you won't be able to stay in this country. I'm sorry."

No, this can't be. It will cause great shame. I'm the only one in my family to ever study for a graduate degree. I cannot fail. This is the worst thing that's ever happened to me. Am I going to pass it on to Mai? And our children? I've never felt this terrible in my entire life!

I finally picked up the phone on the fifth ring. Hussam, his voice jumpy, spewed forth the awful news in a rapid-fire monologue: "Do you think it could really be true that I have tuberculosis? It just cannot be. What do you think, Dr. Barber? Is this going to prevent me from continuing my studies? How could I ever tell my parents or Mai? Well, I cannot, they would be terribly worried. I cannot go home as a failure. Everyone is expecting me to succeed."

This was the first of four nearly identical calls Hussam placed to me that same day. He called each of his new friends multiple times as well. He was desperate for someone to give him hope.

Hope finally came when he had his required follow-up visit to the county health department. The nurse who saw him told him plainly: "It seems the test at the university health clinic was a false positive. You do not have tuberculosis, young man." Just as Hussam had never felt as terrible as when the clinic doctor first told him the test result, he now felt like screaming for joy.

The ensuing challenges Hussam faced that year in Utah were more to his liking. They were the stuff of substance, ideas, and principles.

It was midmorning during the first semester, and Hussam was preparing for his classes. Most of them were in the evening because several educators were in the program and could come only at night. The phone rang. "My name is Devin. A friend of mine told me that you are from Palestine, and that you are a Muslim. There are very few Muslims here at BYU. I wondered if you could help me with an important class assignment I have."

These Americans get right to the point! No time to exchange kind greetings.

"Well, of course, I will try to help you. What would you like to know?"

"Part of the assignment is to discuss the question of who has a right to the land where you live: Jews or Muslims. What is your opinion?"

Hussam felt both pleasure and frustration with the question. He was pleased that he was being sought out for information. He had always enjoyed helping people understand things, ever since "Palestine across the Ages." He was a teacher, after all. But he was frustrated at being caught off guard with such a weighty question.

"My answer is that the land belongs to us, the Palestinians." Hussam noticed that the student had phrased the question with the words *Jews* or *Muslims*, alternatives he found odd and unsatisfactory. Perhaps, Hussam thought, the student did not know that up to 20 percent of Israelis are not Jewish, but rather Arab Palestinians, and that while a vast majority of Palestinians are Muslim, 10–15 percent are Christian. So for the sake of accuracy, he substituted *Palestinians*.

But he did so primarily to place the focus on the real issue: Do Palestinians or Israelis have the right to the land? For Hussam, it had nothing to do with religion on the part of Palestinians, but rather on their rights as an

Arab people who have inhabited the region called Palestine for thousands of years—whether they are Muslim, Christian, or any other religion.

"Why do you say that?" pushed the student politely.

Hussam gave the history as he knew it from "Palestine across the Ages," including the fact that Palestinians were descendants of the Canaanites and that when the Prophet Abraham came to the region more than 3,500 BCE, he said he found a people already living there.

Devin found the information fascinating and asked endless questions. Sensing that he was bright and genuinely curious, Hussam relaxed. They talked for almost two hours. At the end of the phone call, Devin wanted to do something for Hussam in exchange for all the help he had given him.

"No, no," said Hussam politely, "you don't need to do anything for me. It was my pleasure. In fact, it is my duty to share information I have with others."

Frustrated by Hussam's refusal to accept his offer, Devin pushed on. "I insist, Hussam. You took a lot of your time to help me. Let me please take you out to lunch sometime."

"Oh, no thank you, Devin. Please, you don't need to do anything for me. Perhaps sometime in the future we could meet and have another discussion. How about that?"

Of course, Devin had no way of understanding Hussam's reluctance. In Palestinian culture doing something in exchange for a favor—a quid pro quo, as it were—is *haram*. You provide help out of a sense of kindness and duty and are offended if the recipient of your help wants to pay you back.

Something clicked inside Hussam's head during the conversation. He wasn't sure he'd ever referred to himself as a Muslim. Of course, he knew he was a Muslim, but his prime identity was Palestinian. Living in Gaza—under Israeli occupation—it's natural to think of yourself as Palestinian first, he reasoned, because the nature of life there was to struggle for the right to be called a Palestinian and for the world to recognize that Gaza, along with the West Bank and East Jerusalem, should be autonomous and recognized as the nation of Palestine.

But although some people at BYU who had studied the issues between Palestinians and Israelis wanted to get his take on the conflict, most—students and faculty alike—referred to him as a Muslim and wanted him to teach them about Islam.

An example of this way of seeing Hussam occurred early on, during another phone call. Professor Bowen of the political science department called and asked him to give a lecture to her faculty providing an overview of the Islamic religion—and if he liked, to then provide his insights into the Israeli-Palestinian conflict.

Hussam lowered his head as he set the phone receiver down. He started sweating, and he felt sick to his stomach. *I've never had to give a lecture on Islam before. I wish they'd just ask me to talk about the conflict. That would be so much easier!* he thought. *I've studied it and lived through it.*

In fact, although he observed some of the traditions of Islam, Hussam had never been a devout Muslim. He didn't pray five times every day. He had read the Quran, of course, but since his research for his posters he'd always focused his attention on its political implications for Palestine. Nevertheless, with his characteristic thoroughness, Hussam dove into researching the religion and prepared a thorough lecture that not only compared Islam with both Christianity and Judaism, but also explained his own religious values, practices, and beliefs. The day before he delivered his lecture, he worked late into the night. He had heard of PowerPoint but didn't know how to use it, so he wrote out note cards for his lecture.

Hussam's presentation to the political science faculty was well received. Personally, he felt satisfied that he had acquitted himself well in preparing for it. But what he was not prepared for was how that lecture would change him. The more he studied, the more he became "converted" to the principles of Islam. Ever since he had felt betrayed by some of the leaders of his political faction years ago after learning about their social and moral failings, he had been bereft of a system of meaning to guide his life. In Islam he finally found one—a system that would never betray him. Thus, ironically, it was when Hussam was living among Mormons that he finally became a Muslim. As much as he devoured and savored what he had learned in his scholarly studies at BYU, the most important consequence of his time in graduate school was that when he left Utah, he was truly a Muslim. Hussam had become a more complete person, one who was better equipped to deal with the burdens to come.

A Bombshell

(2000, age twenty-seven)

Hussam sat with his mother in the back of the old-model taxi. His side of the bench seat had long ago lost its springs and was pitching him toward the window. Fares was sitting up front with the taxi driver as they made the twenty-minute drive from the Rafah crossing back home to the al-Nuseirat camp. The brutal June heat hadn't set in yet, but it was plenty warm, and Hussam opened his window. Eyes closed, head tilted out the window, he inhaled the aromas of Gaza, using his arm to divert as much of the air to his nose as possible. He felt so relaxed, so at peace, lost in random thoughts about his life in Gaza and his past year in the United States.

Once they got home, as everyone was relaxing in the salon, Fares and Rasmeya dropped a bomb on Hussam. They wanted to talk marriage—his marriage—and announced that it would take place on July 18, just twenty-nine days away.

"No, you can't be serious, Baba and Mama!" exclaimed an astonished Hussam. "There's no way I can be ready by then. Please, I just arrived home after a year away. I need time to rest and get my bearings. I have so many people to see, so many things I need to do before I return to my job. And, I mean, there's also everything we need to do to prepare for the banquet, for the wedding hall, not to mention everything that needs to get done for our new apartment. There are so many things to do! Maybe Mai wants to buy some gold. We can't possibly do all these things in one month! That's crazy! I prefer waiting until October."

Following tradition, Fares called Yousef, Mai's father, and asked him, his wife, and Mai to come over to discuss the wedding date. But when he heard his siblings giggling in the background, Hussam quickly realized that this discussion was a ruse; both families had been in cahoots for months, deciding together on the July 18 date. "We have already set the wedding date, Hussam," his parents said, "Please don't resist this plan. All of us have waited a very long time for the wedding and there is no reason to delay it. There has been no marriage in the Abushawish family for years! We'll take care of all of the details." Hussam really had no choice but to accept what everyone wanted, even though he didn't like this immediate pressure on him just as he arrived home.

Soon Mai, her parents, and her brothers arrived to greet Hussam. His face lit up when he saw Mai. It had been a year since they'd laid eyes on each other, with only phone conversations while he was away. "It's so nice to have you here, Mai. It seems that we will be married soon and begin our happy life together," Hussam said in front of everyone. They shook hands. After formalities, they went to a side room, both feeling awkward, unsure what to say in private. But Mai's big smile told Hussam that she still felt the same way about him. He certainly did about her.

The remaining days before their marriage were chock full of tasks: signing the marriage contract, selecting witnesses, hosting and attending luncheons and parties, buying clothes and jewelry, and so on. Despite the time pressure, Hussam was able to relax enough to sense a growing happiness inside him. This was a crucial next stage of his life, one that he and Mai had waited a long time to share. The elaborate wedding went off without a hitch.

In 2001, one year after their marriage, Hussam and Mai welcomed their first child, Montaser, a boy. Over the following ten years, they had four more children, all girls: Lama in 2002, Shaden in 2004, Shahd in 2007, and Layan in 2011.

During these first years of his marriage, Hussam continued to thrive at his job at the Palestine Technical College. The work was relentless: each year more enrollees, more classes to staff, more administration. He taught more courses than anyone else at the college and would work long into the night on his syllabi. He loved his students and delighted in teaching them everything he had learned about effective leadership.

Hussam received successive promotions: Immediately after his return from the United States in 2000, he was promoted from instructor to lecturer; the following year, he became chair of the education department; and in 2006 he was promoted to vice dean for academic affairs. But life became increasingly difficult in Gaza. Classes were often canceled during the civil war that followed Hamas's election in 2006. Then the Israeli blockade took hold, severely restricting basic goods that Gazans needed in their day-to-day lives. Taxi fares went up, food prices increased steadily, electricity was intermittent, and health care for his kids was harder to get.

December 2008 brought Operation Cast Lead, the three-week Israeli assault on Gaza for the stated purpose of eliminating Hamas in the face of its launching of hundreds of makeshift rockets into Israel. Israeli ground forces also made incursions into numerous places in the Strip, targeting the power plant near Nuseirat, political offices, the Islamic University, and UNRWA compounds and schools. This was the greatest level of violence that Gazans had experienced since 1967. At the time, they couldn't have imagined anything worse.

Malaysia

(2010, age thirty-seven)

In 2010, a full decade after he had completed his master's program, Hussam didn't want to admit it, but he needed an escape from the incessantly squeezing pressure of life in Gaza. And he felt as if he was stagnating professionally. So he began applying for PhD programs in educational leadership, a process that was expensive and required a huge amount of paperwork. He received a couple of offers, but they were untenable: The one from the UK had very high fees, and he couldn't imagine his family living in the freezing weather of Estonia.

Fortunately, a feasible offer finally arrived, this time from the Universiti Sains Malaysia on the island of Penang, a one-hour flight north from Kuala Lumpur, the capital of Malaysia. Penang seemed several worlds away. What sold Hussam on the offer, however, was that Malaysia is a Muslim country. He and his family would feel more at home there.

Eventually, Hussam needed to take four separate trips to Malaysia to complete his degree. The first month-long trip was in late 2010 to begin coursework. The second trip in 2012 was for eight months to complete coursework. On this trip, Hussam brought the entire family with him. That trip was momentous: the first, and it turned out, the only trip for Mai and the kids outside the Gaza Strip. They delighted in the island's vast expanses of nature, with its seemingly endless species of birds and varieties of trees. It was so beautiful and felt so safe, unlike their intense and dangerous life in Gaza. They bought a car and took rides to the sea daily. Penang was just an island, but it seemed massive compared with their little Gaza. There were so many restaurants with such varieties of food. They loved the unknown tropical fruits. And then there were the huge shopping malls.

Back home in 2012 and early 2013, he collected data for his dissertation research surveying leadership practices in Gazan universities, and he began drafting his dissertation. He took his third trip to Malaysia in mid-2013 for a month to discuss his dissertation with his advisors and his fourth trip in late 2013 through early 2014 to complete his dissertation and then defend it.

On all these trips, Hussam had to postpone flights because the Rafah crossing was suddenly closed on the days he needed to leave. But for this final trip he had to postpone them at the last minute three times. Travel outside of Gaza through the Rafah crossing to Egypt had become much more difficult during those years. Egypt had erupted in revolution in 2011 during the Arab Spring. President Hosni Mubarak was deposed, Mohamed Morsi of the Muslim Brotherhood was elected to replace him, and by 2014 General Abdel Fattah el Sisi had staged a successful military coup and been elected president. El Sisi disliked Hamas because it was an offshoot of the Muslim Brotherhood, and he made entering Egypt through the Rafa crossing extremely difficult for Palestinians.

War

(2014, age forty-one)

The shrill ring of the landline interrupted the still dawn. Fares shuffled into the front room to answer it. Hussam was there preparing for his morning's lecture at the college—he often studied downstairs in a back room of the mostly unfinished ground floor of the house to escape the noise of his own apartment, what with the kids and all. As he watched the color drain from his father's face, he could hear the deep voice speaking loudly in Israeli-accented English.

"Mr. Abushawish, is your front door open or closed?"

Such a strange question, thought Fares.

"It's closed, of course; it's five in the morning."

"Leave, and close the door behind you," ordered the Israeli commander.

"You mean we have to leave our home?" replied Fares, alarmed and perturbed at having to play this guessing game.

"Yes, you must go. Right now!"

"Why?" Fares challenged.

"Your house is scheduled to be bombed in ten minutes."

So Fares's family had finally gotten the call that Hammam's family had received, along with thousands of others. It was now thirty days into the fourth war, Operation Protective Edge, in eight years between Israel and Hamas. This war had already lasted nearly twice as long as the 2008–9 war that had seen eighteen days of devastating bombardment from Israeli jets and drones from the sky, tank shelling from the east, and missiles from the Israeli war ships that constantly patrolled six kilometers from the shore.

Fares raced to the stairwell and screamed the news so that all the families in the house would know what was about to happen. By now, the house had four stories above the ground level. Each level had two apartments, except the top level, which had only one. Fares and Rasmeya and Hussam and Mai lived on the first floor (above the ground level); Hussam's brothers Ashraf and Mohammed and their families lived on the second floor; his brothers Alaa and Omar and their families lived on the third floor; and his youngest brother, Thaer, lived on the fourth.

"Everyone! The Israelis say they will be bombing the house in ten minutes. Everyone decide for yourselves if you are going to stay or leave. Your mother and I will be leaving on foot immediately."

Fares's news set off a wildfire of activity throughout the whole house. From each level came shouts of alarm and protest, as well as loud discussions of what to do. The awakening kids added to the chaos; they didn't know what was happening but screamed in response to the sense of danger. All the parents were asking themselves the same agonizing questions:

Are they really going to bomb us?

Should we leave?

Or barricade ourselves in the stairwell?

If we leave, where will we go?

How do we know if it will be any safer there?

When will we come back?

What will we do if they really destroy our house?

Hussam's mind was racing, with no time to perform his worst-case scenario analysis. He bounded up the bare concrete steps one floor to find Mai already packing clothes. She looked up at him, and they needed no words to convey their fear. They had rehearsed this scenario, but now it was real. At least they knew that they would be going to live in the spare room of Mai's parents' new house, which they'd built in 2012, a few kilometers away on the south side of the camp near the power plant.

"Let me do this, Mai. Please grab whatever we need from the kitchen." Mai rushed about, pulling the plastic containers of olive oil, salt, sugar, coffee, rice, and flour off the shelves, as well as various packets of herbs and spices. A memory suddenly flashed in her brain: "Hussam," she cried, "I just remembered that the spare room has no furniture in it!"

"That means we'll have to take all seven bed mats with us. I'll call Hani (a young cousin) and ask if he could take us in his car. We'll just have to stuff the beds in somehow." Mai also remembered that they had one, mostly empty, tank of propane to run a stove, and she lugged it over to the pile of goods they'd amassed in the middle of the salon.

Hussam paused a second to look at the large battery in the corner of the room—the precious battery he had saved up to buy for so long. Powered by solar panels during the day, it provided basic electricity for his family. Gazans had usually been permitted only six hours of electricity per day during those years, but now with the war, it was much less, even down to only two hours per day. However, the battery weighed nearly eighty kilos, and the car could hold only so much. All he could do was hope to retrieve it later.

Hani arrived quickly, honking repeatedly for the family to hurry up. Hussam and Montaser handled the thin bed mats, the two younger girls each took a small roller bag, and Mai wrestled the larger bag down the steps. Ashraf, Mohammed, Omar, and Alaa, each having decided to hold out with their families at the house, rushed to help Mai with the bag and the remaining items. Hani helped stuff the bed mats into his dinged-up hatchback. The suitcases filled most of the back seat. The kids lay on top of them, and Mai sat on Hussam's lap in the front seat.

Hani's old car rocked back and forth as he turned the key. Thankfully, the engine started, with everyone wondering if the car could actually move. It was so weighted down that the tires were barely visible. Slowly, it did manage to pull away, tires spinning in the sand.

Just then, there was a massive explosion on a neighboring street. Hussam knew it was a bomb from an F-16 fighter jet, having long since learned to identify the sounds of Israel's aircraft and weaponry. Unlike the primitive, unguided rockets Hamas flew into Israel that made a tremendously loud sound at launch, these laser-guided bombs from the American-made fighter jets discharged from unseen heights and were silent until they smashed into the target.

The bomb produced a thunderous explosion, blasting eardrums and pulverizing the target and its surroundings, sending tremors through the earth for hundreds of meters in all directions. Everyone shrieked as the whole car pitched back and forth. The buildings shielded them from much of the barrage of debris—concrete, rebar, wood, powdered cinder block, and glass. But the gray cloud of dust quickly darkened the whole area.

"This isn't safe, Hussam," screamed Mai. "We have to go back." Hussam agreed, and everyone piled out of the car and raced back to their house. They huddled together in the salon on the ground floor under the sofa cushions in anticipation of the next blast.

"What should we do, Hussam?" whispered Mai, trying not to alarm the girls, who were holding one another for dear life.

"I just don't know, Mai," replied Hussam. Should they stay and risk the bombing that they'd been warned about? Or had they just heard the bomb that was meant to hit their house? "We might be safe if we stay. How can we know what to do? Or should we flee just to be sure?"

For both Mai and Hussam, their only real concern was the kids. TV news over the last month continuously showed gruesome photos and footage of the bombardments, both during the day and night, sometimes graphically displaying children being torn apart by shrapnel. Earlier that week a bunker-buster bomb from a B-1 had annihilated a house like theirs, killing all twenty-one members of the family.

Privately, their thoughts were aligned:

We cannot let this happen to our children. They are our responsibility, and we must do everything to protect them. But what is the right thing to do to protect them?

After calming down a little, Hussam and Mai agreed that they should leave again; maybe things would be better near her parents. Everyone packed back into Hani's car, which was still in the middle of the street, engine sputtering. But just as soon as Hani had driven one hundred meters, two bombs in rapid succession struck the street one hundred meters on the other side of their house. The double blast was deafening and mind numbing. The shock waves made the car feel like a ship caught in a ferocious sea storm.

"Cover your eyes and mouths, kids! Immediately!" shrieked Hussam, his own voice sounding to him like a whisper from the far end of a long, black tunnel. The dark cloud of dust and debris was hurtling towards them like a hurricane. It hit the car with tremendous force, lacerating the back end. Miraculously, the monster explosion spared the car's tires and windows, but it enveloped the outside and filled the inside with a sickening dust.

When it was all over, Hussam and Mai wiped off each other's faces, now covered with a muddy mixture of dust and tears. Mai reached back from Hussam's lap and did the same for the girls. Hani reached back to help Montaser. The kids had stopped shrieking. They seemed frozen, almost catatonic. Hussam ordered everyone out of the car, and they all raced back to the house once again, which, praise God, was unharmed by the blasts, other than being covered in the same blanket of gray ash.

The family, including Hani, huddled together in the salon again. No talking, no crying, just paralysis from the terrifying violence of the explosions. After several minutes Hussam asked Mai to join him in a far corner of the room. They were both exhausted from the sheer energy it took to withstand the trauma and to keep themselves in enough control for the sake of the kids. After reviewing the events of the morning, they agreed that it was not smart to keep returning to the house. They had to leave for good and take shelter near Mai's parents' house.

Once they were back in the car, everyone clutched whatever or whoever was in reach, shaking and deathly afraid that another bomb would obliterate them. Hani clutched the steering wheel so tightly it seemed like it would break. Sitting on Hussam's lap, Mai reached down and grabbed his hands. The kids lay entangled together on top of the suitcases. They made the sluggish, bumpy drive to Mai's parents' house in fifteen minutes without incident.

Hugging Mai's parents and siblings was exactly what they all needed to calm down after their horrific morning. Tea, coffee, biscuits, and fruit were already laid out for the kids. It was the middle of Ramadan, so the adults were fasting.

Now settled in the new space, Hussam reached for his phone and discovered what he expected: no bars because the cellular network was down. He desperately hoped that his parents had survived their escape. Later that evening the network popped back on, and Hussam was able to reach them. He recounted the ordeals of the day and assured them that everything was okay now. The kids were still anxious, but they were safe.

For their part, his mother and father had made it safely on foot, dragging one suitcase each to the home of relatives who lived near the main mosque. The first blast scared them badly, but they kept on going, now running. By the time the next bombs exploded, they were far enough away not to be knocked over. They had just reached Ashraf, Mohammed, Omar, Alaa, and Thaer by phone. Everyone there was okay. The house had not been bombed, after all.

Although Hussam's family could hear the constant sound of bombing in the distance, by nightfall no bombs had struck their area. For now, they felt protected by a curtain of safety and stillness, something Hussam's family desperately needed after their nightmarish morning. Mai and the kids instantly fell into a deep sleep.

Hussam had just begun to doze off on his bed mat. Then he shot up, rigid. There it was—that eerie clicking sound—from the Abrams tanks the Israeli military had positioned five miles to the east on the other side of the fence separating Gaza from Israel. A few seconds after every click came the signature whoosh of the tank shell. The whoosh was loud, meaning that the shells were just missing Mai's parents' house, screaming through the black night on their way to puncture other structures, destroying everything and perhaps everyone in them. Thankfully, Mai and the kids did not awaken.

The tank shelling continued every night. It was only a matter of time before a shell exploded right through the wall of their room, which faced directly east toward Israel. And there was the real possibility that the power plant, just six hundred meters away, would be bombed again by the F-16s. After consulting with Mai, Hussam decided that it was just too risky to stay there, and she agreed. With her father's blessing, Hussam, Mai, and the kids went to the house of another relative who lived near the great mosque in al-Nuseirat Camp—not far from where his parents were holed up. Although that location was also dangerous because the mosque had often been targeted, at least they would be closer to family and to their own home. Hani's car was still functioning, and he bravely agreed to pick them up and deliver them to their new refuge.

Just a few days after they had arrived at the new place, Mai noticed that Hussam was getting ready to go out. No longer able to contain her terror, Mai shrieked, "Where are you going?"

"It's Friday, Mai. I must go to the mosque to pray," pleaded Hussam.

"But Hussam, please, please don't go. The bombs have been falling all morning! We need you here. If we are going to die, let us die together . . . please!"

"Mai, you know that I made a commitment to Allah. Don't worry. He will protect us all. I will be gone just one hour. Please, have faith. You know that I must do this. Please gather yourselves in the stairwell. I'll be right back."

Hussam was crazed with anxiety after making this decision. Of course, he wanted to be with Mai and the kids, to huddle with them, to support them, to be supported by them, to die with them. But when he had fully embraced Islam during his year in the United States, he'd promised that he would be 100 percent faithful. God would never betray him. Hussam just needed to be faithful, and Friday prayer was a crucial service.

The mosque was overflowing, so Hussam joined the hundreds of other men in the overflow area, everyone kneeling on an individual rug in the street, fanning out from the main entrance. The imam's sermon went on for at least thirty minutes. He aimed to comfort the faithful and bring some peace to their hearts. This was his central message:

> Praise to Allah, the greatest and most powerful, that you have come to this sacred place. Do not be frightened. Allah will reward you for your devotion. Remember, all is in Allah's hands. He will protect us from our enemy in his own ways. Do not fear. If you must die, it will be because he wills it. Praise Allah forever.

Hussam felt comforted by the imam's preaching, but that feeling was shattered when a bomb from an F-16 landed just a block away. It splintered the silence. The man on his right jumped up as if to flee, but then thought better of it and knelt again, shaking like all his brothers surrounding him. The friend on his left suggested that the blast they had heard was just a warning sign. It wasn't as strong as a full bomb, he reasoned; it probably came from the drones that had been circling Gaza twenty-four hours a day for years now, blighting the air with their relentless, whiny buzz. If that's true, he continued, then it may mean that a full bomb from an F-16 would obliterate the mosque and all of them.

The instant the imam had finished, Hussam rushed back to the relative's house and found Mai and the kids in the stairwell, as he'd instructed. All the kids were sobbing hysterically, no longer able to hold back their tears after the chaos of the past few days. Mai was keeping a steady voice, but Hussam knew that she, too, was petrified. So was he. "How much of this can we take?" they asked each other, away from the kids. Mai said she was desperately worried; she couldn't remember the last time she'd seen smiles on the kids' faces, or sensed any ease in their tone of voice or saw any light in their dark eyes.

"What should we do?" was still the most plaguing question. They had learned that nowhere was safe. Operation Protective Edge was different from the previous three operations, when the Israeli bombardments had been targeted at specific sites and areas, making it relatively easy to find a place to feel safe. This operation would run a full fifty-one days over all of Gaza, eventually destroying ten thousand homes, killing more than two thousand people and injuring more than eleven thousand.[63]

All of them—Mai, Hussam, and the kids—longed for their real home. At least the familiarity of its configurations and smells would help to assuage their terror. "We can't keep running forever," they agreed. "God will protect us." So they elected to risk returning home. There was no time to call for Hani, and it would be too dangerous for him anyway. Bombs, missiles, and shells were exploding incessantly now.

They had to abandon their bed mats, and they simply grabbed whatever piece of luggage each of them could manage as they fled on foot. "Stay close

---

[63] United Nations Office for the Coordination of Humanitarian Affairs (OCHA), "Key Figures on the 2014 Hostilities," June 23, 2015, https://www.ochaopt.org/content/key-figures-2014-hostilities.

to the buildings," Hussam ordered everyone as he charted a course through back alleys in the hope of avoiding a direct hit. The constant explosions disturbed the characteristic serenity of this part of the camp. The family forged ahead, dragging their suitcases, the parents and two oldest kids each holding a younger child's hand. Then they heard a loud blast—it sounded like something less powerful than a bomb, likely a missile from a drone. As they turned a corner, an old woman shrieked at them,

"No, no, don't go that way! I just saw shrapnel tearing someone's leg off. Take this other alley. Hurry! God protect you, dear ones!"

The girls couldn't take anymore. Shrieking and wetting themselves, they just collapsed. There was no time to stop—they were close to home now—so Hussam, Mai, and Montaser dragged the girls the last distance. Finally, they rounded the corner. Their house, coated in dust, was still intact. The neighborhood was now ghostly silent.

There Is No Bottom to Worse

(2017, age forty-four)

Hussam and Mai sat on the big sofa in the front room enjoying the pleasant breeze blowing the sheer curtains slowly in and out of the open windows. It was late morning on the last Saturday in April, one of the most pleasant times of the year in Gaza. The cold rains were over, and the thick blanket of heat had yet to envelop the Strip.

The windows also let in the competing choruses of the weekend street vendors, who were already making their rounds in their wooden donkey carts.

"Sweet water! Sweet water!" (fresh water) chanted the old man with the black-and-white checked *kaffiyeh* wrapped around his neck, one son seated next to him. The wooden cart carried a translucent, one hundred–gallon plastic container of fresh water. The man would have purchased it from tanker trucks that came from Israel. Or he would have filled the container from one of the few remaining wells that were deep enough to draw fresh water from the aquifer, Gaza's only natural source of water. The increasingly thick upper layer of the aquifer had been contaminated by the nitrates leaching from the beds of raw sewage diverted from the camps to empty fields. The aquifer had also become heavily salinized from the sea water that flowed into it because of the over pumping of the top layer. Gaza had gotten relatively little rain during the past winter, so there had been little fresh water to replenish the aquifer.

This man had been peddling water for so long that he had trained his tenor voice to project far. Still, he was outmatched by the farmer who somehow had acquired an old megaphone:

"Cauliflower! White Cabbage! Carrots! Onions! Leeks! Rhubarb! Radishes!"

But the fruit vendor had the real advantage. Recently, he had acquired not just a megaphone but also a small loudspeaker that would send his calls crackling into the air: "Oranges! Lemons! Apples! Pears!" (The famed strawberries from Beit Lahia in northern Gaza would be on the cart in a few weeks.) These vendors were not competing with one another. They each peddled different necessities; their strategy was just to draw in as many customers as possible.

The simple pleasure of a Saturday morning was intensified with excitement on that particular Saturday because all Palestinian Authority (PA) employees get paid on the last Saturday of the month. Hussam and Mai had used the morning to go over their finances, meticulously budgeting everything for the coming month.

As a full professor at a government college, Hussam earned 7,000 shekels per month (approximately $2,000), which was enough to cover all the family's expenses: utilities, food, school supplies, and so on. As a primary and secondary school teacher, also at PA-run schools, Mai earned 2,400 shekels (approximately $700). But according to Islamic law, a wife's salary was strictly for herself. That is, it wasn't automatically added to her husband's salary to spend on the family. Of course, Mai was quite generous with her money—she had no other interest than creating the best life possible for her family with Hussam. But she also held some money in reserve for her parents and siblings in case a need arose.

Mai's financial autonomy gave her an advantage when she and Hussam occasionally disagreed about the best way to spend any extra money they had. For example, Hussam had recently wanted to use part of that surplus to buy the kids some new clothes. He knew they'd be pleased—and he liked them looking their best. But Mai, often more practical, preferred to spend her salary on getting a new water main line—the inch-diameter black plastic tube through which nonpotable water, delivered by small tanker trucks, was pumped up to storage tanks on the roof using Hussam's portable generator. From these rooftop tanks, the water flowed down through numerous smaller plastic lines to every apartment in the house, for every water need except drinking and cooking. Mai had noticed that the main line, which ran up the stucco wall of the house just next to the front door, was getting worn and rigid, likely from constant exposure to the elements. She knew the hardship it would create if that line broke, and she figured that it was the right investment to make to protect her own family—and the other families in the house.

Another time, when Hussam wanted to replace their ancient TV with a smart one so the kids could play video games and watch cable channels, Mai chose instead to use her funds to buy Hussam a new cell phone. His had broken months ago, and he was using a cheap, old flip phone. "How can you operate like that, Hussam? Your students have much better phones than you do!"

It was that new cell phone that started to vibrate on the side table next to Hussam. "Ah, here it is, Mai," said Hussam, assuming that it was the text message he was expecting from the bank announcing the deposit of his salary. Like all the other seventy thousand PA employees in Gaza, they'd been waiting for this deposit confirmation before they withdrew the money to start paying their bills, buying their groceries, and making their other expenditures. "Oh good," replied Mai. "I'll go get the cash." The main branch near the central market had an ATM. She wanted to hurry because there'd soon be a long line of people waiting to withdraw their salary funds.

Just like Hammam, what Hussam he read in the text message jolted him. "What?! There must be some mistake here!" he protested as his eyes burned holes in the phone screen. "They've only deposited half of my salary!" His face scrunched up with both distress and fear.

A minute later, Mai's phone chirped. There it was: Her salary had also been cut in half.

By this time, the tensions between the PA and Hamas had reached an extreme level. Both sides claimed that they wanted to reconcile. Just weeks before, Hamas had agreed to return governmental control of the Strip to the PA, who ran the West Bank. But it wouldn't budge on policing and security, responsibilities it insisted on sharing with the PA. Mahmoud Abbas, the PA president, would have none of it; he demanded that Hamas relinquish all official functions to the PA—essentially to return the situation to what it had been before Hamas's electoral victory and subsequent military takeover of Gaza.

Both Hussam and Mai immediately began calling friends and colleagues, all of whom confirmed that everyone's salary had been cut. In fact, calls were ricocheting throughout the neighborhood as virtually every family tried to get information. The size of the salary cuts varied; Hussam and Mai heard figures ranging from 25 to 60 percent.[64]

"Abbas is doing exactly what Israel is doing to us!" bristled Hussam to Mai. For more than a decade now, Israel—with support from the United States, the EU, and Egypt—had blocked the import and export of food and medicine and had prohibited travel in and out of Gaza. Now Abbas was cutting electricity and salaries. "We're not responsible for his squabbles with

---

[64] Despite the PA's claims that the salary cuts were the result of its own shortage of funds, Gazans were quick to point out that no salary cuts were made in the other Palestinian territories. Most Gazans viewed the cuts as a form of collective punishment on them to pressure Hamas to relinquish control of the Strip. See Amjad Ayman and Chloé Benoist, "'Soon I Will Be Begging': PA Salary Cuts Push Gaza Closer to the Brink," *Middle East Eye*, May 4, 2018, https://www.middleeasteye.net/news/soon-i-will-be-begging-pa-salary-cuts-push-gaza-closer-brink.

Hamas," said Hussam. "We've been loyal citizens and employees. How dare he punish everyone like this! He is *humiliating* us."

Mai had never heard Hussam refer to humiliation as his reaction to the various hardships in their lives. He had weathered many crises over the years—the fear, torture, and imprisonment he had endured during the first *intifada*; the sense of betrayal he had felt when he discovered the shortcomings of some leaders of his political faction; the tuberculosis scare in Utah; the wars with Israel, particularly the 2014 nightmare; and more. But Hussam considered this betrayal by Palestinian leaders far worse. She had never seen him so infuriated.

When Mai awoke in the middle of the night, she realized that Hussam had left their bed. She found him in the front room, just sitting with his arms folded, staring into the darkness. Nestling up to him on the sofa, she quietly pleaded, "Hussam, please tell me what you're thinking and feeling." After a minute or so, he unloaded.

"This is a different type of sacrifice than those we've been forced to make at the hands of the Israelis. I'm very proud of my sacrifices during the *intifada* and my efforts to educate my people ever since. In fact, it's an honor to defy Israel, and I will always do so. They are a foreign enemy who have always treated us as subhuman. They have trampled on our every basic right, even the right to call ourselves Palestinians and to call our land Palestine. I . . . we . . . will always resist this treatment. But to be oppressed and collectively punished by our own people, our own leaders, is repulsive."

Imagining that he was speaking directly to Abbas, he exploded with rage: "I've worked for you for nearly a quarter century. How dare you betray us like this? Sure, I fault Hamas for taking over the governing of Gaza. But I'm not responsible for your infighting. And you don't have the right to manipulate me and our rights to solve your problem with Hamas. We are all Palestinians. You politicians should settle your differences among yourselves. You should cooperate and collaborate on solutions. How dare you trash our dignity with this new layer of collective punishment!"

Of course, Mai felt precisely the same way. Their life had been so full of burdens, and now to be insulted and deprived like this! It was too much. But both of them knew that their rage wouldn't answer the now pressing question, "How were they going to manage financially? Mai went to get the budget sheets they had worked out the day before. Hussam turned on the light, and they began their own slashing of funds.

Hussam would sell his car (at a significant loss). No new clothes for anyone. No more treats for the kids—no snacks, no fancy multicolored notebooks—just basic food and supplies. They would stop paying the water bill, since that utility seemed more forgiving of late payments. They would cancel their cable service. A neighbor had recently offered to share his service by stringing a line across the back alley between their homes. Hussam had demurred out of pride, but things had just changed drastically.

Still, with these and other cuts, it was clear from their calculations that Hussam's salary could not cover the basics. They would need to start drawing down their savings. It seemed that they could make it if they withdrew 700 shekels (about $200) a month. They had saved enough to do that for about eighteen months.

Hussam was greatly relieved when they realized that they could manage financially for the time being. But he knew things would get worse. Abbas had already leaked the rumor that his next "austerity" move might be to force some PA employees in Gaza—maybe all of them, wondered Hussam—into early retirement. He and Mai did the calculations together using the PA pension formula. It would be impossible for their family to survive at this level of income.

Barely even a week into this crisis, Hussam started to seriously contemplate—even plan for—something he had never imagined. They would have to leave Gaza to survive. The writing was on the wall everywhere. Even the private sector was suffering. Restaurants were closing; the few big supermarkets also began to cut employees' salaries by 30 percent. Their profits had plummeted because fewer people could afford their goods. Things were getting worse and worse. *Was there a bottom to worse?* he wondered.

One day Hussam arrived home an hour later than usual. "Where have you been?" asked Mai.

"I'm sorry, I tried to call, but my battery was dead. I was at the passport office."

"Passport office?"

"Yes, I started the passport renewal process for you and the kids. Mine is still valid."

"Are you thinking that we'll leave?"

"Just in case, yes."

That night after dinner, once he and Mai had settled on the sofa in the front room, Hussam continued the discussion. "We've both always believed that Gaza is the best place in the world to live," he began. "It's our cherished homeland, where we both grew up and have raised our children. But conditions have gotten nearly intolerable now. What do we do if the salary cut continues for a long time? We simply won't be able to make it.

"I know that you don't want to go, and I totally understand that. I'm not thinking that we would go permanently, only a few years until conditions improve here. Why should we stay here and suffer like this? We're totally helpless in trying to change any of the horrible living conditions now that our own leader is against us, and I refuse to get involved in this deplorable conflict between Abbas and Hamas. We must be practical. We can't just wait here and weep. Our dignity demands more than that."

Mai understood, of course. As much as she hated discussing even a hypothetical scenario of leaving Gaza, she needed to express her deepest concern about staying:

"I'm very worried about the kids. Montaser will take the *tawjihi* next year, and Lama the year after that. I hope we'll be able to find a way to get the younger girls through high school as well. And they all want to continue their education after high school. But on this half salary, there's no way we could afford to pay for university for all of them, or even some of them."

Her face draped in a sadness, Mai continued: "It's like this salary cut has torn our hearts in two: one part forever fused to Gaza, and this new, ugly part accepting that Gaza may no longer be survivable."

The next day Hussam began his search, a process he was familiar with from his graduate programs. Now it would be for a faculty position abroad. Within a couple of weeks, he had applied to university slots in Brunei, Cyprus, Qatar, Jordan, the United States, and the UK. Friends in Malaysia had told him that it was nearly impossible to find a position there these days, so he didn't bother applying to his alma mater.

And Again

(2018, age forty-five)

"How is everyone? How are your families?" Hussam asked the teachers who had just come into his office. Although he was still teaching several classes, he was now vice dean of academic affairs. It had been nineteen months since the PA had slashed everyone's salary.

"In fact, Hussam," replied one of the teachers, speaking for the group, "we've come to tell you that things have gotten terrible for us with the financial crisis. Believe me, we've been scraping by as best we can during these months of the salary cut, but we're not making it. We're nearly out of money, and we're ashamed to say that if we don't get paid next week, we won't be able to continue teaching at the college."

Another teacher clarified: "Yes, soon I literally won't even have the four shekels to pay for the taxi to get to work. I can't even feed my family."

The exchange turned into a conversation among brothers as Hussam empathized with their plight by revealing that he was struggling too. For an hour or more they sat commiserating as they reviewed their lives over these past months.

"We are human beings, not merely numbers," exclaimed another teacher. "They act as if we are somehow responsible for the failure of the reconciliation talks. Both parties are at fault for this political crisis. The only thing we as people can do is to express ourselves in a new election." (No election has been held since 2006 because of internal Palestinian politics combined with Israeli and regional intervention.) "Abbas probably doesn't even want one, since it might end his regime. Meanwhile, they are violating our basic human rights. This is shameful, and it infuriates me."

Hussam hadn't mentioned to the others that for him, this month had been the worst one ever; that he honestly feared that he would not be able to feed his family any longer; that he and Mai had now fully depleted their savings account; that even if they still got their 50 percent salaries next month, they wouldn't be able to manage; that he felt guilty for complaining because he was actually one of the fortunate ones with a professional, regular job, when more than half of Gazans were unemployed. How awful it must be for them. Many had taken to roaming the streets and alleys in search of metal and plastic that they might be able to sell for a few shekels. And he knew that many Gazans were actually starving.

Hussam didn't admit to feeling nearly beaten by what he had taken to calling a catastrophe. But he did reveal his feelings about the magnitude of the crisis to these teachers. "You know, this is the ultimate oppression. We've suffered all our lives through the Israeli occupation, and now this stupid infighting among our own political leaders. It's like we were born into captivity. Now we're in our forties, and we've been constantly oppressed by the Israelis, the Arabs, so many others. But this is worse; it feels like betrayal."

The crisis was so bad that even Mai's calm faith had been tried. She told Hussam one night, "All our plans for the future, for our children, are blowing away in the wind. There are so many powers toying with us: the Israelis, the Arabs, the US, the EU. None of them really seems to care about us. We're like little pawns in their political games. It is so humiliating."

Hussam echoed Mai's analysis in his discussion with the teachers:

"Have you noticed that this financial crisis started after Trump became president? I think that this is all part of his plan. His stupid 'Deal of the Century,' which left us an afterthought, means that we're forced into ever deeper despair and humiliation.[65] We're being betrayed by the entire international community, just as we've been betrayed our entire lives. We're not human to them, not deserving of even the most basic rights. Every one of their so-called peace plans offers us a little lump of sugar just to get us to go along with their grand plans. All the plans have failed to acknowledge our right to self-determination and independence in a state where we can fully enjoy our rights, dignity, and humanity."

---

[65] Jeremy Bowen, "Trump's Middle East Peace Plan: 'Deal of the Century' Is Huge Gamble. *BBC News*, January 28, 2020, https://www.bbc.com/news/world-middle-east-51263815.

Gaza Forever

(2019, age forty-six)

Nothing had panned out yet for Hussam. He had gotten no solid offers on his countless applications for faculty positions at universities literally across the globe. Meanwhile, the PA had lightened up a bit in the last year. Although Abbas hadn't restored full salaries, under pressure from Washington, Brussels, and Cairo, the PA had made some lump sum payments of past salaries. These payments brought Hussam up to the equivalent of 75 percent of his original salary for the time being. It had made a huge difference in meeting the family's needs—and above all, saved him from the ultimate humiliation of having to borrow money from family or friends.

Still, he was barely surviving financially. He was desperate for a break from all of Gaza's pressures, now even more urgently because the kids were growing up. He wanted them to have a better life—one free from danger, oppression, inadequate health services and medicines, and terrible water. Above all, he wanted them to get a good education and have the freedom to move about, like normal people do—things he had tasted in the United States and Malaysia.

The following timeline shows the progression of the most promising of Hussam's attempts to find a university job and help his family escape their plight in Gaza:

July 1

Mai and the kids had already gone to bed. Hussam was trying to unwind on the sofa after a grueling day at work, teaching and resolving faculty issues. The neighborhood was silent except for the occasional rooster crowing at an odd nocturnal hour. There was no electricity, but he had enough battery left on his cell phone to scroll mindlessly through Facebook. He saw a posting from Khaled, a Gazan friend who had also gotten his PhD at the Universti Sains Malaysia. He recalled that some years ago, Khaled had landed a job at A' Sharqiyah University in Oman, a small country on the Arabian Peninsula, and had moved his family there.

Despite the late hour, Hussam called Khaled and asked if by any chance his university had any openings. Hussam hadn't seen any advertised, but he figured it wouldn't hurt to ask—if only to satisfy his compulsiveness to do everything he could. "It would be fantastic to have you here!" replied Khaled. "Let me check tomorrow."

July 2

Hussam sat alone in his office at the college, the last rays of sun filtering through the dusty windows. It was beastly hot, but the power had been cut off for the rest of the day, so the fans were useless. The other faculty had already gone home. His phone rumbled and slid around on his thickly varnished desk. Although he could tell from caller ID that it was Khaled, Hussam felt no excitement. By now he believed the worst-case scenario for everything. Good things rarely happen in Gaza.

So he was floored by Khaled's report: "Success, *habibi*! The university has at least four openings, one in my own department! I'm sure you can find something. It will be so great to have you and your family here."

Sure enough, the last iota of power left in his laptop revealed these openings. *How did I miss these listings?* Yet his flicker of hope faded as he read the details. One by one he had to eliminate them because his training wasn't a good fit. But wait a minute, that last one . . . Hussam's heart jumped: assistant professor of management in the College of Business Administration. On the surface it wasn't a good fit, but he reasoned that educational leadership is all about management and that he had courses in leadership in business settings.

Hussam consulted Mai that evening, and they agreed that he should apply.

July 3

Hussam woke up well before dawn as usual and hurried to the salon to start his research into the application process. Fortunately, he had charged his laptop because the electricity went off at midnight and wouldn't be turned on again until three that afternoon.

Hussam took a break from his preparations for the next semester and began drafting the letter of intent to accompany his formal application. That night and the next day, Hussam revised his draft multiple times. After Mai approved the final draft, Hussam saved the letter in a zip file with his CV.

The next evening he uploaded the file to the application website so that he wouldn't have to think about it over the weekend. He had applied for jobs countless times, so he felt nothing special about this one, certain that he would be rejected again.

A' Sharqiyah answered a week later with an email from the department head inviting Hussam for a Zoom interview on July 24. Getting an initial interview was the furthest he'd gotten in all his previous attempts to land a position, but he wasn't going to allow himself to get his hopes up, only to be disappointed again.

July 24

The department head indicated that the review committee was impressed with Hussam's application but wanted to ask him some questions. Hussam's knees began to quiver. *What if they criticize or challenge my fit within the department? What if they ask me why an education professor is applying for a job in a business department? What if they ask me how my family will feel about moving to Ibra, Oman?*

They asked him to introduce himself in English. Easy. The committee was impressed that he had identified which of their courses he thought he could teach. They were further impressed by his articulation of the "competence education" approach he used with struggling students. Then they moved on to the expected workload: five courses per semester, one more than his already heavy load. They also expected him to keep up his impressive publication record of four journal articles per year, or three at the bare minimum.

The department head ended the interview by noting that Ibra was a very conservative city, where people have great respect for Islam and dress traditionally.

"That won't be a problem at all," Hussam assured him. "As you might imagine, Gaza is also a very religious, traditional place. As for entertainment, we're used to limited opportunities, whether because of the Israelis or Hamas."

July 31

Arriving early at the office to enjoy some relatively pleasant time before the onslaught of the day's heat, Hussam booted up his laptop to complete a report but immediately saw the notification of an email from Oman.

Dear Professor Abushawish:

It is my pleasure to inform you that the College of Business Administration has selected you as our choice to fill the vacant position in our department. We hope you will be pleased. The next step in the process will be a Zoom interview with the head of the university or his representatives. You will hear from the president's office as to the timing of that interview. I wish you the very best as the process continues.

Sincerely,

Professor Daher, Dean

Hussam knew from his own college's hiring process that the upper-level review was typically a rubber stamp of the department's decision. What matters most is that the department wanted you. And this department verifiably wanted him.

Hussam felt as if he had received an infusion of energy and hope, as if a bright ray of sunlight had broken through the dark clouds smothering Gaza. He cancelled the morning's faculty meeting, printed out the email, and raced home to show it to Mai.

"*Alhamdulillah, Alhamdulillah!* Thanks be to God! Thanks be to God!" she exclaimed after reading the letter. Embracing Hussam, she whispered in his ear, "You made it, my love! Congratulations! This is wonderful news."

They sat down on the sofa and tried to appreciate the wonder of this moment. Mai didn't need Hussam to caution her that this was only the first step. Somehow she knew inside that this was real. They both immediately recalled their experience in Malaysia—how wonderful it had been to see another part of the world, to learn new customs and try new foods, all among people of their faith. They recalled how thrilled the kids had been at the beauty of Malaysia—the parks, zoos, beaches, swimming pools, and mostly the simple freedom of being able to go wherever the family wanted. Not to mention twenty-four hours a day of electricity!

Hussam and Mai decided that it would be prudent to wait before laying so much hope on the kids. Meanwhile, they had plenty of work to do. Together, they needed to have a detailed discussion about what each child had to do or acquire before moving abroad. It was easiest for Montaser, now seventeen and having just passed the *tawjihi*. They simply needed to research where in

Oman he could pursue his bachelor's degree in information technology. Hussam would handle that.

It was trickier for Lama. She was sixteen and slaving away to prepare for the *tawjihi* next spring. Mai would try to investigate the *tawjihi* process in Oman. Presuming that Lama were to pass the exam in Oman, then there was the question of where she would begin pursuing her medical degree. Hussam would take that on.

The planning was easiest for the youngest girls—Shaden, now fourteen; Shahd, eleven; and Layan, seven. Although Mai would need to confirm, both parents presumed that it would be straightforward to enter the girls in the public schools in Ibra.

And then there was the travel aspect. Hussam already knew the procedures to leave Gaza. Although he had never done it, the most efficient option would be through the northern Erez crossing into Israel. Since Gazans were not allowed to fly out of Israel's Ben Gurion airport, he would need to travel through Israel to Jordan and fly to Muscat, Oman's largest city, from Amman. To do this, he would need visas from Oman and Jordan and a permit from the Israelis. The other option would be to travel through Egypt, a process that Hussam knew intimately by now.

August 14

Present in the interview were the same three people from the first interview, along with an additional three people representing the university administration. The university president was away and couldn't join the interview, which was virtually a carbon copy of the first one.

That night he and Mai decided to inform the children. Mai gathered them all in the salon for a family meeting.

"Kids, listen, we have something very important to discuss. Your father might have a job offer to teach and do research at a university in Oman. How would you feel if we were to move there for a few years?"

Montaser vaulted off the sofa. "You mean like Malaysia?" he exclaimed. "We loved that so much. I'd love to travel again and see another part of the world. I could do my university work in IT there for sure. Definitely, 100 percent, let's do it!"

"Oh, please take me!" followed Lama in a softer-spoken version of Montaser's excitement. "I could finish my preparations and take the *tawjihi* there. Then I could study medicine. They offer medicine there, don't they, Baba? Oh, I can't wait! Please, let's go!"

The three younger girls were literally jumping up and down, yelling, "Yes! Yes! Yes!"

August 26

"Oh my god, it's real!" Hussam shouted over the phone to Mai two weeks later, perched all the way forward in his high-back desk chair after he'd slammed his office door closed harder than he'd intended. Really, it didn't matter. All noise transferred completely through the half-glass doors. Everyone in the office would hear his call. "I just received a formal offer from the university: $4,300 a month! Can you imagine it? That's more than double what my salary was before the PA cuts."

"Think of all the things we'll be able to do," said Mai. "We could even start making serious plans to build our dream house."

August 27

By now, Hussam had received visas from Oman and Jordan, but Israel had rejected his application for a permit to travel through Israel to Jordan, using the ubiquitous two-word explanation: "Security Reasons." So he'd need to travel to Oman through Cairo. The problem with passing through Egypt now was that the crossing might not be open on the desired day. Because of political instability, it had been closed much more often than open since 2013. And even when the crossing was actually open, Egypt set a daily quota of people allowed to cross—a seemingly arbitrary number. It could be fifty, it could be three hundred. Hussam didn't have the thousands of dollars that some people paid to bribe their way to the front of the line. Moreover, with all of the hostilities going on in the Sinai at the time between ISIS and Egyptian forces, what had once been an eight-hour excursion had become a three-day ordeal of navigating more than three dozen Egyptian checkpoints.

September 3

Hussam set out to tackle the other key issues. Mai had learned that enrolling the younger girls in the public school system in Ibra would be no problem. But what about Montaser and Lama? The dreams of an IT program for Montaser and a medical degree for Lama seemed increasingly distant as

Hussam navigated a maze of possible universities. He learned that A' Sharqiya University didn't have an IT program for Montaser. So he did an online search of every college and university in Oman, looking for one that had a bachelor's program in IT. It turned out that there was only one public university in all of Oman—Sultan Qaboos University—that had such a program, and it was in Muscat, the capital, far away from Ibra. There were IT programs at private universities, but they were unaffordable.

As for Lama, Mai wasn't able to find information on the *tawjihi* process in Oman. Regardless, she was skeptical about the plan. It just seemed problematic that she could finish her preparations for the *tawjihi* and pass it there. There was no way of knowing how well teachers prepared students or whether the exam itself would be modified to fit nuances of the Omani culture or education system that were unfamiliar to Lama.

But even if she passed, what would Lama do then? A' Sharqiyah didn't have a medical school. Although he wasn't crazy about the idea of having Montaser study IT in Muscat, Hussam thought he could deal with it. But neither Hussam nor Mai would be comfortable with Lama being so far away. She was unwaveringly committed to studying medicine. Persuading her to pursue another path would be even harder than getting Montaser to give up his dream of studying IT.

With these concerns about the kids in mind, Hussam and Mai began contemplating other options in nightly sessions after the children had gone to bed. Hussam's original plan was to take the entire family to Oman for two years and stay for another two years if things were working out. Hopefully, conditions in Gaza would have improved by then.

But what if they couldn't achieve the full dream? Perhaps Lama could stay in Gaza for a year with Hussam's parents until she passed the *tawjihi.* Or maybe both older kids wouldn't go at all but would instead pursue their degrees in Gaza, while Hussam, Mai, and the three younger girls lived in Oman for the four years. Or maybe only Hussam should go.

Every of those options felt like an unhappy downgrade of the dream.

And then there was the huge issue of how things would work with his current position. Hussam had every intention of returning to Gaza, and of course he wanted assurance that he'd have a job when he returned. He needed to get a leave of absence.

September 4

Hussam consulted the PA policies to find out whether he could get an unpaid leave, but they were not completely clear. He needed to call and have a discussion with the authorities.

"No, Hussam, I'm sorry, but you may not. We don't offer such leaves if your intent is to be employed at another job during the leave. I'm afraid the only thing I can think of would be to take a leave as a visiting scholar at another institution. If your college has a policy for that, we'll honor it and grant you the leave."

"Thank you very much, sir." Gratefully, this was not a Zoom call, thought Hussam, or else the official would have seen the disappointment on his face.

September 5

"I want to discuss Hussam's situation regarding his job in Oman," said the dean during a faculty meeting. "As you know, after tremendous effort and patience, Hussam has landed a great job in Oman. This is a fantastic opportunity, and I want to support him in every way I can. But it seems there's a problem with how to arrange for his unpaid leave from his current job here at our college, since he definitely wants to return after a few years. In fact, we wouldn't support him if he wanted to leave us for good!"

The discussion was confusing and disheartening. The dean and faculty brainstormed a range of strategies, each more unworkable than the next. Finally, Hussam realized that there was no good solution.

September 8

"Have you heard anything from Sultan Qaboos about Montaser?" asked Mai during their evening session.

"No, not a word, even after several requests. I'm really starting to feel very troubled about this whole thing. And now it turns out that there are serious complications about getting a leave from my job."

Hussam relayed the whole situation to Mai, including the discussion with the dean and faculty that morning. And plans for their children's education seemed hopeless. "Mai, I'm starting to hope that something falls through with the last steps of the application. My only motivation in pursuing this was to make life better for our family. But now it seems like there is no way to have the whole family there."

"All that happiness and hope we had just a few weeks ago seems to have turned into worry and struggle," said Mai. "But maybe this will help. After our talk last night, I called Fadia, Khaled's wife in Oman. I wanted to get a sense of what it's like to live in Ibra. She was very clear, and not in a positive way."

Fadia had been blunt. Ibra was terribly hot, like a desert, with only a few trees. It has just one small mall; the only thing to do in winter is go the National Park, which is really just a bunch of bushes; the dialect was very hard for their kids to understand; the education system is so different in Oman that she actually brought their daughter back to Gaza to focus on the *tawjihi*.

"I'm sorry Hussam, I should have called her much earlier to learn what it's actually like to live there. If I can be frank, I really don't want to go to Oman now. But I realize that your salary increase will be so helpful, so as much as I hate to say it, maybe the best plan is for you to go and visit us here in the summers. I'm very sorry, my love."

"Don't worry, Mai. When you left the room to make that call, you actually had the speakerphone on, and I heard every word Fadia said. And, frankly, what she said eased my mind a bit because she made it clear to me that Ibra is not the place for us to live."

September 17

"This is just not going to work, Khaled." Hussam explained in a phone call, listing all the obstacles blocking his path to Oman. "I'm seriously considering writing a letter withdrawing my acceptance of the position. What do you think?"

"I'm so sorry to hear this. I would love to have you here, but that's selfish of me. This is your future and the future of your family. If you don't think this is a good choice, then clearly you should not come."

The next day Hussam sent his withdrawal letter to Oman.

Feeling relieved after making their decision, Hussam and Mai began building their own house, a sanctuary they had dreamed about and worked toward for nearly twenty years. The only property they could afford was near Mai's parents' house—virtually adjacent to the power plant that has been a prime target of Israeli bombing over the years.

PART 2

OCTOBER 7, 2023

We may not meet again after today. We may all die at any time, my friend. May we be a beautiful memory in your life. If we die, remember that we lived dreaming of peace, that we were innocent, and that we were always peaceful.

—Hammam al-Faqawi, October 13, 2023

Introduction

In the early hours of October 7, 2023, in what they called Operation Al-Aqsa Flood, Hamas militants from Gaza breached the security fence with Israel in more than a dozen places and attacked Israeli military outposts, various nearby kibbutzes, and the Nova music festival. They killed hundreds of Israeli soldiers and civilians. Exact figures are disputed, but the consensus seems to be that there were approximately 1,200 total deaths, with a few hundred of them reportedly caused by Israeli forces themselves when they belatedly arrived to handle the crisis.[66] In addition, Hamas forces took 251 hostages into Gaza. They abducted mainly civilian women, men, the elderly, and children—Israelis and non-Israelis, including US citizens—but some were Israeli soldiers and security personnel.[67]

Various hypotheses as to the timing of the Hamas assault include the following: the fiftieth anniversary of the 1973 Yom Kippur War, the last time Israel was invaded; Israel's ongoing violations of the Al-Aqsa Mosque in Jerusalem; increasing violence by Jewish settlers against Palestinians in the West Bank; and the apparently imminent deal to normalize relations between Israel and Saudi Arabia that, like all previous Middle East peace accords, ignored the Israeli occupation and the plight of Palestinians.[68]

---

[66] Liza Rozovsky, "Families of Israelis Killed in Be'eri Home Hit by IDF Tank on October 7 Demand Probe," *Haaretz*, January 6, 2024, https://www.haaretz.com/israel-news/2024-01-06/ty-article/.premium/families-of-israelis-killed-in-beeri-home-hit-by-tank-fire-on-october-7-demand-probe/0000018c-de77-daf6-a5df-df7f22d60000.

[67] "Hamas Hostages: Stories of the People Taken from Israel," *BBC News*, October 7, 2024, https://www.bbc.com/news/world-middle-east-67053011; Matthew Mpoke Bigg, Ephrat Livni, and Aryn Baker, "Dozens of Hostages Remain in Gaza: What We Know," *New York Times*, October 25, 2024, https://www.nytimes.com/article/hostages-in-gaza-hamas.html.

[68] Aamer Madhani, "Biden Says Hamas Attacked Israel in Part to Stop a Historic Agreement with Saudi Arabia," *AP News*, October 20, 2023, https://apnews.com/article/biden-israel-hamas-saudi-arabia-war-1c376cf1497acd0df05a98721bf88fae.

The extent and violence of the assault was startling, but the unpreparedness of the Israeli military was equally surprising. The highest-tech security fence was breached. Troops guarding the West Bank took hours to get to southern Israel by vehicle and helicopter to quash the assault. Moreover, the Israeli military had apparently intercepted the precise details of the attack more than a year before it occurred and had observed Hamas practice exercises near the fence—but they disregarded both warnings.[69]

In an unwitting admission that the Israeli military exercises full control over Gaza's basic resources—even after it had removed Jewish settlers in 2005 and redeployed the Israeli troops guarding them to the perimeter of the Gaza Strip—on October 9 the Israeli defense minister, Yoav Gallant, ordered a "complete" siege of Gaza, including curtailing the supply of electricity, food, and fuel.[70] "We are fighting human animals and we are acting accordingly," said Gallant.[71]

Other Israeli current and past politicians and military officers expressed similar views, including that Israel's goal should be to wipe Hamas "off the face of the earth,"[72] to "burn Gaza" because there are no "innocent people

---

[69] Ronen Bergman and Adam Goldman, "Israel Knew Hamas's Attack Plan More Than a Year Ago," *New York Times*, November 30, 2023, updated December 2, 2023, https://www.nytimes.com/2023/11/30/world/middleeast/israel-hamas-attack-intelligence.html.

[70] In addition to restricting resources, the IDF has controlled Gaza in other important ways. In addition to forbidding a seaport and an airport, they have imposed a buffer zone ranging from fifty to three hundred meters inside Gaza on the border with Israel, depriving Gazans of some of their most fertile agricultural land. They have also imposed maritime buffer zones of up to six nautical miles that have resulted in a reduction of the total fish catch by 90 percent. Violators of these zones are shot. See Roy, *Gaza Strip*, xlvi-l. Finally, for decades, the IDF has flown drones day and night over Gaza to surveil the population and to assassinate individuals. The incessant, disturbing whine of the drones is inescapable. See Jonathan Cook, "Gaza: Life and Death Under Israel's Drones," *Al Jazeera*, November 28, 2013, https://www.aljazeera.com/features/2013/11/28/gaza-life-and-death-under-israels-drones.

[71] Emanuel Fabian, "Defense Minister Announces 'Complete Siege' of Gaza: No Power, Food, or Fuel," *Times of Israel*, October 9, 2023, https://www.timesofisrael.com/liveblog_entry/defense-minister-announces-complete-siege-of-gaza-no-power-food-or-fuel/.

[72] "Israel's New War Cabinet Vows to Wipe Hamas Off the Earth," *Reuters*, October 11, 2023, https://www.reuters.com/world/middle-east/netanyahu-gantz-agree-form-emergency-israel-government-statement-2023-10-11/.

there now,"[73] to cause the "total annihilation" of Gaza,[74] and to "erase the memory of [Palestinians] . . . erase them, their families, mothers and children."[75]

On October 7, 2023, the Israeli military began its Operation Swords of Iron with a bombardment of the Gaza Strip, followed some days later by the first stage of what became a full ground invasion of Gaza. The bombardments and ground operations have not stopped since.

Here are some relevant statistics as of October 9, 2024, about the consequences of the Israeli retaliation on Gaza, both for the Israeli military and for Gazans (all of whom are Palestinians):[76]

- *Reported number of Israeli soldiers killed in Gaza during Operation Swords of Iron*: 348
- *Reported number of Israeli soldiers injured in Gaza during Operation Swords of Iron*: 2,319
- *Reported number of Palestinians killed*: 42,010 (men, women, children, and the elderly). Additional killings have included aid workers [307, including 7 foreign nationals], health workers [986], journalists [167)], and civil defense staff [85]).
- *Reported number of people reported missing or under the rubble*: more than 10,000
- *Reported number of Palestinians injured*: 97,720
- *Internally displaced Palestinians*: approximately 1.9 million (90 percent of the entire population), many of whom were displaced multiple times

[73] "Ahead of ICJ Genocide Case, Likud MK Doubles Down on Call to Burn Gaza to the Ground," *Jerusalem Post*, January 10, 2024, https://www.jpost.com/israel-hamas-war/article-781618.

[74] Noa Shpigel, "Israel's Far-Right Minister Smotrich Calls for 'No Half Measures' in the 'Total Annihilation' of Gaza," *Haaretz*, April 30, 2024, https://www.haaretz.com/israel-news/2024-04-30/ty-article/.premium/smotrich-calls-for-no-half-measures-in-the-total-annihilation-of-gaza/0000018f-2f4c-d9c3-abcf-7f7d25460000.

[75] Jean Shaoul, "How the Israeli Army Used 95-Year-Old Veteran of Deir Yassin Massacre Ezra Yachin to 'Motivate' the Troops," World Socialist Web Site, January 17, 2024, https://www.wsws.org/en/articles/2024/01/17/zzih-j17.html.

[76] United Nations Office for the Coordination of Humanitarian Affairs (OCHA), "Reported Impact Snapshot: Gaza Strip, 9 October 2024 at 15:00," https://www.unocha.org/publications/report/occupied-palestinian-territory/reported-impact-snapshot-gaza-strip-9-october-2024-1500. OCHA collects data from UN agencies, as well as from numerous international and local nongovernmental organizations, the Palestinian Ministry of Health, the Israeli news media, and other sources.

- *Percent of Gaza under Israeli-issued evacuation orders: approximately 84 percent*
- *Persons facing crisis or worse levels of food insecurity*: 96 percent, including 745,000 people facing emergency level food insecurity (IPC Phase IV) and 495,000 facing catastrophic level food insecurity/famine (IPC Phase V).[77]
- *Disease* (estimates as of July 7, 2024): acute respiratory infections (995,000), acute watery diarrhea (577,000), acute jaundice syndrome (107,000), polio (1, as of August 16, 2024)
- *Damage and Destruction*: housing units (87 percent), commercial buildings (80 percent), school buildings (87 percent), road network (65 percent), UNRWA facilities (190), ambulances (130), cropland (68 percent), meat and dairy producing livestock (60–70 percent), fishing fleet (70 percent), water desalinization plants (2 out of 3), water supply (70 percent), hospitals (53 percent), primary health care centers (57 percent), UNRWA health centers (70 percent), and the total road network (68 percent)
- *Education*: students with no access to education: 625,000
- *Rubble and debris*: As of August 15, 2024, Gaza is burdened with 42 million tons of debris, mostly from destroyed housing. It will take years to remove it. Rebuilding Gaza could cost more than $80 billion, according to one estimate.[78]
- *Cultural heritage*: As of February 2024, the Israeli bombardment has destroyed approximately 60 percent of Gaza's cultural sites and monuments, including archaeological sites, historical monuments, artifacts, archives, and museums—all symbols of collective identity and links to past peoples.[79]

---

[77] Integrated Food Security Phase Classification (IPC), "Fact Sheet: The IPC Famine," United Nations website, March 2024, https://www.un.org/unispal/wp-content/uploads/2024/03/IPC_Famine_Factsheet.pdf.

[78] Fadwa Hodali, Fares Akram, Jason Kao, Jennah Haque, and Jeremy D. F. Lin, "Gaza Reduced to 42 Million Tonnes of Rubble. What Will It Take to Rebuild?" *Bloomberg*, August 15, 2024, https://www.bloomberg.com/graphics/2024-gaza-who-will-pay-to-rebuild/.

[79] Salah al-Houdalieh, "The International Order Is Failing to Protect Palestinian Cultural Heritage," *SAPIENS*, June 6, 2024, https://www.sapiens.org/archaeology/cultural-heritage-gaza-destruction/.

- *Humanitarian aid*: Before October 7, 2023, Gaza received a daily average of 500 truckloads, including fuel. The monthly average beginning in November 2023 has ranged from 83 to a high of 165 (April 2024) and a low of 13 (October 2024).[80]

The extent and breadth of this assault have led many human rights organizations and legal scholars,[81] UN officials,[82] and Middle East scholars[83] to conclude that Israel is committing acts of genocide in Gaza. In response to a case brought by South Africa alleging that Israel had violated the Genocide Convention in Gaza, the International Court of Justice (ICJ) issued a provisional ruling in January 2024 that South Africa's allegations were "plausible."[84] Some scholars have also accused Hamas of genocide for its October 7 attack,[85] and in November 2023 the families of nine Israeli victims of the attack brought a war crimes case against Hamas to the International Criminal Court (ICC).[86]

In January 2024 the Office of the Prosecutor of the International Criminal Court applied for arrest warrants against Israeli Prime Minister Benjamin Netanyahu and Israeli Defense Minister Yoav Gallant, as well as Hamas leaders Yahya Sinwar, Mohammed Deif, and Ismail Haniyeh "for war crimes and crimes against humanity committed in Israel and in the State of

---

[80] OCHA, "Reported Impact Snapshot."

[81] University Network for Human Rights, et al., *Genocide in Gaza: Analysis of International Law and Its Application to Israel's Military Actions Since October 7, 2023*, May 14, 2024, https://static1.squarespace.com/static/66a134337e960f229da81434/t/66fb05bb0497da4726e125d8/1727727037094/Genocide+in+Gaza+-+Final+version+051524.pdf.

[82] "Rights Expert Finds 'Reasonable Grounds' Genocide is Being Committed in Gaza," *UN News*, March 26, 2024, https://news.un.org/en/story/2024/03/1147976.

[83] Marc Lynch and Shibley Telhami, "Gloom about the 'Day After' the Gaza War Pervasive among Mideast Scholars," Brookings Institution, Center for Middle East Policy website, June 20, 2024, https://www.brookings.edu/articles/gloom-about-the-day-after-the-gaza-war-pervasive-among-mideast-scholars/.

[84] International Court of Justice (ICJ), "Summary: Application of the Convention on the Prevention and Punishment of the Crime of Genocide in the Gaza Strip (South Africa v. Israel): Request for Provisional Measures," January 26, 2024, https://www.icj-cij.org/sites/default/files/case-related/192/192-20240126-sum-01-00-en.pdf.

[85] Bruce Hoffman, "Understanding Hamas's Genocidal Ideology," *Atlantic*, October 10, 2023, https://www.theatlantic.com/international/archive/2023/10/hamas-covenant-israel-attack-war-genocide/675602/.

[86] Agence France Presse (AFP), "Israeli Families Bring War Crime Complaint to ICC: Lawyer," *Barron's*, November 3, 2023, https://www.barrons.com/news/israeli-families-bring-war-crime-complaint-to-icc-lawyer-ed3aec98.

Palestine, specifically in the occupied Gaza Strip, from at least 7 October 2023."[87] Israeli forces assassinated Haniyeh, the political leader of Hamas, while he was in Tehran, Iran, on July 31, 2024.[88]

****

The following chapters record the WhatsApp text and voice messages that Hammam, Khalil, and Hussam sent to me over the one-year period from October 7, 2023, through October 7, 2024, the stopping point for this book. I have edited out extraneous messages and otherwise edited their messages only slightly for clarity. I have also removed my own parts of the message threads unless my questions or comments are necessary for the reader to understand their statements. For all those cases, I have used italics for my messages. Explanatory words or comments, as well as English translations of Arabic words or phrases, are enclosed in brackets.

---

[87] "Israel/OPT: ICC Applications for Arrest Warrants for Netanyahu, Sinwar and other Senior Israeli and Hamas Officials Crucial Step Towards Justice," Amnesty International website, May 21, 2024, https://www.amnesty.org/en/latest/news/2024/05/israel-opt-icc-applications-for-arrest-warrants-for-netanyahu-sinwar-and-other-senior-israeli-and-hamas-officials-crucial-step-towards-justice/.

[88] See Ronen Bergman, Mark Mazzetti, and Farnaz Fassihi, "Bomb Smuggled into Tehran Guesthouse Months Ago Killed Hamas Leader," *New York Times*, August 1, 2024, https://www.nytimes.com/2024/08/01/world/middleeast/how-hamas-leader-haniyeh-killed-iran-bomb.html.

Hammam

WhatsApp Messages: October 7, 2023–October 7, 2024

October 7, 2023

How are you all?

Hello Brian, everyone is fine, thank God. It was truly an unexpected surprise, an amazing thing, extreme horror and madness, what happened. I hope you are always well.

October 9, 2023

9:00 a.m. Everyone is fine, but the situation is getting worse. We are all afraid because there is shelling everywhere. From the early morning hours until ten minutes ago, the electricity returned. It's very difficult. We hope everyone is safe.

1:00 p.m. The situation is really unbearable.

October 10, 2023

More destruction than you can imagine in Khan Younis. Very large destruction. It's not far from our home.

October 12, 2023

The situation is very, very, very bad. Shelling everywhere. I am in my house now and there are thousands of refugees in the neighboring houses. Many Gazans came to Khan Younis, people are sleeping in the streets. Trucks transporting people and homeless people. The truth is, it is so terrible that it is unbearable. No electricity, No water. No food. Very severe headache. We can barely find the queue to buy bread. This is hell. 50 shekels for 500 liters of water.

My parents are living in terror. Very, very afraid and worried. Brian, the situation is terrifying. We are dying a slow death. Oh my God, what's going on? Today I went to the hospital to charge my mobile phone. Thousands were found in shelters there. I was only able to charge the mobile 10% after waiting 3 hours. 4 days without electricity.

October 13, 2023

Water only 2 hours. Nothing in stores. 2 hours to get bread. Habiba is very terrified; Mohammed is trying to find safety. Omar is always afraid. Fuad only sleeps during the day.

We may not meet again after today. We may all die at any time, my friend. May we be a beautiful memory in your life. If we die, remember that we lived dreaming of peace, that we were innocent, and that we were always peaceful. I am writing to you while crying because we no longer expect to live a single minute. The battery is gone.

October 18, 2023

Hey Brian, electricity for five minutes, we're fine.

October 19, 2023

9:00 a.m. But, my friend, you have more stories to write after this cursed war. I forgot to tell you some good news. I became a manager in Gaza on 9/10/2023. Director of one of the largest schools in Gaza City. Jaffa School. The number of students is 1200.

Fuad became a student at Al-Aqsa University, specialization in information technology. This is some good news that has been waiting for you.

Do you have any food and water?

O Allah, you're talking about something difficult. Today, Mohammed, Omar, and I stood for 3 hours to get a loaf of bread. Today I bought 250 liters of drinking water for 25 shekels, each person is allowed to buy bread for only 5 shekels.

Can I send you some money?

I have 1,500 shekels left from my salary, which is enough. Now all my sisters are here and their children. We host about 6 other families, more than 50 people. Just a moment and I'll come back.

1:00 p.m. All of the people in our house are children and women. Everyone is in a difficult situation. We barely provide food, and you can only provide food one day at a time because there are no refrigerators to store food.

We buy vegetables available in the market. Chickens are sold live without cleaning, without slaughter. There is no meat. Vegetables are available at fantastic prices. There is no fruit except some of what is left over from last week. Acceptably available, but prices are high.

A kilo of tomatoes costs 4 shekels. A kilo of onions costs 4 shekels. Cucumbers and eggplant are fairly cheap. Tomatoes are 5 quid [kilos] for 10 shekels. Onions 4 kilos for 10 shekels. Canned meat and canned fish.

Displaced people in UNRWA shelters do not receive any aid, only some bread. Where is Hamas? They actually melted like salt. There are no police, no institutions, no employees, and no oversight as in previous wars. Very, very simple aid from UNRWA and some individual efforts. People in the shelters buy their needs from the market with the money they have. They are just in a place they think is safe.

What's happening is terrible. Forbidden, forbidden, forbidden.

I'm getting ready for the party. Looks like a hot night, Brian. Yes, the night party is like every day. Bombing, news, and martyrs.

October 21, 2023

Good morning. Yesterday, one of the students of my school where I work in Gaza City ran towards me in the street and greeted me warmly and says to me, Professor, we immigrated from Gaza [City] and we now live in the school. He points with his hand to a school that is about 100 meters away from us and says:

> You will come to teach us again. There are many students from our school in Gaza with me, but we lost the books. We came from Gaza with only our clothes on. It affected me and left a strong impact when many of the students of our school said their homes were bombed, and they were martyred, and some of them were pulled out in pieces from under the rubble. Their homes.

I accepted his speech with great pain, but what hurt my heart more was the brother of this young student, who was not nearly seven years old. He said to me, "You are the teacher who teaches Mahmoud in the school. I know you. Come on, come to the school. We now live there. Come and teach us there."

I cried when I found out that this child wants to learn even in these very, very difficult circumstances. This child conveyed to me, with the innocence of childhood, that knowledge is a message and that there is a future.

3:50 p.m. Three martyrs and 13 wounded next to our house, only 50 meters away. Thank God, we are fine. Everyone is afraid. Terrifying, but without injuries or damage. Thank God. The home belonged to a very peaceful family, and they have no connection to any [political] organization at all. We are very surprised so far. Maybe the bomb missed its target.

October 24, 2023

Here are the families in our home now:

My sister Hana's family of 7; My sister Wafa's family of 6; My sister Hadeel's family of 5; My brother Hani's family of 4; My brother Waseem's family of 5; My family of 6; My father Fuad, my mother Fatima, and my sister Heba.

36 family members, plus 50 refugee women and children.

There is no electricity or water. Heavy bombing now. The house is shaking. Many raids. So far 7 raids in about a kilometer in circumference.

11:54 am *Urgent* | Targeting a house on Street 5 in the Western Sattar area in Khan Younis. [from a news group on WhatsApp]

By raids, I mean targeting by aircraft. I don't mean that there are soldiers on the ground. Now 10 raids in the last 15 minutes. When night comes, the planes come. But today since the beginning of the night. Looks like a rough night. So far about 15 strikes.

12:03 p.m. *Follow* | **6:55 p.m.** Occupation aircraft launched several successive raids in the Bani Suhaila area, east of Khan Younis. [from the same news group on WhatsApp]

It seems to be a very difficult night from the beginning. The bombing is frequent and in many places. It is severe and the number of attacks is more than usual. I want to go now and come back to you later. I will check on you when I return.

5:34 p.m. Thank God we got out safely. There has been a bombing next to our house. It is 15 meters away. Thank God we are fine.

6:52 p.m. Very violent artillery shelling. We are all near our house.

Why this area?

I don't know I don't know. What an injustice. Now me and the kids will go home. We will sweep out the glass. We try to sleep. Everyone is now on the street. I will go home now. Don't worry.

October 25, 2023

5:56 a.m. My uncle, his wife, his son, and his daughter-in-law died today after being injured on the night of her brother's death.

6:23 a.m. One loaf of [pita] bread per person.

3:14 p.m. We have not had internet for 5 days. So far, we are fine. OK but till now no internet in our area.

November 4, 2023

5:59 a.m. Good morning. After 10 days. No internet. Today it's back. Till now we are OK. But there is a severe shortage of everything. The situation is getting very bad. It is very difficult to get water. There is no potable water. They bottle nonpotable water. We have to buy it at fantastic prices. It is for washing. But unfortunately, it seems that we will have to drink it.

No electricity at all for 27 days. Darkness is deadly. The night is terrifying. Sounds of explosions everywhere. The whistle of shells is terrifying and unprecedented. Everything is difficult. Queues everywhere for bread, water, some canned food. Yesterday I was able to get four bags of macaroni. The shops are almost empty. Today there are tomatoes, onions and potatoes on the market. But the prices are terrifying.

Shelter centers have become infected with skin diseases.[89] The dawn hours are very cold. We have enough blankets now. But for the displaced there are none.

I try as much as possible to calm the children down. I try to release myself and my emotions for them. I ask myself who is having the hardest time? Omar and Habiba. Anxiety before bed. Anxiety during sleep. I try to lift their spirits. I tell them don't worry, the bombing is far away, we only hear the sound. I tell them some stories. We have a puzzle game. We think about solutions together.

We all had bad coughs three days ago. Now we are better. Something yellow comes out of the throat. The doctor said this was due to inhaling dust. We actually inhaled a very large amount of dust. We haven't showered in days. Once a day, we make coffee. Cooking gas must be supplied, my friend.

---

[89] For example, severe skin rashes, scabies, psoriasis, and hepatitis A. See Mahmoud Issa, "Skin Diseases Afflict Gaza's Children as War Drags on without End," *Reuters*, August 8, 2024, https://www.reuters.com/world/middle-east/skin-diseases-afflict-gazas-children-war-drags-without-end-2024-08-08/.

There are no gas suppliers in the region. Whoever has cooking gas is a person of high prosperity. Now we started trying to delay lunch time.

Going out of the house for the purpose of bringing home needs and searching in depth to obtain them. And standing for too long to get what you need. The boys come out with me one at a time. Today for example I have a problem with the lighting battery. I spent 3 hours looking for a new battery. After much suffering, I was able to obtain a used battery at a price of approximately 50 dollars. When I left with the battery, someone followed me who wanted to buy it for 55.

My salary is about to run out. I am waiting for the salary. We do not know if it will come. But everyone needs money now, the beginning of a new month. War a month ago. Some of the prices are terrifying.

When can I send you some money?

When the time comes, I will tell you. Don't worry. When I start maintaining the house because I need a lot of glass and re-maintenance of windows.

How will I send money?

Western Union, MoneyGram, things like this. For some you wait for days to get it. Depends on the internet. It is not easy and I have to wait a long time. Shada's brother transferred money to his parents from Belgium. I tried for 8 days until I got the money. Don't send me anything now. When I need to, I will ask you without shame.

I want to tell you something important. It might be strange, I don't know. In fact, I don't talk to anyone but you. Do you know why? I feel strong after talking with you. Your words are wonderful and your articles are wonderful. In fact, I derive my strength from you. I don't know why, but your words always make me more determined and stronger.

What is your biggest worry right now?

That we all die innocent.

11:19 am After waiting for 4 hours since I left you. I was able to get 50 loaves of bread. 4 hours of waiting in a line extending for hundreds of meters. Absolutely delicious.

No dinner tonight because we delayed lunch by one hour, so the kids will eat some cookies. In the morning, everyone eats a cheese sandwich. We wait until lunch and each person eats one or two loaves of bread at most.

November 11, 2023

Still unharmed?

November 14, 2023

OK till now. A lot of bombing. But life is unbearable. Everything is difficult. There is no water or electricity and food is starting to diminish. Prices are difficult. Bakeries stopped working.

November 16, 2023

Today the internet isn't available so I went out to get some household needs.

I am now looking for any temporary humanitarian asylum in any country because I really can no longer bear the situation, it is absolutely unbearable. Try to help me with that if you can.

November 20, 2023

Still OK. Life and situation are sooooooo bad 👎. Still tons of bombing.

What are you eating?

We are on a diet.

November 23, 2023

Still OK. I want to ask about you because for many days you didn't ask about us. Are you OK? Brian! Are you OK? I don't want to worry anymore.

It is very difficult to describe the situation now. Each day gets worse than the day before. Everything is difficult and stressful. Everything is missing.

Typical day?

I sleep every night after months of exhaustion. Wake up from sleep. It's half past four in the morning. I go to my father and mother and sit with them until six in the morning. Then my father and I go out to the market to buy our daily needs. We search for necessary things everywhere. Flour, for example, a bag weighing 25 kilos costs $50. And not available. Bread must wait from two to four hours to get it. Yesterday we were in severe suffering. We were looking for table salt. We walked about 5 kilometers asking about salt, but there was none.

We buy vegetables available in the market: eggplant, potatoes, tomatoes, onions, green pepper. There is no chicken in the market. Ricc, but poor quality.

I bought a bag of flour a week ago from one of my relatives, with difficulty, for 150 shekels. The price then rose to 250 shekels. My wife makes the bread and I bake on wood.

Prices have doubled.

After shopping, we return home, watch the news, and continue charging the batteries and mobile phones.

Hani charges his battery in the supermarket. Waseem is charging at the hospital. I charge the battery with solar energy.

47 days since the electricity was cut off.

The water was cut off for 10 consecutive days

The children did not bathe for two weeks. The house smells very bad. All the water is not completely clean, the purification rate is 30 to 50 percent

We light the fire and start cooking food for the children. After cooking on the fire and eating lunch we take a break for two hours so we can stay up at night.

Then we begin the second journey. Wash laundry. There is no washing machine, so you wash the laundry by hand.

How is Shada doing?

She's very, very sad. Housework is very stressful because everything requires effort. It's not like before. She washes without a washing machine, cooks on firewood, and prepares bread without bakeries.

November 27, 2023

We are fine so far. The humanitarian truce made us feel temporary relief. Now we are at home quietly. Thank God. I hope that you are well.

At least we are able to cook food. This is Friday. I was able to buy meat from the market. So wonderful that is. I cooked it on firewood.

Chicken?

What are you saying man? Chicken? Chicken is thing of the past. Cow meat.

Tomorrow is Habiba's birthday. She will be 11. We celebrated it today. I bought 2 kilos of turkey meat. We try to bring happiness to the hearts of children. The children are very sad, always afraid.

The humanitarian truce is wonderful!

I was able to talk to the children and lift their spirits. I told them that every storm is followed by a beautiful day. The hurricane comes and destroys many things, but it makes us think about how we will come back again. I tried to deliver a beautiful message. Unfortunately, there are no beautiful phrases. I directed the children to read.

Mohammad is reading the novel Les Misérables, Victor Hugo.

Fuad is reading a beautiful book: 100 men who changed world history.

Habiba reads some stories.

Omar creates beautiful things like an airplane. He has great drawing talent.

Fuad draws beautiful things every day.

I'm trying to change reality.

November 28, 2023

Good day, we are OK.

We are still at home, but after the end of the humanitarian truce, the bombing is very intense in Khan Younis. The bombing does not stop at night and intermittently during the day. The situation is getting dangerous.

Heavy attack beside our home 50 meters far, many people killed. We have to leave to our old home in the camp where you lived with us.

All children are OK. Fuad and Fatima are OK. Wasseem and Hani and their children are OK.

December 3, 2023

Brian, I want to explain to you what happened today, this morning. The Israeli army published maps on its Facebook site. We are in square 57. Look at the check marks on the boxes that show which areas they are going to bomb tonight. Our area has a check mark. There is a check mark on square 57. We must leave.

Now we are in the old home in the camp. No bombings here now.

Brian it's so hard. Soooooo hard.

What is the hardest part?

First time I feel that I am not strong. It was hard to take the children to the camp. It was hard to hear that our home was damaged severely after we left. For the first time in my life, I feel very weak. I was forced to leave my home. It is hard for me to remain strong in front of my children. I don't have any words to encourage them. They are strong. I am helpless.

The boys are very, very upset. They moved from a house with all the amenities. They feel very anxious. They don't feel safe. In all honesty, what is happening is indescribable. I can't find a definition for what's happening.

When do you think it will end?

I expect it will end with us being displaced from Gaza. I am almost certain of that.

December 8, 2023

How are you?

9:00 a.m. Sooo bad. We had to leave the camp home to stay with relatives in Rafah.

First time I am crying with sorrow. We have nothing. We are waiting for aid to feed our children.

3:00 p.m. Today we got a carton of humanitarian aid from the UAE: 3 cans of beans, 3 cans of beef, some rice, salt, sugar, biscuits, and some tea.

A strange cough haunts me and Omar. Dandruff appears on the head, very bad, and we have not showered for 8 days. Today, I and the children had to shower with very cold and unclean water. The internet is very bad.

December 9, 2023

Hi Brian. How are you? Hope you are good. Today is hard.

I'm OK thanks. How is it hard today habibi?

Dear Brian, I know that I have become annoying to you with the bad news that I deliver to you every day. Indeed, I feel ashamed sometimes, but I would love to talk to you today. I was able to reach our house with very great difficulty. I wished that I had not gone there when I saw our house and

Habiba's room and the children's rooms and my room when I saw the house empty and upside down. Upside down, I cried a lot. I felt very sad about what had been a day full of life and activity. I controlled myself and wanted to take anything, everything with me, but I took one blanket from your room, the room you always stay in when you visit us, and left quickly. I carried a cooking gas cannister that weighed 28 kilograms on my back and left and walked. A distance of 10 kilometers while carrying a very heavy load. I am so tired.

Tell me when we can talk.

December 24, 2023

How are you all?

December 27, 2023

How are you?

December 29, 2023

Hi Brian. We are in Al Mawasi area now. Near the sea. We are in a tent. Nothing. It's so bad. Nothing. No connection.

What kinds of food are you eating?

Hahah. What do you mean by food? Just canned food. Today we bought meat. 70 shekels for a kg [kilo]. Life so bad. After 17 days we can buy 2 kgm [kilos] of meat.

January 11, 2024

How are you?

January 18, 2024

Another week and nothing from you! I'm worried!

January 29, 2024

Still OK 👍

February 18, 2024

I'm very worried!!!!!

February 25, 2024

Still OK till now. Such a bad life

March 19, 2024

Wayn enta? Kifku? [Where are you? How are you all?]

Still OK. Waiting for peace

March 24, 2024

I am in Rafah. Searching for money 💰

When are you going to let me help you with money?

Not yet. But soon.

I am so tired, and afraid. Death smell everywhere.

How do the children spend the days?

They play chess, they read some books. Many of them are sold at very cheap prices. Many books are lying on the streets.

Food?

Canned food is available. Vegetables, only tomatoes, potatoes, eggplant and cucumber. There are some other types, but they are difficult to buy. The water is very bad. We buy water from trucks.

When was the last time you had chicken or meat?

Last Friday after a 4-week hiatus. Chicken weighs 1100 grams, 70 shekels. 1 kilo of meat is 150 shekels. One cigarette costs 15 shekels.

Our life is difficult. I wish to leave the country. I want to protect my children. The situation is unbearable.

Where?

Any place where there is calm and peace where my children can live in peace. In whatever country I can find work. Gaza has become hell. Even if we return to our homes, the situation is unbearable. There is no water and no infrastructure. All of Khan Younis is destroyed. I hope that you are well.

Why do you want to finish the book? There are still other chapters of life that have not yet been completed. A life of misery and misery. We are no longer what we used to be. Our lives became worse than we expected. I will leave you to go to sleep.

April 6, 2024

Good morning from our tent. After 6 months we have internet! Some young people in the area have signed up for an antenna internet subscription. But it's bad.

April 9, 2024

Will you go back to your home?

I go home every day. I started cleaning the house yesterday after the withdrawal of troops from Khan Younis.

April 11, 2023

How are you?

Still OK

April 18, 2024

Hello my friend. I'm still in Al-Mawasi. After the army withdrew, I went home and cleaned every day to get ready to go back. But there is no electricity or water in the area so we still can't return home. We walk around all the places in the city and move freely. But there is no life. Everything is destroyed or bombed. The smell of gunpowder on the first day here was deadly. The internet is so bad. Life in tent.

April 20, 2024

Now we are at home 🏠. All of my family SHADA, FUAD, MOHAMMED, OMAR, HABIBA, FATIMA AND MY FATHER. We are very happy.

April 30, 2024

Now a new suffering has begun. Providing water and food is a problem. I want to provide an opportunity for education for children. Reality is difficult,

Brian. I became unable to think. I need your help in understanding reality, what is happening.

We are dying every day. Everything is destroyed. Khan Younis is destroyed. There is no education, no universities, and no future for the children. For the first time in my life, I feel helpless. I want to change my children's lives. I want them to learn.

Mohammed is in the tenth grade, Omar is in eighth grade, Habiba in sixth grade. Fuad is in his first year of university. A year of school has now been lost. There is no life here. It will take years before education can be built here. Therefore, leaving Gaza has become inevitable.

First: I need $30,000 to be able to leave. Exiting from Gaza to Egypt is difficult, as you must pay $5,000 for each person. Second: I need an apartment in Egypt. Apartment rent, exit expenses from Gaza, and school registration fees. Just thinking about it makes me very nervous. Shada feels helpless like me.

Leaving Gaza is not the best solution, but I fear for the future of my children. That's what made me think about leaving Gaza. I will be a stranger in another country. The children are my problem now. I want to protect them and their future. I can live in all circumstances and in any place, but I must protect my children. You know that I am very opposed to receiving money from anyone. I try as much as possible to save what I can.

I need to get out of Gaza and immigrate to any country. I want to apply for immigration to Australia, Canada, or another country. I can live there with dignity. After a short time, the internet will be cut off. If I go out suddenly, you will know that the internet has been cut off.

We have had two family meetings about leaving. I asked each one to study the issue from his point of view. The third meeting will be to give the final decision to everyone. The third meeting I think white smoke will come out.[90] Hahahahahaha.

I remember Virginia Woolf's novel To the Lighthouse. Actually, this is what happens to us.

Now I leave you to enjoy your sleep. Sorry I bothered you. Don't worry, we will check on you.

---

[90] A reference to the process of selecting a new pope in Rome.

I wish you a happy day. Good Bye now. Don't worry, many things were dreams in my life, and with persistence and determination I turned them into realities, my friend. Money has never hindered me from achieving my goal.

May 4, 2024

I decided to hold a meeting for our children to be our final decision to leave Gaza for an indefinite period because we are all looking forward to a better future after the war cut off all hope of remaining on this land, even though there is something on it that deserves to remain. It contains beautiful memories and years of life that we spent building a future for our children until this war came and destroyed and wiped all of that off the face of the earth.

It was a quick and strange meeting. It was in my room. I called the children and told them that there is a difficult decision that we must make now. I have decided that we will leave Gaza to any other country for your sake and for your future to complete your studies and live in dignity. Mohammed asked for permission to speak and said, "You have made a right decision, and I am with you for our future, but where to?"

I told him to Australia, Canada, or any Arab country, and perhaps America. He said, "Where there is safety, there is the future," and we all want safety and the future. I agree, but for a limited time and we will come back.

It was Omar's turn to talk and he said, "I am with you, despite my love for Gaza, but because the situation is getting worse, and there will be no studies for years, and we want to live in safety as well. I agree, and the same question is repeated, but to where? He told me that he would prefer it to be an Arab country. I told him OK but why? He replied, so that we do not waste more time studying the language and other things and be closer to the culture.

It was Habiba's turn to talk and she agreed and everyone did as well, no one objected.

May 8, 2024

When do you want to register to leave? Do you have a family member in Cairo to receive the money to pay Al Hala?[91]

---

[91] The Egyptian travel agency that, at that time, had sole authority to arrange for Gazans to leave for Cairo. Fees were $5,000 per adult and $2,500 per child. Would-be travelers had to find a way to have the required fees in US dollars (in cash) delivered to the agency's Cairo

I will organize that and call you soon.

May 19, 2024

Where are you man? Everyone is missing you. I'm still waiting for Al Hala response.

May 22, 2024

We returned to our house. The house is in good condition. There are some hits. The situation is very bad, everything is difficult now after returning home. Now we buy water as we used to in Al-Mawasi, but the price is many times higher. In any case, it is better than living in a tent.

Brian: Our decision to leave Gaza is irreversible. The future of my children is more important than anything.

May 27, 2024

Salamat. Kaif halak? [Many greetings, how are you?]

We are in our home and have nothing. The internet is so bad. Today was the first day we have internet.

Don't worry, I will find a way and I will wait, but in any case, I and my children will leave Gaza.

June 12, 2024

What is your news!?

Still OK 👍 No new news. Still wait for the Rafah terminal to [re]open.

June 19, 2024

Now we have entered a very bad stage, the stage of stealing aid. After we returned home, many people began to come to Salah al-Din Street, wait for the aid trucks, and steal their contents. Stupid and disrespectful.

---

office. They were then put on a waiting list, which was—and currently still is—many weeks' long. In May 2024 Israeli forces took over the Rafah crossing, and as of October 2024 they have permitted very few Gazans to leave. See Adam Rasgon, "When the Only Escape from War in Gaza Is to Buy a Way Out," *New York Times,* June 20, 2024, https://www.nytimes.com/2024/06/20/world/middleeast/palestinians-gaza-gofundme-egypt.html.

We are all fine so far. Eid al-Adha was the worst day. For the first time, there is no holiday aspect.[92]

June 24, 2025

Hi Brian. HOW ARE YOU? We're still OK. Everyone misses you. Let me know how are you.

July 3, 2024

The internet is so bad. Every day we think about the battery and the charger. At the beginning of the war, we had bought a solar panel that provided us with 150 watts of solar energy to charge a small battery that we had previously purchased. We were able to charge mobile devices to keep in touch with friends but the battery, unfortunately, had ended its lifespan and its malfunctions increase every day. We sit and watch this battery until it can charge only one mobile phone at a time. Every day is the same and in the end there is no internet. I had to go to the sea area so I can use the internet.

Life has become unbearable. Every day is different from the day before. A life without planning.

July 11, 2024

Our news . . . still waiting for a ceasefire. All of us are very tired. Everything is very expensive. The biggest problem is to find water. I buy 1,000 liters of water every 6-7 days. It costs 80 shekels. And every day I buy sweet water for drinking, 40-50 liters. It costs 10-20 shekels. You need to coordinate to buy water a day ahead with the man who is selling water; even washing and cleaning water.

Food now, it's a bit better because the goods start to enter from Kerem Shalom crossing, and the prices starts to lessen. I get 50% of my salary, 2,000 shekels. But I must pay 10-20% commission to get the money in cash.

My mood is very bad. I'm afraid every second. There is no safe place; constant attacks on civilians. I most fear losing everything, children, and home. They are still bombing everywhere on many days. Just an hour ago, they bombed a humanitarian area just 7 meters from my home: 7 martyrs.

I can't understand anything . . . I can't think. Every day I'm just thinking about how we can find water, food; the prices and life protection. Now I face a new problem. My kids are asking me questions I can't answer. They are asking

[92] A major Islamic holiday commemorating Abraham's willingness to sacrifice his son.

about their future. They've lost one year of learning, and the second year will start soon.

FUAD: What we will do after the war? Nothing can live in Gaza.

MOHAMMED: When can I live normally?

OMAR: Why are we in Gaza? We need to be in another place to be active in a society without war.

HABIBA: How can you protect our life?

SHADA: When will we leave Gaza? Our children's future will be destroyed. Don't hesitate to find the way.

All people in Gaza are searching for safety. It will be hard to live outside of Gaza, but at least we'll have safety.

July 12, 2024

Do you imagine that you would leave Gaza and never return?

I can't imagine that, after 49 years of relations, friendship, my job, my big family, and my character as a known man. The situation is different because there is nothing in Gaza. I feel that we are waiting for nothing. Starting a new life will be easier than daily or yearly suffering that leads me to think about my children and their future. So, I will get my retirement and leave Gaza for a long time, and see the changes. If it's good and Gaza is livable, I will return, after assuring that all of my children's futures are good. I lived in Sudan for a year and made a new life in that different society easily.

July 16, 2024

I'm starting to feel tired. There is nothing to do.

What is a typical day?

Get up at 6 o'clock. Turn off any lights. Make sure the battery is still connected to the solar panels on the roof. Breakfast: tomatoes. Start searching for water. Go to the market to buy something for lunch. Walking in the heat of the sun. Thirsty. It's killing me because there is so little water to buy and drink. 33 degrees [94 Fahrenheit] during the days; 24 [78] at night. Insects and mosquitos, we've never seen before because of the sea of raw sewage covering the market area.

Then I find frozen meat, chicken that came from the Kerem Shalom crossing. 1.5 kilos for 51 shekels. We made Fattet Hummos.[93] I got three cans of chickpeas from EU aids.

After lunch, I went to Khan Younis camp, walking again. As mukhtar I had to solve a problem. Two men had fought over water. I took two respected men with me. There is only one source of water for 100 families. Each family can fill only 60 liters per day. Each family knows when their time is. But one man, who had been away for some days visiting family, cut in line and the fight started.

We convinced them that this is not the time for making problems and that you are good people and that you must apologize to each other. They apologized.

July 18, 2024

Living with garbage, rubble, and remnants of war is a scene repeated every day. Today we were able to get water. 1000 ltr [liters] for 7 days.

July 19, 2024

Marhaba [hello], Kaif halak ya raajel [How are you, man]? Ana zaalan minnak [I'm sad because of you].

Laish [why]?

I am asking about you every day. You didn't reply. Sometimes we are worried about you. Fuad, Mohammed, Omar and Habiba all asking: How is Brian? I want to talk about the amount of sadness I feel when my children lost their education and the difficult decision to emigrate. I want to write to you something from the seventh of October until this moment, and the ideas that came to me and the topics that the children and I discussed during this period. I think it's important.

Yes, please do.

July 23, 2024

Good morning. Leaving home again. On 21st of July early morning the IDF called with a recorded message that our area is not a humanitarian area

[93] Typically, a breakfast dish made of toasted pita bread, hummos, and whole chickpeas.

from now on. And included a map of new safe zones. So, we leave our home again toward another area where a friend is.

July 25, 2024

New instructions to leave again. Now I don't know where I can go.

July 27, 2024

Greetings to you . . . this is our latest news. We're staying in the basement of a home this time, not in a tent. Today is very bad.

August 1, 2024

We moved back to Al-Mawasi after the army announced the end of its work in Khan Younis. I decided to stay in Al-Mawasi for a short time so that the children could feel some comfort. I felt that the children needed some rest. They are very tired.

The first day in a tent, but the heat is unbearable and insects are everywhere. So, a friend found two rooms in a house and I rented them, a very large amount, $500/month.

Why did the army enter Khan Younis again and displace you twice?

Bodies of hostages.

Did you know the bodies of the hostages were there?

No. They found them in one of the cemeteries. You get a call from the army, you must evacuate immediately all residents of the areas, according to the sector numbers mentioned by the army. We of course must follow orders. Let's escape with our lives.

What is the temperature?

33 during the day [99 Fahrenheit]. 25 or less at night [80]. But it is 40 in the tents [110].

We are all okay, very tired.

How does it feel?

Frustration, feeling of oppression, a desire to die, hate everything, constant anxiety about the news, the truce, our house, and the children, providing needs, not having enough money, it all makes me frustrated.

I wrote you part of my war memoirs:

> It was the morning of October 7th, that day, when I woke up at exactly six in the morning, as I have been accustomed to for many years due to the nature of my work in education. On that day, I wanted to finish some late work before going to work in the morning and my daughter Habiba, that 11-year-old girl, was getting dressed to go to school, and my wife was preparing breakfast for us, when I heard loud noises coming from everywhere. I could not distinguish where these sounds were coming from, the sounds of missiles being launched intensely from everywhere, and from here the story began. I thought that it was like every other time, but this time it was different. Time stopped at that moment, and I wish it would go back to before. Everything really changed for the worse. We stayed at home from October 7th until December 3rd, 2023. Every day we see displacement from one place to another, but the most difficult moment was when we decided to evacuate after we were informed that our area was a dangerous area, when the plane dropped leaflets containing a map specifying the areas that had to be evacuated, including our area. Here came the fatal decision, which was to leave our house to a safer place. I gathered some important things, which were my school certificates, my children's school certificates, my wife's certificates, and my passport, all those important papers, and put them in a bag. My wife put some clothes in another bag, as the weather was very cold at this time of winter. I left the house and left everything. We got into the car, and I looked at the house with a farewell look, as if I was saying goodbye to a part of my body that carries my memories, dreams, and years of fatigue. I said goodbye to everything and hoped to return and find the house as I left it. All the neighbors were saying goodbye to each other, and in their eyes was one sentence that I could read easily: will we return. I moved the car towards our old house in Khan Younis camp, and the sounds of shells and explosions were in all directions. It was a very terrifying sound, and I was trying to appear strong. In front of my children who were trembling with fear as they went with me to the unknown, heading to that old house that was not fit for habitation that we had left about 20 years ago,[94] here I felt that I had lost everything. I looked at the children where the first meeting of the family council in this cursed war was taking place inside the

[94] Their original home in the Khan Younis refugee camp.

> car, and I told them that now everything would be more difficult than what we were used to, and I explained to them thc difficulty of living in the old house and explained the situation to them quickly, and I found that everyone accepted to go to any safe place. We arrived at the house and got out of the car and entered the house and one of our relatives came, who is one of my father's very close friends, and he said I will not allow you to stay in this dilapidated house, you are my guests and you will sit in my house and he insisted on his request and to please him we went with him to his house and he gave us his son's apartment, the people of the house were very happy with our presence, but I was not happy, my heart was broken and my mind was distracted, because everything is different, going to the bathroom, eating, using the kitchen, getting dressed, even showering is difficult, there is no water, everything is difficult, so I decided to look for another place.

August 8, 2024

8:34 a.m. See this map. The red areas must evacuate immediately, thousands of people, to humanitarian areas. The heat is very intense.

Thank you for sending the money. I can't thank you enough, I'm in desperate need of it or else I would have never asked. It is at the bank. I am trying to find one of the thieves who sells us money through the banking application, where I transfer the amount from my bank account to his account, and he gives me the money in cash dollars minus a 15 or 20 percent commission.

There is no longer any bank in Khan Younis for me to go in and get the money directly. The bank has been destroyed. The banks in Deir al-Balah or Nuseirat are very difficult to reach. And you need a reservation. Your turn may not be until a week later. Everything is difficult.

What is the news on the ground about getting out of Gaza?

Waiting for the crossing to open and to get out of here. Enough torture.

What are the worst aspects of this torture?

Repeated displacement. Everything is difficult: No food, no water, no electricity, and no decent life.

9:39 p.m. This is an hour ago, new instructions to evacuate Khan Yunis. Areas circled in red must evacuate immediately. Thousands of people. The heat is very intense.

Another order to evacuate??!! Why this time?

I don't know

So, 3 evacuation orders in the last two weeks.

Right. As my son jokes, it's like a weekend trip to the sea [referring to the displacement camp in Al Mawasi near the sea].

A weekly trip costs 500 shekels each way for hiring transport and for fuel. I swear to you, this is the first time in my life that I feel poor and unable to do anything. Salaries are not enough for your daily needs. But I'm better off than a lot of people.

What is your first priority for the funds I sent?

My first priority is to pay the rest of the apartment rent. My second priority is to fix my mobile phone. The third priority, and I am ashamed to mention it, I want to buy some cleaning supplies and underwear for the boys. I hope to find shoes for them too.

August 15, 2024

What is your news, Hammam? I'm worried.

I found one of the damned thieves. He took 15% to get me the money you sent.

Are there screens available to buy for your phone?

Nooooo. You have to buy a used mobile phone at several times the real price. Exploitation in everything. The screen cost no more than 100 shekels before the war. Today's screen price: 650 shekels.

Where do you buy food?

There are new markets in different places. For example . . . the Attar area . . . has a market that did not exist before. Al-Aqsa University area did not have any markets. Now there is a new market. All the places where the displaced gather have become new markets. One million and one hundred thousand people in the Mawasi area now. Scary numbers and very heavy congestion.

August 26, 2024

What is your news, please.

Still OK. Busy solving a bunch of family problems, different families, not just my family.

August 27, 2024

I have a lot to talk to you about. The internet connection is so bad. This is the first night at home, after one month and three days, just to try to see if we can stay home or need to go back to rental house.

September 5, 2024

We have had difficult days. I finally got close to finishing reading my story from your book. I have some very minor modifications to some details and place names. Your writing really touched my heart and I often read and cried while reading. The details and the way of writing are heart touching. Very accurate in detailing. Very good at connecting events. Thank you very much from the bottom of my heart. It is one of the great pleasures of my life.

September 30, 2024

What is your news? I'm worried. Tell me about your life.

Hey Brian I've been really late talking to you, don't worry. Now a lot of things keep me busy: People's problems are increasing day by day, providing children's needs and household needs. There are many things we need every day, like filling water buckets and providing food. Everything has become very expensive. Now cleaning materials such as soap and shampoo are available, but their prices are very, very expensive, double the previous.

How long was shampoo not available?

At least 5 months. A piece of soap costs 25 shekels. A 450 ml bottle of shampoo costs 80 shekels. People's problems are increasing day by day.

There are a lot of killings. Lots of thefts.

What are the main reasons for the killings?

Getting revenge. Some are killed because they stole aid supplies. When some people try to steal the aid, one of the individuals assigned to protect the aid opens fire. This is how injuries occur. Some of them die.

How often does aid come?

It depends on the coordination, whether from UNRWA or a trader. According to the days that the Israeli side allows entry.

Where are you living now?

I am home now. I sit in the street in front of the house so I can get the internet.

Do you have electricity and water in the house now?

We buy 1,000 liters of water every 5 days for 35 shekels. No electricity. Just battery.

How long does the battery last?

It barely lights up the night, possibly 6 hours, and in the best-case scenario 8 hours. A good battery now costs about a thousand dollars.

October 7, 2024

Hi Brian, how are you? I know I'm late in writing to you, but circumstances are difficult and the internet is always bad. Everyone is always asking about you, every day.

Thank you! So, now it is one full year of this nightmare. What do you think about it all?

This nightmare and this day are the worst of my life. We were happy to be home, but a few moments ago these idiots launched their absurd missiles. These Hamas and Israeli fools do not realize the extent of the disaster that has befallen humanity because of them. Now there is another evacuation map because of this stupidity. We have to leave the house for the tenth time.

I don't know what to do now. Should I leave to the Al-Mawasi area again? The house I rented before is now rented to someone else. I think I should stay home despite the danger because there is no shelter, no home, no place to go to.

I have become unable to think. I don't know where these idiots will take us.

Khalil

WhatsApp Messages: October 7, 2023–October 7, 2024

October 7, 2023

Is your family OK?

So far yes. What is coming will be unpredictable. There are two possibilities from my point of view, ending Hamas or enabling Hamas. I hope everybody will be saved.

October 9, 2023

Everyone OK?

Hi Brian, so far, we are good. Hopefully we will be safe. The war has started to be more aggressive. It seems that they decide to invade. Now it is an operation to kill more civilians. More than 100,000 citizens have been evacuated. Every single minute we hear about more victims. Nobody can predict what will happen, but it seems like the worst has not come yet.

October 12, 2023

How are you?

October 18, 2023

Still unharmed?

Yes, so far. It seems it will take a long time. I am afraid to go more to the south. They target it from time to another. Do you think the USA and Western world will continue the war? The situation is very indescribable. Much worse than before. Will they push us to migrate to Sinai? They want to finish Hamas, why do they target civilians?

October 21, 2023

Are you still unharmed?

Yes, and hopefully we'll continue to be safe.

October 26, 2023

Some news from you, please. Only brief, since your battery power is precious.

October 27, 2023

I am still alive. The internet does not help now.

October 29, 2023

We are not good but we are strong enough.

November 3, 2023

Still unharmed?

Yes. What do you expect after the Blinken visit?

I fear there will be no change, no pause.

But do you think it will be another forced migration to Sinai?

Definitely not, I think.

That is good. But they want to reach Al-Shifa Hospital. It seems they know something is there.

Are they correct when they say that there is a major Hamas command center underneath Al-Shifa?

Personally, I do not know. But they talk a lot about this.

November 12, 2023

Still unharmed physically?

Alhamdulillah [praise God]

November 19, 2023

Still unharmed physically?

Alhamdulillah. The Canadian government said they would evacuate us to Canada. If we are still alive after the war, I will think seriously of leaving Gaza.

[Khalil sent me a link to an article he wrote titled "Gaza Is the Graveyard of Human Rights" that he had just published on an independent online news publication focusing on Palestine.[95] Here are some excerpts:]

> An apology is required.
>
> I have come to that conclusion through witnessing this holocaust in Palestine.
>
> The mass killing of innocent children, women and men.
>
> Destruction that no human mind can imagine.
>
> I have come to that conclusion after observing the inability or unwillingness of the "international community" to help the children and people of Gaza.
>
> The failure to help is a failure of humanity itself.
>
> I hereby apologize for all the concepts, values and principles of human rights that I have worked hard to promote over the course of 25 years. . . .
>
> I had thought that law would always prevail. . . . We have been stabbed in the back by the "international community."
>
> We have to turn away from our children when they ask us questions . . . International law seems to have excluded us from its provisions.
>
> I apologize to my children . . . [and] to my friends and colleagues for promoting human rights and the principles behind them.
>
> I apologize to every child, woman and man who has become a victim in Gaza.
>
> I do not have answers to their questions at this time . . . I promoted and sincerely believed in human rights. I was wrong.
>
> Gaza is now the graveyard of human rights.

---

[95] Khalil Abu Shammala, "Gaza Is the Graveyard of Human Rights," *The Electronic Intifada*, November 8, 2023, https://electronicintifada.net/content/gaza-graveyard-human-rights/40191.

November 24, 2023

[Here are some excerpts from another article that Khalil published on the same website[96]:]

> The question that 2.3 million captives in Gaza are now asking is:
>
> What's next? What is to come after all this cold-blooded killing and genocide? . . .
>
> All beauty has been robbed from us. Gaza has been reduced to heaps.
>
> What comes after the Israeli planes and tanks obliterate Old Gaza and New Gaza? It is as if they want to erase and wipe the memories of the people of Gaza, the landmarks of the cities and towns we have loved and lived in for years. . . . The whole world did not even succeed in saving a single child from bombing, a single infant from facing death in a hospital for lack of electricity and medical supplies. . . .
>
> How will more than a million Palestinians who have lost their homes and businesses behave?
>
> What of the hundreds of thousands of students whose schools and universities have been destroyed? . . .
>
> What next, when the world has destroyed the lives of the people of Gaza? The planes bombed our hearts before our homes, streets, markets, hospitals and hotels. . . . How will we rebuild our lives?
>
> What's next, when the world has left the Palestinians to face their fates alone?
>
> History will be written for years about this war and what happened, because those who were killed are not just numbers. Each one of them constitutes a story of ambition, pain and hope.
>
> Can anyone provide the Palestinians in Gaza with any answers?

---

96 Khalil Abu Shammala, "What's Next?" *The Electronic Intifada*, November 23, 2023, https://electronicintifada.net/content/whats-next/41591.

December 1, 2023

Still OK?

Yes, my friend. The bombing continues.

December 8, 2023

I am still waiting for an end of this foolishness.

January 2, 2024

How are you?

January 22, 2024

What's your situation now? Are you eating at least once a day?

January 28, 2024

I'm fine. All is OK. I'm eating three times a day. The problem is not the food, even though it is no good. We are waiting for the end of this crisis.

February 17, 2024

[There was a possibility that I could join a delegation going to Gaza, but the trip didn't materialize.]

Let me know when you are coming. I will receive you and will know where you should stay. Sahar and I and sometimes the kids [go] to the UN headquarters in Rafah, where all of the international NGOs work.

Brian, the price of the cigarette is so expensive. It is unpredictable and unbelievable. One pack, 20 cigarettes is 2,000 shekels. If you can, bring some cigarettes. It would be a wonderful gift.

I hope to learn soon about whether I'll be accepted to join the delegation. What brand of cigarette do you favor? Are there other small things I could bring to the family?

I will ask Nour and Nesma to come up with a list. Coffee would be good and maybe dry food for our cat because it is difficult to find suitable dry food. Marlboro red. If you can, two cartons.

You should visit our tent. It is in a safe place.

March 10, 2024

I was evacuated from Gaza City to Khan Younis. My apartment in Gaza City has been destroyed. We live in tents in the Al-Mawasi area. Life here is so difficult it's hard to think about the future. I need to help my family. My children have many things to do in their lives.

May 14, 2024

Today I succeeded to get 5 chickens for my family and my brother's family. It will be a happy surprise. Can u imagine? You need to fight in order to get such. One of my friends who works at the ministry of economy arranged to get them for the ordinary price not the black market, 150 shekels. In the market if you find them, you should pay 500. Sahar and the kids will celebrate. They will make a party because of the chickens. Today there is no time to cook.

How will you keep them cool?

The chicken is frozen. The weather also is cold.

March 18, 2024

Hi Brian, how are you? I'm in Rafah now, going back to Al-Mawasi. The news is not good because of the continuing attacks against Al-Shifa hospital and the bombing in Rafah terrifying the people.

March 21, 2024

I have the flu. It is because of the weather. It is not covid, I tested. Don't worry. I am good. It takes three to 7 days.

March 26, 2024

I am OK now. I took vitamin C.

April 7, 2024

I am OK. No changes, just waiting for any hope to stop what we are living with.

April 13, 2024

We are good. Waiting for an end to this war. But it seems no end soon. They bomb by air everywhere. They continue killing. There are no specific areas for targeting. There are so many bodies, no one can reach them. They destroy very widely. I continue [to] think and ask, what is next?

The bombing is not close to me, but I move from Khan Younis to Rafah every day. No one can say confidently that a place is safe or not. No war continues forever. But this is a long war, we did not expect it, and we have no power to face it.

April 23, 2024

The news about Rafah is not good. They may invade Rafah soon. Cairo is warning about a Rafah invasion. Here the UN staff is planning to rent in Zawayda, middle of the Gaza Strip, due to the hot talk about Israel invasion of Rafah. If they control the Rafah border, they will be in control of all of Gaza. And they will stop thousands of Palestinians to travel.

April 30, 2024

How is Mohammed doing? [He had contracted hepatitis A.]

He is better today. It is 4 days now. But I think he will start recovering from today.

How is the food situation now?

The problem is not the food, it is the prices of the good food. Most people depend on the aid that comes from international organizations, like WFP, UNICEF and UNRWA.

May 9, 2024

Let us now wait until we see what will happen at the border. I think many things will be changed concerning the operation of the border. Do you agree with me?

It's still unclear to me. I think no one knows, even the IDF.

Yes, this is right.

Is Mohammed better? Anyone else ill?

He is OK. Today is his best day of the last week. Still he needs to follow the program of food. The problem is that this kind of disease has no specific medicine. Sweet without oil, potatoes, and so on.

And the rest of the family?

We are OK. The hepatitis hasn't transferred to any of the rest of us so far. I hope we will be safe. Due to the high pollution and the crowding, we have more than 80,000 case of hepatitis A.

And how are you, physically and emotionally.

After the war we will need a long time to treat many things, including diseases, and morale among the society. It's unbelievable, unbelievable, Brian. We appear not to be normal human beings. We are not normal because we live this war for a long time and nobody can predict when it comes to the end. It is a real nightmare. Nobody can imagine the stories of killings everywhere in Gaza.

May 11, 2024

Good morning. The war goes as if it just started. During the last night the bombing did not stop.

May 15, 2024

Everything OK with you?

Your voice sounds like you're ill. I hope not seriously.

Yes, I am tired, Brian. I swear I am so tired because, imagine that you sleep, wake up to face the unknown, you don't know when this nightmare will reach its end. It is so difficult.

What is the difference between us in Gaza and animals? Animals, they eat, sleep. We do the same now.

May 16, 2024

My energy sometimes betrays me. We are no longer 20 or 30 years old to face these troubles as we were in the past. Your body, your heart, what about people who live in tents for more than five months with minimum conditions of life? We sleep, wake up and we don't know what will happen for today and tomorrow and after a month.

You look at your kids' eyes with no power to make them happy or to help them survive or get them out of Gaza. This situation gives you different feelings that contradict themselves. You ask yourself many questions and have no answers. Why all of this? Why have we been left isolated like now? Why the people, the governments all over the world don't raise their voice and ask Israel to stop the genocide?

May 17, 2024

Can you imagine that you continue your long years of life keeping your secrets the private matters of your life with your family. Now there is no privacy. Leave aside poverty and hunger for the moment. All of us are equal now. Even your privacy you can't keep it. You become an open book for everybody. They hear everything and tell it to others. This is the life. Can you imagine? You cannot keep your secrets as something personal. Wow.

I want to give you a life example, and it is not a joke. Some of our neighbors in the tents are my cousins. My cousin, one of them is a female teacher. She punished her kid, "I was a teacher for 200 students, all of them were under my shoes, how can I teach you and you don't obey me?" Her voice is very loud. When they shout, it is because they have conflicts and we follow by listening.

In tents, no husband can approach his wife, or she, her husband. Very severe punishment. Who punishes. If anyone just breathes, the neighbors hear.

May 19, 2024

I have the flu and the weather is very hot. I took medicine and I'm waiting for any developments.

May 20, 2024

I'm still suffering from the flu. The summer flu is worse than the winter flu.

May 21, 2024

Is there clean water to drink?

I'm still sick. I drink mineral water.

We have developed water after they recycled it from the sea.

May 22, 2024

I'm feeling better, but I still have the flu. I visited my sister today, after her fourth forced evacuation.

May 25, 2024

They are starting to talk about opening the border to allow aid to enter Gaza. Egyptian government said they will not leave their responsibility for the population of Gaza. This might be an introduction to decide to reopen the border for individuals.

May 26, 2024

I'm still very sick, getting worse day by day. Today I took two kinds of antiflu medicine. I expected that I would recover sooner. I'm isolating in this tent. Sahar and the kids are in another tent.

May 29, 2024

Now Sahar, Nour, and Nesma are also suffering from the flu.

May 30, 2024

Khalil, I'm worried about you.

I'm still suffering. It seems that I am getting old, that is why I suffer from simple flu. When I said this to Nour, she said, "Finally, you admit that you're getting old!"

May 31, 2024

I'm feeling better today. It seems like I am really recovering.

June 1, 2024

I'm still taking medicine. It makes me sleepy. The flu is very severe. I don't know what this is.

June 7, 2024

I don't hear any improvement in your voice.

Yes, Brian. This is the fact. I am still suffering and struggling. I just took one course of three tablets of antibiotics. I don't want to repeat it. I want my body to resist. There are so many reasons for a slow recovery: (1) the situation, (2) the stress, and (3) no quality of food. Gazans are used to having meat on Fridays. Can you imagine that there is no meat in the markets for long weeks? In fact, the pain of the body is nothing compared with the pain of the mind and the heart, thinking and emotions.

June 9, 2024

It was bloody yesterday, more than 210 have been killed while they recovered the hostages. The news focuses on the hostages and ignores the innocents who were victims for both Israel and Hamas.

June 11, 2024

Nour published a poem titled My Mother Once Said.[97] She surprised me. I discovered she is a potential poet.

[Here are the last two stanzas of the poem:]

I will recognize you by your voice,
by your prayers
for me and for the martyrs.
I will not lose my way in the darkness,
for the fires of their hatred
have lit up the sky.
Oh, mother,
You lied, mother,
you lied for me and to yourself,
and for a homeland you loved.
But no one loved us,
Oh, mother,
no one loved us,
except God.

[97] Nour Khalil Abu Shammala, "My Mother Once Said," *The Electronic Intifada*, June 10, 2024, https://electronicintifada.net/content/my-mother-once-said/46996.

June 13, 2024

Two of my friends, they passed away.

Allah yarhamhum [God have mercy upon them].

June 14, 2024

There are hundreds of thousands of people in Al-Mawasi. We wash our hands and shower and cook sometimes with polluted water. Nour suffers a lot because she's very sensitive and she cannot continue with such a life under the hot sun as if we are in a desert. The population in the world is more than 8 billion. Gaza's two million are nothing.

Sahar also suffers because she goes every two days from Khan Younis to Deir el-Bellah to the office they rent to continue the work of their NGO center where they provide services for evacuees as wide as they can.

Anyhow, we started summer intense and this is, you cannot imagine how difficult it is to live in tents under the very hot sun, even the water is polluted. Mohammed my son suffered from hepatitis A because of the polluted water and because of the vegetables. We depend on him to bring the needs of the family.

Israel has now closed the southern border. We're fed up. It is an unbelievable condition of life. We have been here for five months now and we don't know when this will end. We love our country, but we don't love suffering. We need to stop suffering.

Al Azhar University started the semester online. Nesma had registered, but she suffers until she gets an internet connection to download the lectures. And of course she follows the lectures under the intense heat. I'm talking to you while all of my clothes are soaked with sweat. She needs to continue waiting [until] the early hours of the morning because this is the suitable time to download.

I cannot talk about myself. I can talk about others. Because I live simply in the middle of all this suffering. I feel that I am responsible for this. I want to save my family. I sometimes escape from their eyes because I'm very weak in getting them out of this. But the reality says that I am a failure to save and protect them and a failure to give happiness.

Hopefully the border will open and according to the news they are discussing [with] Egyptians, Americans and Europeans to reopen the border and to bring PA or UN people to manage the exit of people and the entry of goods.

Our eyes look at the border. We are waiting to listen anytime that the border will reopen because once they open, we can proceed to leave Gaza.

Due to the war we see more than 60 percent of Gaza is completely destroyed. We need many years to restore conditions of life. Now we suffer from the lack of the minimum conditions of life.

As a father my investment is in my kids. That pushes me to think how to save them and how to provide them the conditions to continue their lives because the future should focus on this generation.

June 22, 2024

How are you feeling?

I cannot tell how I am doing. This is the most difficult question with only difficult answers. No one can know if s/he will survive this genocide. We live until when? Who will be next? To get water is most difficult, to get food is most difficult, to get covering from the heat is most difficult, getting answers for thousands of questions about the war is most difficult. The time is going very slow. Every hour we hear of massacres all over Gaza. It is unbelievable. We are in deep crisis. No solution.

Is there anything that relieves the pressure on your mind, even for a moment or two?

I am trying to put myself in any place, I mean to manage the time, I focus on the small garden I started outside the tent. Peppers, eggplant, cucumber, watermelon. I try to escape by taking care of this growth. Every day I give water in the morning and the evening for this small farm.

June 28, 2024

Nour is suffering from hepatitis A. I do not know what to do in this life. I see my kids one after one suffer from pain and I feel very weak. I have not had food since the morning. I do not like to see Nour suffering. I am crying now, Brian. I have never told anybody that I cry. But I feel satisfied when I talk to you.

June 29, 2024

Salamat Khalil [many greetings, Khalil]. How are you feeling?

June 30, 2024

I'm feeling better, thank you.

July 13, 2024

The bombing today was just 700 meters from our tent. The area that was targeted was very crowded with people, the main street where most of the people in Al-Mawasi move about. There are so many shops for the evacuated people: drinks, sweet water.

Last night I was with my friend. We were walking along the street very close to the awful bombing. This is the confusion that we feel. They say we're in a safe place. But there is not a single safe place in Gaza. I think Israel will commit more crimes in the coming days. Many Hamas are staying here. We can't tell these people to leave.

July 14, 2024

I'm watching two parents bringing their two sons' bodies. It's unbelievable Brian. Very horrible.

How are you?

I'm okay, but I have a strange feeling that something will happen. I'm so, so afraid of what may come.

How is Nour?

Nour is good. She's healthy now. But she is fed up. She is energetic, strong, powerful but now sometimes she says she hopes to die because she doesn't want to continue suffering. Mohammed and Nesma are strong, but Nour is very sensitive, she cannot understand why we have to suffer this long.

July 17, 2024

Nour just wrote this poem[98]:

> The earth yields its fruits,
> Defying siege and hunger,
> Defying the occupation.

---

[98] Nour Khalil Abu Shammala, "The Land Fights, Too," *The Electronic Intifada*, August 5, 2024, https://electronicintifada.net/content/land-fights-too/47811.

Tomatoes sprout,
Peppers and eggplants,
Despite cut-off water,
Despite forbidden shells.

Mint and basil's fragrance wafts,
The scent of homeland
In the land of peace.

Despite the tents' heat,
Children's displacement,
The loss of dreams,
The earth yields its fruits,
Feeding its children,
North and south,
Refusing starvation.

The earth brings forth vegetables,
And fruits,
Watered by martyrs' blood.

It fights with its soil,
Holding warriors' remnants,
Steadfast in death,
Defying forces,
Defying weapons.

Our people plant,
And eat from our land's soil.
The earth fights side by side,
With its sea, with its brave resisters.

It grows patience,
Quelling children's hunger,
Silencing mothers' tears,
Easing men's burdens.

Only in Gaza,
The earth fights with its people.

I suffer from pain in my back. They took a CT at the hospital. They said I need to rest and to not carry heavy things. The pain goes from thc bottom of my back into my legs. I don't know if these doctors are good enough to deal with this.

By the way, we are moving from Al-Mawasi to the area between Zawayda and Nuseirat because my kids and Sahar are so tired of the heat in the tents. I don't know if this will be a good step or not. I'll have to leave my brother and his family. I'm not sure that area is safe. I don't know if we are going somewhere better or to the unknown. I will keep the tent in case they invade Nuseirat. We are moving to a concrete place, not tents, just to protect ourselves from the heat.

July 20, 2024

Now it's difficult for us to think about the future because the border is still closed. We are waiting for another announcement about reopening the border.

I have started to lose my passion for life. And I feel sad that I have such feelings. The situation is very, very difficult. You cannot describe it even if you use both Arabic and English dictionaries.

There are some things that we can't talk about on WhatsApp or even phone because of the security situation, everything is controlled. Yes, Israel kills civilians and targets civilians and targets everything, against international law. At the same time, some of the targets live among or between the civilians. They think that they protect themselves, but they don't. They consciously expose civilians to danger and death.

I wrote this essay:

> A Message to Humanity
>
> By Khalil Abu Shammala
>
> I hope that everyone, wherever they are in the world, is well and experiencing happiness and continuous fulfillment in their work, family, and friendships. However, I invite all of you, while you enjoy the details of life, to take a few minutes to contemplate my words and questions:

Has it ever occurred to you that you might be forced to leave your home, leave behind everything connected to you, including your own memories and the memories of your children and family?

Have you ever considered what it would be like to be forced to leave your own home and not know where to go or what to do next?

Have you ever imagined living in a poor makeshift tent or pergola tents, through the bitter cold of winter or the oppressive heat of summer?

Can you imagine losing your entire family as a result of your home being bombed while eating, sitting, sleeping, walking in the street, riding in a car, or simply going about your daily life?

Has it ever crossed your mind to be a doctor in the emergency department, treating the injured, only to find that the patients brought in by the ambulance are your own family members among the wounded and dead?

Have you ever had to watch your son or a family member suffer an injury and find no doctors, no ambulance, or even basic medical treatment available?

How many of you can imagine living in conditions where there is no drinking water or water to wash clothes or kitchen utensils?

Has it ever occurred to you that you might lose your brother, your son, or anyone you love and trust without getting a chance to say goodbye?

Can you imagine a friend, neighbor, son, or daughter being killed, head detached from their body or wounded with one of their body parts amputated or blown off yet they are still alive as a result of a direct or indirect injury?

I do not think anyone anywhere in the world would imagine living in circumstances where they lose everything: their work, studies, home, family, friends, memories, along with their personal belongings including their clothes, photos, albums of their children and family, without the ability to recover any of these precious things.

Everything mentioned, and more, is happening in Gaza as a result of a systematic genocide. It represents the complete destruction of lives and is being carried out mercilessly by Israel with American weapons, without any regard to the slightest international intervention and human rights.

Everything mentioned above has happened and is happening in Gaza, which has been calling upon and still pleading for the world's attention since October 2023 until now. The international community has failed to protect children, women, the disabled, the elderly, and the youth. It has not upheld the principles of international law and human rights.

Contemporary history has not witnessed crimes more heinous and ferocious than those we are witnessing in the Gaza Strip. There is no doubt that the international community has failed to honor human rights conventions and has tacitly allowed the continued bloodshed and endless barbaric suffering in Gaza.

At the same time, the Palestinians in Gaza are grateful for and thankful to all those who have participated in solidarity activities against genocide, whether demonstrations, rallies or encampments led by students in North American and European universities, by activists, by civil society members, by ordinary women, men, and children worldwide. These free people of conscience worldwide act out of duty and responsibility, believing that injustice will not prevail and that humanity will ultimately reject anyone who perpetuates this genocide.

July 22, 2024

While I am writing now, the Israeli forces ordered the people from the east and middle of Khan Younis to evacuate to the west of Khan Younis. Many people have been killed since last night. It's not just the war and the bombing and the killing but the forced evacuations. How many times can people can be evacuated, and to where? So many people can't pay for evacuation. Things are very expensive, money is useless. Even if you have a million dollars, you can't do anything with them.

Just now we received news of another evacuation. For many people this is the tenth time they've had to evacuate.

July 28, 2024

This is the third night in Nuseirat. The IDF ordered the population of al-Bureij camp to evacuate, and part of Nuseirat as well. I am confused and worry that they will tell us to evacuate also. This is a massive moment where you feel so weak and incapable of protecting your loved ones.

Can you imagine that most of our conversations are about the news of the bombing, killing, destroying, evacuation. My sister comes to visit and instead of talking about good times we talk about the options we have if they force to evacuate again.

Mohammed, my nephew, is an engineer. He owns an alternative energy company in Nuseirat. He is afraid that the IDF will invade and he'll lose $80,000, all of his solar panels. He doesn't know what to do. Should he try to move the equipment elsewhere? Should he leave it where it is?

August 1, 2024

Assassination of Haniyeh. This is a very dangerous development. This means that Israel does not respect any country. I don't know what's going to happen. Israel knows no red lines. Netanyahu would not have done this without the full support of the USA. These are the people who talk about human rights and claim that they protect international law. They are creating extremists in the world and then they come later and present themselves as the good boys. The international community should feel shame. They just watch how creative Israel is in killing the Palestinians.

We have completed the paperwork for Nour to study in Jordan.

August 21, 2024

Death is the only certainty for the Palestinians in Gaza.

Israel just invaded Al-Mawasi from three kilometers north of us. I can't think now. I need to see what will happen. The shooting continued until 10 pm.

You cannot imagine the situation that we face.

August 26, 2024

I was thirty seconds away from death today. Five people were killed in a bombing just 40 meters from me. They targeted a Hamas person standing behind his car.

August 27, 2024

I am still thinking about yesterday's bombing. I'm having nightmares.

August 28, 2024

It was 2:00 p.m. when I left the tent where coffee is served, just 50 meters from a friend's tent. I was the last of three friends. I was delayed a few seconds because I met a friend of Nesma. Just 30 seconds later I heard a huge explosion. It was right on the path I took from the coffee place to the tent. People started to shout. The scene was very dramatic. A man I know, a journalist, was working installing access to internet with his 5-year-old. The child started to shout Baba! Baba! But his father was dead. Another one was standing in front of the coffee tent and he died immediately. Mohammed is a very famous TikToker, speaks English very well, very intelligent. He had two million followers. Nesma actually trained him to code. He would sit at the coffee place to work on TikTok because of the internet. They started to pick up the bodies. At the moment, 5 people have been killed. Mohammed is one of the intellectual youths among the evacuees I know. I'd say hello to him every day. I imagine the nightmare, you see the child shouting, crying at this father while his father doesn't respond. People started to shout. Nobody knows who was killed and who was injured. The scene was very confused, everybody shouting and the ones who found their relatives safe, they calmed down. On the other side people run after their fathers who are being taken to the hospital.

This is what happened two days ago. Many cases like this. Some of it you hear about, some you witness.

When I say nightmare, I imagine the darkness of this life. I am one of the Gazans who expects to die at any moment. I am one of those who doesn't know what is next.

September 1, 2024

There is good news. Nour has been accepted in the master's program at the University of Jordan. She is so happy.

They started to vaccinate today.

Will there be a pause in the fighting?

They have designated specific places for the vaccinations, but I think that if the IDF has a target in those places they will not hesitate to bomb.

September 10, 2024

Last night the bombing in Al-Mawasi killed 50 people. It was just 200 meters away from the tent of my sister.

October 7, 2024

Now it has been a year. What are your thoughts today?

I am thinking of the day before 7 of October 2023, and what we have become now. I am thinking of more than 40,000 who have been killed, 26,000 who lost their fathers or mothers. More than 70,000 who have become disabled. 80% destruction of buildings. The massive poverty, the tens of thousands who have passed away due to the difficulty of life and lack of treatment. The destruction of education, homes, infrastructure, the absence of life.

And I ask myself a question: Does what Hamas did on Oct 7 merit this terrible price?

I don't believe it does. Nothing is more valuable than human life.

Hussam

WhatsApp Messages: October 7, 2023–October 7, 2024

October 7, 2023

Salamat. I'm so sorry to hear about Omar [Hussam's younger brother]. This is horrible. Is everyone else OK?

Many thanks for your sincere feelings. They are OK and I hope they will continue to be. The hardest part, I am out of Palestine in Egypt and heading to Lebanon, and thinking of getting back [to Gaza] right now, but not sure if that is possible.[99]

After praying Fajr, Omar went jogging as he is used to do every morning. He was hit with a missile with a surrounding female student passing by.

October 9, 2023

How are things now?

Terribly bad. Still out of Gaza.

October 12, 2023

Thanks for asking. Everyone is OK, but terrified. Things are getting even worse, and I am still out of Gaza.

Still unharmed?

So far, and hope everyone will stay unharmed. The worst thing I am still out of Gaza and cannot get back. This is very harmful to me. Also, I cannot bear the horrible scenes coming out in the news.

October 20, 2023

I am fine, but still stuck in Egypt. Communication with the family is too difficult.

---

[99] Hussam had left Gaza on October 4 to travel through Egypt to Lebanon to present a paper at an academic conference. He returned to Gaza on November 26, 2023, during the ceasefire.

Any idea when you can return?

No, unfortunately.

October 22, 2023

Please read this remembrance I wrote about my brother Omar, beginning with his words:

> "In times of war, exceptional circumstances unfold. It is the unique paradox of living life while being spiritually detached, of confronting death while being physically present and awakening each day with gratitude that the walls haven't crumbled upon a body harboring the dreams of a peaceful slumber."
>
> These words were spoken by a man named Omar, who would become the first in the family to taste the consecrated earth with his blood. Omar, a Gazan in his thirties, was a writer, a poet, and a graduate of Al-Azhar University with a passion for sports, faith, homeland, arts, and music. He also represented the Arab youth as an ambassador.
>
> Omar was known for his grace, his warm countenance, his impeccable manners, and his elegant appearance. He had aspirations, dreams, and a bright future ahead of him. However, his journey was tragically cut short by an Israeli missile while he was out for a jog along Gaza's coastline, an area he affectionately called the "Capital of the Nuseirat."
>
> That missile the very one that didn't grant him the opportunity to continue his pursuit of knowledge, work, and poetry. It robbed him of the chance to embrace fatherhood to a three-year-old daughter named Elena.
>
> Omar's debut novel, titled "Living on the Edge of Death," was released in 2016. In it, he recounted the Israeli aggression on the Gaza Strip in 2008, which resonates with the conflicts of today. He portrayed the war as a life teetering between existence and nonexistence, a life where vitality emerged from whispers of love, from the mountains of resilience, from patience under the rain of rockets and bullets. Nevertheless, death would soon snatch life away and scatter destruction like relentless volcanic eruptions that ceaselessly burn and never subside.

According to Omar, life was a fleeting experience, as he expressed, “You live to die within minutes or hours, whether beneath precarious walls or in the path of a missile that tears through your very core.”

Omar was accustomed to the scenes of death in Gaza, yet he embraced humanity, volunteerism, creativity, hope, and dreams. He forged a path to be and become, receiving several international awards in the fields of culture, media, and poetry, all while serving as an exemplar of the ideal Palestinian youth.

For the departed are more than mere statistics; they are embodiments of dreams, bearers of light, authors of narratives that have been tragically extinguished. Our martyrs represent ideas, and ideas never truly perish.

Omar, the one who, in describing the martyrs, said: “Death does not despise you, O little ones, for God loves you. He took you on a long journey with no return.”

And here is Omar, embarking on that long journey without a return. His innocent little Elena continued to wait for him, as she did every day, expecting him to come back laden with sweets, so she could steal a kiss on his forehead and cheeks.

Elena, who bid farewell to her martyr father with a heart-wrenching gaze, will grow up, and she will neither forgive nor forget those who stole her father. She will ask the world: By what sin was my father killed? Or can practicing the sport of running be lethal when war unleashes its weight at any time?

The sea still asks, where is the one who used to greet me every morning? Where is the one who used to talk to me and woo me with his stories?

It’s the Palestinian seagull, the martyr of sports, Omar Fares Abu Shaqra, known as Omar. We are all Omar, living on the edge of death, but with different timing.

I wrote this amidst the sound of falling missiles, shattering glass, and broken homes. I wrote this amid the scent of rubble and the touch of the martyrs’ blood. I wrote this in the hope that Palestine will one day be free, not knowing if we will witness its liberation or join the ranks of the martyrs.

Even if they killed Omar, they will never be able to kill the pen.

October 26, 2023

What is the hardest part for you?

Keeping track of the news to make sure the family is safe. Connection is lost most of the time and I spend substantial time worried until I get a reply. This has been happening to me every single day, most of the day. No place is safe there. This one is 100 times harder than the last ones [previous Israeli bombardments of Gaza], according to Mai and the family.

Death is soaring around, in a literal sense. I hope every member of the family will be safe. No place to escape death. People were targeted in streets and shelters in the south.

October 29, 2023

Family still unharmed?

Alhamdullilah. But still at risk.

November 3, 2023

Thanks for asking. They are still OK. Great suffering. You may have many more chapters to add [to your book], if we are to live more. Really thanks for keeping asking about the family. I really appreciate that.

November 15, 2023

Now, there is no connection with Gaza. This is killing to me.

Has the house been damaged at all?

No. Alhamdulliah.

And your parent's house?

Still OK. Hope all ends soon. I wish I was there. It is now 43 days since I travelled. I expected it to last for 50 days. I guess the goals are not achievable. That's why it may end with a bargain. I also believe the US and Israel have different agendas.

November 25, 2023

Everyone still unharmed physically?

Yes! Alhamdulilah.

December 10, 2023

Currently, I am back to Gaza. They opened the borders during the ceasefire for a few days and I barely managed to cross. But have no internet connection due to the damage of the network. I am visiting my parents and found some weak connection. Hope you are doing well!

December 23, 2023

I hope this war ends soon.

January 2, 2024

Alhumdulliah, we are still OK, but my house was bombed by an artillery shell this morning and there is some damage. An errant missile. The bombing is very heavy sometimes.

I abandoned my house according to IDF's orders to evacuate the area. We're now at my parents' house. I managed to get food adequate for some time but at four or five times the normal price. Hope not to be forced to be displaced once again. Crazy things are just happening around. Frequent displacement of people. People just keep moving from one place to another with no shelter or food.

Yesterday, the house just next to my family's was bombed and it was a horrible night. Alhumdulliah, no one was hurt. It was deliberately targeted. People do not explain, but it seems the house owner may be wanted.

Has your college been damaged?

Our branch in the north is probably damaged. Our main campus in Deir el-Balah is taken by people displaced from northern Gaza. It was reported to be damaged due to the huge number of people living in it. It will take a long time to handle the consequences of this war. Unprecedented consequences.

Weak [internet] connection and is repeatedly disconnected. Sorry for this inconvenience.

January 9, 2024

Salamat Habibi. Once again, forced to be displaced, along with all the extended family. I am in Rafah right now! 😔😟 I am in a friend's house. He offered me the guest room with a separate toilet. My brother Mohammed is in tents. My parents are in the house of our relatives. The rest of my brothers are in my sister's home in Deir el-Balah.

And Mai and the kids are with you in that guest room?

Yes, this is the best I managed to offer my family. I visited those tents. Even some people do not have the privilege of having a tent. They make their own with wood and plastic covers.

Two questions please: 1. What do you envision for Gaza once this horrible onslaught stops? 2. At the moment, what is your greatest fear?

The first question is hard to answer. Nobody can imagine what will happen after this genocide ends. Generally, a nonstop misery and suffering is awaiting Palestinians trying to restore their lives. Losing beloved ones; demolished homes; impoverished economy; destroyed electricity, communications, and water networks; explicitly violating the right to education by destroying schools and universities are not easy things to live with or handle. Palestinians have been suffering the Israeli blockade; now they have tortured souls with no basic life rights along with the lasting savage blockade. Above all, they have been betrayed by both the international and the Arab communities. I do expect people to have a bitter struggle with basic life needs. In sum, the future of Gaza is very dark.

The psychological and the social consequences of this horrific genocide will be catastrophic to Palestinians and the world alike.

I believe there is no chance for peace in the Middle East after this mass killing. Both the US and ISL [Israel] only instilled seeds of anger and hatred and just provided the proper environment for these seeds to grow. Such consequences cannot be cured even in the long term.

The whole world has just failed to prove their abidance with the core human principles they have been calling for years. All is proven to be big lies; the world is just as savage as the jungle: even the jungle itself has governing rules.

Of course, this is just a quick answer for the first question. I think we need to have a long conversation to cover it. My mind is brimming over but cannot express my deepest thoughts. I have so many issues to handle for now for securing my family.

What is a typical day for you, what types of things do you do?

The day starts with tormenting bewilderment; is it OK to stay in Rafah or do we need to go back to Nuseirat regardless of the consequences? Usually, I talk to my family and our conversation ends with no decision because we are uncertain of what is best for the family. The decision is really fatal.

After that, we track the news on the internet or radio for any beam of hope that ends this misery. Then, we spend most of the day attempting to secure food and drinking water. Next, we visit nearby family members in the tents or those living with relatives. Always, we are home by sunset, because being out after that risks our lives.

The biggest fear is making a decision that puts my family at risk. One is never certain about his or her decision nowadays. A decision is simply as fatal as choosing between two cups, one filled with water and the other with a strong poison.

We are responsible not only for ourselves but also for our families and beloved ones.

Decisions: Which part is the safest place to stay at home: the staircase or another room, which one? To stick to our homes or to follow displacement orders? Where to stay? Where to go for displacement? To go back to Nuseirat or to stay in Rafah, or just go for an interval period in Deir el-Balah then to Nuseirat? Where would ISL's next attack be: Nuseirat, Deir el-Balah, or Rafah? Where is the safest shelter for the family? To go out to buy food or not? To leave the family members home or to take them with you when you go out? And many other decisions that seem simple to other people but fatal to Palestinians. Every normal life decision is fatal now.

You know, the decision to go back home after the first displacement to check if it is OK was probably one of the most endangering decisions I have ever taken. I went back several times: sometimes with Mai, with the whole family, or with one or more of the kids. We could simply be targeted by drones or aircraft for being there. When I think back on this, I go crazy. How could I simply do that?! What consequences could I just have brought to my family?

Today, I was thinking of going back to Nuseirat but got scared when thinking of having the north Gaza scenario in Nuseirat. Yet, I am not sure if staying in Rafah is the best option.

January 10, 2024

We fear to send the kids out when an air strike is being executed. This is one kind of those fatal decisions we have been talking about. We cannot leave them by themselves home alone either. So, Mai or I have to stay home with them. Or, we go out together.

In addition, where to go to buy stuff is another difficult decision to take. We have to decide how safe is that place before we go. Then, we have to do the purchasing task as quick as possible because staying longer than expected could be dangerous.

What kinds of food are available?

Mostly canned food, like mortadella and canned beef or chicken, beans, canned fish (tuna). Sometimes vegetables at high prices. Of course, we have no fruits coming in. Nor any kind of sweets or biscuits other than those coming with the relief mission trucks. Sometimes, we bought stuff at 6-10 times the normal price. Salt was sold at 20 shekels, while it was sold at 1 shekel before this genocide. One kg of cucumber is sold at 12 shekels although it was normally sold at 1-3 shekels before. Rice for 20 shekels while 5-7 shekels before. Recently, in Rafah, we have apples coming in that are sold at 25 shekels/kg, and oranges at 12 shekels/ kg.

People have no liquid money to buy food.

Are people angry at the sellers for charging such prices?

Sure, they have to buy basic stuff for living. This is some sort of an internal betrayal. This is due to greedy sellers at the top of the supply chain who take advantage of the war. Retailers are supply resellers who try to make some money for living. They add a few shekels as a proper profit margin. The top greedy sellers are the real problem. We cannot blame retailers. After the war, I assume people will take revenge on these greedy sellers.

Some of the goods are originally sent to people for free as relief packages. Some people steal and leak goods to greedy sellers to take advantage of the control and security gap created by the war. Some of them are protected by corrupt officials. They share profit.

Yesterday, I wanted to secure a tent for my family just in case I have to leave the house. They wanted 2,500 shekels for it! This is so crazy. I am talking about retailers who got the tent one way or another and wanted to make good money for living. Tents are sent to people for free. Presuming some people managed to build up their own shelters the old way, they sell tents to secure money for living. But these guys told me they bought it for 2,400 shekels, which means the tents were stolen by some guy and sold at a high price.

Although not a common practice, this is what I personally experienced with tent issues. At war times, some people are competent opportunists. But they affected the whole society due to their influence.

I have to go to catch Maghreb (sunset) prayer.

February 1, 2024

Salamat. Alhamdullilah we are OK. We are back to Nuseirat. We don't have regular food. Mostly canned food. Almost no meat or chicken. Vegetables are so expensive. No fruits.

Please take some photos of you and your family depicting the circumstances you are in.

We think photos of us in our current conditions would not be nice. Psychologically speaking, we do not feel OK. I am just now talking to Mai and the kids and they are not in favor of taking photos. Maybe later. They are so deeply hurt. All are not in favor of having their photos published during such a tragic misery. Really, they are not feeling OK. They feel betrayed by all. They have been going through many tragic events like losing beloved ones to being displaced more than 7 times. Not to mention many close heavy bombardments.

This time is way different from 2014. Then, we only left on the last day to avoid errant rockets. It was our choice. We could stay home. This time the war is way more savage. It is a genocide. You had no choice but to leave for weeks or months.

Death is literally soaring over our heads. We feel our kids are in real danger all the time and there is no safe place in Gaza. The worst ever is that we are helpless with all this cruelty.

February 16, 2024

I may have the chance to join a small medical delegation within weeks bringing medical supplies into Gaza, arranged by WHO. If I'm able to join, I would of course want to see you and the family. Would that be feasible?

Nice to know that and I hope you will be able to do it. Of course, you are welcome to visit us. We just cannot wait to see you.

Are there some small things I could bring?

Many thanks for your kindness. I do not know if it is possible to get two power banks for laptops and one power bank with 100,000 ml ampere capacity. Mai also wants to know how much does an iPhone that supports eSIM [a digital SIM card that allows you to activate a cellular plan without needing a physical SIM card] cost in the US? We bought Samsung Galaxy A54, but found out this version does not support eSIM.

Also, we would be very grateful if you can get two wireless ear pods of any brand available.

Also, coffee is almost gone. And if available poor brands are sold at nearly 100$ per kg. So, you need to get some coffee, and please get us one kg if you can.

But I still think it's too dangerous for you to come. The situation here is beyond description.

February 17, 2024

See this item of news from a local Agency:

> Ministry of Health in Gaza:
>
> –Israeli occupation forces detain an aid convoy from the World Health Organization 50 meters from Nasser Medical Complex, which includes high-ranking international figures.
>
> The convoy consists of two trucks, one loaded with fuel and the other loaded with water and food, and has been detained for 7 hours.
>
> –The Israeli occupation set up holes in front and behind the UN aid convoy to prevent it from reaching the Nasser Medical Complex. (Google translated).

I hope Allah will choose all that is good for you. We lost internet connection for a while. It's back now.

February 29, 2024

I really do not know if it is a good idea to join the delegation. Hope you can make the choice that works best for you. I know coming here is a unique opportunity to witness and document the reality of what's going on but, meanwhile, your safety matters. [I did not join the delegation for health reasons and for fear of burdening my friends in Gaza.]

March 10, 2024

Last night was a terribly tough one in our neighborhood. Heavy bombardment with more than 13 air strikes in just two minutes. Internet connection is lost now and I am writing using a poor local network which is unstable. So, I am not sure if we can keep our connection.

March 11, 2024

I returned home on 26/11/2023. The family changed residence in the following sequence:

1. Our home to parents' home
2. To relatives'
3. To parents' home
4. To relatives'
5. To parents'
6. Back to our home on my arrival on 26/11/2023
7. Displaced to parents' on 24/12/2023
8. Then displaced to Rafah on 3/1/2024
9. Back to parents' on 22/1/2024

The main cause of changing residence was heavy bombardment of the neighborhood or displacement orders by the IDF.

March 27, 2024

As you may know, I have had a long discussion over the past weeks with Mai and the kids, and we concluded with the necessity to get the older kids out of Gaza to save their lives and future. Yet, we had a further extensive discussion over the past few days and we think that the whole family needs to get out of Gaza for a while for several reasons: it does not look like the war is coming to an end in the near future; we are being at great danger and our lives are at stake; and we need to save our kids' lives and future. Of course, we realize that this needs an urgent sum of money, nearly USD 40000, to cover the exit fees. That's why we are also thinking of selling our house.

Both the campaign and selling the house need a considerably long time to accomplish. The Rafah invasion or at least controlling the Philadelphi Corridor at the borders with Egypt is very likely. The consequences of the invasion will be unimaginable; the only exit will not be allowed anymore and we will be trapped in. This thought is evidenced by the fact that the US and I*sr@el are establishing a seaport, which will replace all the land ports of Gaza, and which, with the technique of planned large-scale starvation, will enforce the immigration of Palestinians through it, while claimed to be used for humanitarian aid.

April 9, 2024

I hope you are doing great! Just checking in.

April 15, 2024

9:02 a.m. The situation is so terrifying in my neighborhood. Most of the houses were either hit with errant missiles or hit purposefully with F16s. It is terribly catastrophic there, and all warned me of trying to get there. I almost know nothing about my house. Some tall buildings were leveled to ground there.

9:19 a.m. Iran is taking the attention away while the situation here is getting worse. [There was an exchange of attacks between Israel and Iran in April.]

I remember you saying once, "There is no bottom to worse in Gaza."

True. This the best lesson for Gazans. I am at my parents' now. We are not feeling OK, especially Mai, fearing an overnight invasion of Nuseirat. So, you should not get sad because the situation can be worse. This is what I am trying to tell Mai and kids all the times. Just say alhamdulliah whatever the situation is. Meanwhile, we trust Allah is always there to help.

They [Israeli forces] are already in northern Nuseirat, just few hundred meters from our neighborhood, along the line of wadi Gaza [Gaza Valley] from east to west. There are two brigades at the moments. They may invite more troops. Mechanized brigades. But so far, they say they are there to enlarge the buffer zone.

What is the food situation?

Better, but never like usual. Mostly canned food and little meat, fruits. The usual delicious meals are rarely made. Now, food is getting cheaper, but people have no liquid money at hand. I really hope we can meet again in our new, peaceful home to share those meals again.

1:32 p.m. I just came from my home. It was a real risk to go there with Mai. It is destroyed out of a massively huge pressure out of a missile that hit a nearby house. All the windows with their frames, the doors, some walls, the outer walls, the furniture . . . etc. all are destroyed. Could not take photos 'cause it was terrifying to be there. If we had been there, no one would have survived the strike.

I hope this is the bottom to worse this time. We have no hearts for more suffering.

Even the trees in the garden, that I have been looking after for three years, are destroyed. Specially in the southern side of the garden. Evil people!

I just cannot imagine how passionate these people are and how evil is the way they satisfy their lust for killing and in torturing other people like this, regardless of race, color, or ethnicity. What mindset drives them to be so cruel?

2:39 p.m. Do you remember when we talked about the most difficult part of this war? I answered: decision. The decisions to go or not to go to our home was that of a fatal consequence. Going there has a 50% possibility of being hit by a drone. Nevertheless, we decided to take the fatal challenge. Words cannot express the killing horror moments we experienced all the way to and back from home.

April 22, 2024

2:44 p.m. Salamat. Just few hours ago, Mai's family's house was bombarded on purpose. Her brother, his wife, and his son and two nephews (of her two other brothers) lost their lives. Two of her brothers were injured.

How terrible it was to dig the rubble with bare hands to try to save the lives of the people still under it, in vain. How painful it was to all of us when we finally could pick up the corpse of a 10-year-old girl before the eyes of her helpless father. How tormenting it was to all of us observing a helpless father who can do nothing to pick up his little daughter from the rubble before it was too late. How grieving it was when we had to leave the site because it became so dark and dangerous to stay there, leaving behind people under the rubble, who could be waiting a window of hope to be picked up.

Do you remember visiting this house? We went there to see the kid with autism. You helped with purchasing the medicine called Speak from the US, and brought it in through the WHO. In fact, you sat at the same spot where the missile precisely hit.

Can you imagine that we go there regularly to see my mother-in-law. Two days ago, we visited them. We could have been out of the picture by now.

3:21 p.m. Tomorrow, we will be resuming our search for the people under the rubble.

April 29, 2024

3:19 p.m. The situation in Gaza is way beyond human capacity to bear. Mai and the kids are still thinking of the exit regardless of the ceasefire. To me, I may think of staying behind to secure my house and meet any work requirements on my part before leaving. The discussion within the family is about whether the older kids should accept to leave earlier than us. Mai and I are trying to persuade them to do so.

They have plenty of family in Egypt to help them.[100]

Yeah, they do, fortunately. That's why we are pushing the older kids to leave. To save their academic year, and to seek postgraduate opportunities afterward. Now, they are registered at West Bank universities as visiting students. In Egypt the resources will be much more available than in Gaza, particularly the internet. Another option is to move to Turkey. They are offering Gazan students free opportunities to pursue their degrees. But there will be a credit transfer process that may end up with losing some credits. So, the best option is to stick to the WB [West Bank] initiatives carried out by universities there. Visiting students have no credit transfer processes. I mean Turkish universities.

May 3, 2024

7:16 p.m. Just two hours ago we received the sad news of the death of Mai's second brother in his parents-in-law house bombing. We cannot go out to see what happened or to go to hospitals to confirm it. The local news pages on social media confirmed it from neighbors. You can say word of mouth spread via social media, most likely true. Mai is in the worst condition I have

---

[100] With assistance from one of Fares's nieces in Egypt, Fares and Rasmeya left for Egypt in April 2024. Rasmeya also has a niece and family in Egypt.

ever seen. She has lost two brothers and two nieces and one nephew. Now, we hope Mai can bear these catastrophic conditions. She has been preferring death to hearing the sad news of her family. I am confident she is strong and resilient, but the shock was huge.

My mother-in-law is here too and she knows nothing yet.

5:24 p.m. It is confirmed and we've just buried him. This is a massively sad day. The task of finding a way to pass the sad news to Mai and her mother was one of the toughest in my entire life.

As for her mother, we managed to hide the news until morning. Then, I sat with her with the presence of my brother's wife. Mai could not bear it and stayed in her room so as not to reveal it and cause a shock to her mother. She also was still in a shock. We began talking about general issues in the past, and we had our breakfast together, only she and me. We had to make her eat because she would not eat anymore for probably days out of her grief. From time to time, I used to mention the great number of martyrs the family introduced, and how we said farewell to many relatives, friends, and neighbors. We also talked about the rewards Allah bestows people accepting his destiny and to those who are patient and to those who trust that. Allah will let martyrs into paradise, making them lead a pleasant and comfortable eternal life.

At this point my mother-in-law became aware that [relatives] were trying to say something sad. She kept asking if anything happened, and I replied with a negative answer, believing that she is being more and more prepared to receive the sad news without causing a shock that may cause a stroke to her. Mai's sister arrived home after an hour. I received her by the door and told her that I had not had a chance to tell her mother yet. But her presence too meant that something was not OK. Then a close female relative came in, which caused for sure that my mother-in-law figured out that we are about to tell her sad news. We, and Mai, all approached her very close and passed the sad news to her. We were about to lose her too despite of all the preparation we made throughout the past hour. She grieved like a slaughtered bird. Now, she is accepting the judgement and destiny of Allah, but still feeling massive pain.

May 10, 2024

We hope a ceasefire will be agreed on soon. In shaaAllah [God willing]. This is what the Egyptians claimed. I have an interrupted connection. Sorry for the delayed responses.

May 14, 2024

How close to you was the residence that was bombed yesterday killing 30+?

They are our neighbors who were displaced last Jan. due to bombing their original house. The bombing this time that hit their rented home was 300 meters away from my home. Lost connection. I have a poor mobile data connection.

June 9, 2024

How close to you was the latest onslaught?

It was an unprecedented, horribly terrifying attack with many bombardments using F16s, helicopters, drone quadcopters, tanks, warships, and special forces on the ground, just 600 meters away from our home. 250 Palestinians were massacred and more than 400 were wounded in just 1.5 hours.

Helpless people were escaping the cruel attack, trying to seek protection. Many were killed in their homes with their children. Many martyrs were torn into pieces in streets in the central market; the same road we repeatedly used to take when you visited our home. Two or three days before that, they attacked an UNRWA school at 1:20 a.m. and killed more than 43 Palestinians with the assistance of the American and British hi-tech drones.

Did you know anything about the hostages being there?

Only after the attack ended. But we figured out that such an attack could be targeting a top Hamas leader or an attempt to free hostages. We know the behavioral patterns of the Israelis. In fact, nobody knew. This is a central area which is usually overcrowded.

I hear more and more Gazans who've gone to Egypt say how horrible life is there, some regretting having left Gaza. How are your parents doing?

Whenever we talk to them, my mother starts crying. My father cannot hide the signs of worry and concern.

What is your thinking now about leaving?

It is not about me. It is all about my family. Mai and the kids want to leave. They see no future in the coming ten years. I agree with them, but I am in between: staying or leaving. Above all, I seek to secure their future by facilitating the opportunity for them to pursue their education, and even to start a new life outside. Mai, in particular, has undergone a severely terrifying experience. I believe she needs a new start, even if temporarily. I care a lot about her and the kids. To me, I want to die in Gaza. So, if I leave, I will come back whenever the kids are doing well. If the war comes to an end, I may send them out by themselves and stay here.

But, you know, I am still uncertain about that. It is a hard decision. One of the thoughts that come to my mind is to seek a new academic position in another country for 4 years and then return to Palestine.

Are you still receiving your salary?

Yes, at different percentages. Now 50% of the salary is being paid to PA employees. Like 2017–18. But it seems that Smotrich [Israel's finance minister] with the intentions of the fanatic Israeli wing is trying to end the PA. They want to take over the West Bank. This is one of factors that support leaving, besides this cruel war.

June 20, 2024

[I sent some photos I had taken of the family years before.]

This is really amazing! We loved it a lot. 😂😂 You made all of us happy, seeing these memories. The kids laughed at them so much 😂. Especially that they looked so young 😁 Please share [more photos] with us whenever possible.

July 9, 2024

[I sent another photo.]

Shaden says: the photographer is wanted, alive or dead 😉. She is just joking. She was shocked with her photo 😂. Montaser, Lama, and Shahd are laughing at their photos. Layan hadn't been born yet. Please keep sending photos. We love them. It is a wonderful documentation of our history.

July 24, 2024

How is everyone?

Alhamdulillah, we are OK. Thanks a lot for asking. How are you doing?

How shameful it is that they are warmly receiving him [Netanyahu] at the Congress 😩 I heard every single word in his empty speech. I am really shocked at how these representatives and legislators are standing every 30 seconds to applaud and greet him. This is ridiculous. All are clear lies, but these people are blinded by their bias and prejudice.

August 3, 2024

Salamat habibi [many greetings].

I scanned my narrative in your book, and it was fantastic and catching. What a literary masterpiece! I really loved it. I will read it thoroughly soon. Tentatively, I have some notes that I hope you will take into consideration. I will provide you with the details after my second reading.

How is everyone?

We are all okay, but things are frustrating for the family, and I keep calming everyone down. There are rumors that the IDF may invade Nuseirat or the middle region at any time. Meanwhile, I'm trying to keep the kids focused on their studies as they have started the summer term.

August 20, 2024

Salamat Hussam. I'm just checking how you're doing.

Alhamdulilah, we are all OK. Many thanks for asking. How are you doing?

Our main concern is to not have the kids trapped here with no hope for their future, while there is no end in the horizon for this genocide. They are studying at their original institutions, with Montaser having more credits at An-Najah University [in the West Bank]. The study is online.

There is no power except from our solar power system which was partially damaged during the attack on northern Nuseirat, but it works well. I moved it to my parents' house. The internet connection is OK but sometimes it is not stable.

September 9, 2024

Salamat habibi. What is your news?

Salamat habibi, many thanks for asking. Alhamdulillah, we are safe for now, but the situation around my own house is worsening. I haven't been able to go there for the past three weeks due to ongoing military operations in the area. The neighborhood has been hit multiple times by artillery and mortar missiles, and one of the strikes directly hit my house's garden. What is even worse, 6 innocent people were murdered in cold blood. Today, I attempted to go there, but the conditions were too dangerous. I got as close as 300 meters to my house before I had to turn back. This short open distance was impossible to cross, with tanks, drones, and quadcopters nearby. 😔

The past few weeks have been busy with preparations for resuming education at our college. It is incredibly challenging to manage this in the midst of this devastating deadly conflict. I hope our life conditions will improve soon.

I've just sent you the edited part of the book. I had an amazing time reading it. Thanks a lot.

September 30, 2024

What is your life like these days?

A significant portion of our time is spent securing water, both for daily use and drinking. We also spend a lot of time buying food, as there's a constant shortage of goods, and prices often go crazy high overnight. So, we dedicate considerable effort to searching for essential items, particularly hygiene products. Another challenge we face is waiting in long queues at ATMs to withdraw our smashed salaries. To manage this, we need to register our names through pre-arranged Google Forms and wait for the list of names to be announced. Once it's our turn, we go to the bank—usually once, and rarely twice, a month—to get a portion of our deposited salaries after standing in long lines.

Personally, I spend a lot of time planning and coordinating with our staff to ensure the smooth resumption of college education. Leading the continuous preparations for the new semester is quite complicated, especially with the frequent disruptions in cellphone and internet services. Some staff members don't even have internet access and have to walk several kilometers just to get connected. Additionally, I make and receive long phone calls daily to ensure that preparations are on track as we approach the semester start date of October 12, 2024.

After 6 p.m., I usually gather with friends to relax and have some fun. By 9 p.m., I return home to spend time with my family, and we usually go to bed after 1 a.m.

October 1, 2024

We really wish to get our life back. It was wonderful and peaceful, despite the blockade.

October 2, 2024

How do you feel about the Iranian attack last night?

We hoped a bargain would put an end to this genocide in Gaza. With this strike I believe people have paradoxical feelings; from one side it puts Israel in a serious situation to push it to choose between a destructive regional war in the Middle East or to make a deal to stop the genocide. I hope it chooses the latter option. Yet, on the other side, it forms a serious escalation causing an unfavorable everlasting war in the ME. We need to get back to normal and get our life back.

The joy and celebrations last night were due to the fact that Gazans feel that they are not left alone to face their destiny now, after a year of betrayal from the Islamic, the Arab, and the international community. The strike stirred a beam of hope in each one as they perceive it as a significant factor to help end their suffering.

Israel's increasing the genocide is one of the greatest fears here. Yet, the Israelis were already increasing the genocide even before the strike. So, the strike may either stop the genocide or set the ME and maybe the world on fire. Either way, it creates a massive pressure on all parties as well as on the leaders of the world to stop the genocide, otherwise all will suffer, which is not a wise option. They have to stop these fascists from burning the world.

After a year of unimaginable suffering, killing, and betrayal, Gazans have nothing to lose now, and when they have nothing to lose, they lose nothing. So, the strike gave them some hope to restore the normal life, and even more to end the disgusting occupation.

Also, please note that, generally, Palestinians are rather cautious talking about such issues on social media, including WhatsApp. All are targeted for surveillance, which makes them avoid opening up on any issue like this. I bet face to face communication will expose much deeper attitudes and feelings.

October 7, 2024

What are your thoughts on this grisly anniversary?

Deep concern for the lives of the family and agonizing uncertainty about their future. I earnestly pray to God to bring a swift end to this genocide.

Epilogue

December 20, 2024

Washington, DC

I stopped recording the narratives and relevant events on October 7, 2024, the one-year anniversary of Hamas's attack on southern Israel and the Israeli military's response in Gaza. Here I will provide brief updates—first on some relevant events and then on the lives of Hammam, Khalil, and Hussam since October 7, 2024.

Today marks the 440th consecutive day of Israel's bombardment of the Gaza Strip (except for the 7-day ceasefire at the end of November 2023). The Rafah crossing to Egypt has remained closed since May 7, 2024, essentially locking all Gazans into the Strip except for approximately two hundred severely ill or severely injured people.

The IDF killed Hamas's leader, Yahya Sinwar, in Rafah on October 16, 2024, and claims to have killed Hamas's military commander, Mohammed Deif, in Khan Younis on July 13, 2024. On November 21, 2024, the International Criminal Court (ICC) issued arrest warrants for Israeli Prime Minister Benjamin Netanyahu and Defense Minister Yoav Gallant for war crimes and crimes against humanity. On the same day, the ICC also issued an arrest warrant for the same crimes for Mohammed Deif, concluding that there was not enough evidence to confirm that he had been killed.

Hammam and his family remain in their home in eastern Khan Younis. On the evening of November 9, Hammam's next younger brother, Hani, was severely injured while he was driving in his Save the Children car and an Israeli missile struck a tent next to the road. The shrapnel from the blast severed an artery in one of his legs and sliced into his liver, stomach, spleen, and intestines. He underwent seven hours of surgery and has survived, finally leaving the hospital in Deir el-Balah on December 3. Hammam has begun volunteering as executive director for an educational center affiliated with UNICEF. In November, his children Fuad and Habiba wrote me poignant messages describing how their lives and education have been shattered through the terrifying destruction and multiple displacements. Fuad closed his message saying, "Sharing this pain reminds me that resilience is all we have when everything else is stripped away."

Khalil and his family still split time between their tent in al-Mawasi and a rented, unfinished apartment in al-Nuseirat Camp. Nesma is continuing her studies online in computer engineering with Al-Azhar University in Gaza City. To get an adequate internet connection, she has to make the dangerous journey to another camp. Nour has been accepted into a master's program in governance and anticorruption at the school of law at the University of Jordan. She will complete her coursework online from Gaza until she is able to travel to Amman—so for now, like Nesma, she must take the daily risk of traveling to another camp to find an adequate internet connection. Mohammed and some friends received a grant from the Goethe Institute to develop a podcast series in which Mohammed interviews Gazans about their experiences during this war.

Hussam and his family remain in his parents' home in the al-Nuseirat refugee camp that is the daily target of severe bombardments. All five children are progressing as well as possible in their university and school studies online. That progress is regularly frustrated by the instability of an internet connection, the lack of electric power (the house's solar panels have been destroyed), and the astronomical cost of repairing or replacing phones and computers. For months, the family has been unable to visit their own home near the power plant because of the constant danger of bombardment. They have received news, however, that their house has sustained further damaged.

Afterword

Some people have asked me over this past year whether *No Way but Forward* is still a relevant title for this book, given the ongoing colossal destruction, displacement, death, starvation, and injury in Gaza. I would never think to speak for Palestinians because I am not one. But based on my lengthy experience knowing Palestinians, and particularly Gazans, my answer is unequivocally yes. How many more decades of evidence do we need to realize that there is no extinguishing the human drive for dignity, self-determination, and identity?

Some years ago, I told Ashraf, a good friend in Gaza, that Americans continually ask me how it is that Gazans keep going through all the brutal setbacks. He looked perplexed, even a bit bothered, by the question.

“What other choice do we have?” he said. “Wouldn’t they do the same?”

Acknowledgements

I would never have gone to Gaza if I hadn't accepted the invitation to consult on the study of Palestinian families that Brigham Young University started in 1994. Therefore, my first thanks go to administrators, faculty, and graduate students at BYU, including (in alphabetical order) the late Bruce Chadwick, Camillie Fronk, Tim Heaton, Ray Huntington, Clayne Pope, and the late J. Bonner Ritchie. Equally, I express thanks to the administrators, faculty, and graduate students at the University of Tennessee, where I moved in 2001. They include Will Barnes, Loren Crabtree, Haleigh Craig, Mary Jane Moran, Mick Nordquist, Clea McNeely, Serene Murad, Paul Page, Bob Rider, and Carolyn Spellings.

My deepest thanks go to the more than ten thousand Palestinian youth and their parents who participated in our research projects over the decades, as well as to my many Palestinian research colleagues, including Adnan Abed, the late Abu Ali Hillis, Yasser Abu Jamei, Mohammed Abu Mallouh, Tarek Abu Mallouh, Yehia Abu Mallouh, Cairo Arafat, Mahmoud Daher, the late Eyad el Sarraj, Rita Giacaman, and Khalil Shikaki.

I am grateful to many other institutions that have supported me over the decades, including the National Institute of Mental Health, the Social Science Research Council, the Rockefeller Bellagio Study Center, the BYU Family Studies Center, the Jacobs Foundation (especially Simon Sommer), New America (especially William Gerrity, Peter Bergen, and Anne-Marie Slaughter), the Foundation for Middle East Peace (especially Matt Duss), the US Institute of Peace, United Palestinian Appeal (especially Saleem Zaru), the Middle East Policy Council (especially Bassima Alghussein), and the Institute for Palestine Studies (especially Walid Khalidi, Michelle Esposito, Julia Pitner, Steven Bennett, and Jehad Abusalim).

My sincere thanks go to the many colleagues and friends who have supported this book project by offering ongoing encouragement, providing various kinds of technical assistance, and reading parts or all of the manuscript. They include Yasser Abu Jamei, Dorgham Abusalim, Khaled Alostath, Tareq Baconi, Cathy Baker, Peter Bergen, Todd Cox, Gwyn Daniels, Janine di Giovanni, William Gerrity, Hal Grotevant, Walid Khalidi, Rami Khouri, Nancy Murray, Penny Mitchell, Alice Rothchild, Sara Roy, Jeffrey Sachs, Avi Shlaim, Anne-Marie Slaughter, Sterling Van Wagenen,

Doug Wick, and Jim Youniss. My sincere apologies to all those I may have overlooked.

I am further grateful to the many staff at Amazon Publishing who helped produce this book (especially Max Connor) and to editors Ethan Goffman and Pam Ozaroff for making this a much more polished work.

Above all, I am eternally grateful to the al-Faqawi, Abu Shammala, and Abushawish families for their respect, devotion, patience, and love. I am a better person because of them.

Appendix 1

A Partial List of Books on Gaza in English

Baroud, Ramzy. *My Father Was a Freedom Fighter: Gaza's Untold Story.* New York: Pluto Press, 2010.

Butt, Gerald. *Life at the Crossroads: A History of Gaza.* 2nd ed. Nicosia, Cyprus: Rimal Publications, 2009.

Downey, Glanville. *Gaza in the Early Sixth Century.* Norman: University of Oklahoma Press, 1963.

Filiu, Jean-Pierre. *Gaza: A History.* New York: Oxford University Press, 2014.

Finkelstein, Norman G. *Gaza: An Inquest into Its Martyrdom.* Oakland: University of California Press, 2018.

Hass, Amira. *Drinking the Sea at Gaza: Days and Nights in a Land Under Siege.* Translated by Elana Wesley and Maxine Kaufman-Lacusta. New York: Metropolitan Books, 1999.

Macintyre, Donald. *Gaza: Preparing for Dawn.* London: Oneworld Publications, 2017.

Meyer, Martin A. History of the City of Gaza: From the Earliest Times to the Present Day. New York: Columbia University Press, 1907.

Murphy, Dervla. *A Month by the Sea: Encounters in Gaza.* London: Eland Books, 2013.

Roy, Sara. Failing Peace: Gaza and the Palestinian-Israeli Conflict. London: Pluto Press, 2006.

Roy, Sara. *The Gaza Strip: The Political Economy of De-development.* 3rd ed. Washington, DC: Institute for Palestine Studies, 2016.

Roy, Sara. Hamas and Civil Society in Gaza: Engaging the Islamist Social Sector. Princeton, NJ: Princeton University Press, 2011.

Appendix 2

Publications on Palestine by Brian K. Barber and His Research Teams

Book

Barber, Brian K., ed. *Adolescents and War: How Youth Deal with Political Violence.* New York: Oxford University Press, 2009.

Chapters

Barber, Brian K. "Political Conflict and Youth: A Long-Term View." In *Emerging Trends in the Social and Behavioral Sciences*, edited by Robert A. Scott, Marlis C. Buchman, and Stephen Kosslyn (consulting editor), 1–15. Hoboken, NJ: John Wiley and Sons, 2015. https://doi.org/10.1002/9781118900772.etrds0253.

Barber, Brian K. "Glimpsing the Complexity of Youth and Political Violence." In *Adolescents and War: How Youth Deal with Political Violence*, edited by Brian K. Barber, 3–32. New York: Oxford University Press, 2009.

Barber, Brian K. "Making Sense and No Sense of War: Issues of Identity and Meaning in Adolescents' Experience with Political Conflict." In Barber, *Adolescents and War*: 281–311.

Barber, Brian K. "Adolescents and Political Violence: Recommendations for Continuing Research." In Barber, *Adolescents and War*, 315–22.

Barber, Brian K. "The Palestinian Intifada." In *Youth Activism: An International Encyclopedia*, edited by Lonnie R. Sherrod, Constance A. Flanagan, Ron Kassimir, and Amy K. Kyvertsen. Vol. 2, *K-Z*, 450–54. Westport: CT: Greenwood Publishing, 2005.

Barber, Brian K. "Politics, Politics, and More Politics: Youth Life Experience in the Gaza Strip." In *Everyday Life in the Muslim Middle East,* 3rd ed., edited by Donna L. Bowen, Evelyn A. Early, and Becky Schulthies, 207–23. Indianapolis: Indiana University Press, 2014.

Barber, Brian K. "Youth Experience in the Palestinian Intifada: Intensity, Complexity, Paradox, and Competence." In *Roots of Civic Identity: International Perspectives on Community Service and Activism in Youth*, edited by Miranda Yates and James Youniss, 178–205. New York: Cambridge University Press, 1999.

Barber, Brian K., and Joseph A. Olsen. "Positive and Negative Psychosocial Functioning after Political Conflict: Examining Adolescents of the First Palestinian Intifada." In Barber, *Adolescents and War*, 207–37.

Barber Brian K., and Joseph A. Olsen. "Adolescents' Willingness to Engage in Political Conflict: Lessons from the Gaza Strip." In *Tangled Roots: Social and Psychological Factors in the Genesis of Terrorism*, edited by Jeff Victoroff, 203–26. Amsterdam: IOS Press, 2006.

Barber, Brian K., and Julie M. Schluterman. "Adolescents and Political Violence: A Review of the Empirical Literature." In Barber, *Adolescents and War*, 35–61.

Barber, Brian K., Julie Mikles Schluterman, Elizabeth Senter Denny, and Robert J. McCouch. "Adolescents and Political Violence." In *The Psychology of Resolving Global Conflicts: From War to Peace*, edited by Mari Fitzduff and Chris E. Stout. Vol. 2, *Group and Social Factors*, 171–90. Westport, CT: Praeger Publishers, 2006.

Peer-Reviewed Journal Articles

Barber, Brian K. "The Politics of Development." *Human Development* 57, no. 6 (2014): 319–21.

Barber, Brian K. "Youth and Political Conflict: Where Is the Politics? Where Are the Youth? *Child Development Perspectives* 8, no. 3 (January 2014): 125–30.

Barber, Brian K. "Annual Research Review: The Experience of Youth with Political Conflict: Challenging Notions of Resilience and Encouraging Research Refinement." In "Annual Research Review: Resilience in Child Development," special issue, *Journal of Child Psychology and Psychiatry* 54, no. 4 (April 2013): 461–73.

Barber, Brian K. "Contrasting Portraits of War: Youths' Varied Experiences with Political Violence in Bosnia and Palestine." *International Journal of Behavioral Development* 32, no. 4 (2008): 298–309. https://doi.org/10.1177/0165025408090972.

Barber, Brian K. "Political Violence, Social Integration, and Youth Functioning: Palestinian Youth from the Intifada." *Journal of Community Psychology* 29, no. 3 (May 2001): 259–80. https://doi.org/10.1002/jcop.1017.

Barber, Brian K. "What Has Become of the 'Children of the Stone'?" *Palestine-Israel Journal of Politics, Economics and Culture* 6, no. 4 (1999): 7–15.

Barber, Brian K. "Political Violence, Family Relations, and Palestinian Child Functioning." *Journal of Adolescent Research* 14 (1999): 206–30.

Barber, Brian K. "Palestinian Children and Adolescents during and after the Intifada." *Palestine-Israel Journal of Politics, Economics and Culture* 4, no. 1 (1997): 23–33.

Barber, Brian K., Clea McNeely, Chenoa Allen, Rita Giacaman, Cairo Arafat, Mahmoud Daher, Eyad El Sarraj, Mohammed Abu Mallouh, and Robert F. Belli. "Whither the 'Children of the Stone'? An Entire Life under Occupation." *Journal of Palestine Studies* 45, no. 2 (2016): 77–108. https://doi.org/10.1525/jps.2016.45.2.77.

Barber, Brian K., Clea A. McNeely, Eyad El Sarraj, Mahmoud Daher, Rita Giacaman, Cairo Arafat, William Barnes, and Mohammed Abu Mallouh. "Mental Suffering in Protracted Political Conflict: Feeling Broken or Destroyed." *PLOS ONE* 11, no. 5 (May 27, 2016): e0156216. https://doi.org/10.1371/journal.pone.0156216.

Barber, Brian K., Carolyn Spellings, Clea McNeely, Paul D. Page, Rita Giacaman, Cairo Arafat, Mahmoud Daher, Eyad El Sarraj, and Mohammed Abu Mallouh. "Politics Drives Human Functioning, Dignity, and Quality of Life." *Social Science & Medicine* 122 (December 2014): 90–102. https://doi.org/10.1016/j.socscimed.2014.09.055.

McNeely, Clea A., Brian K. Barber, Rita Giacaman, Robert F. Belli, and Mahmoud Daher. "Long-Term Health Consequences of Movement Restrictions for Palestinians, 1987–2011." *American Journal of Public Health* 108, no. 1 (January 2018): 77–83. https://ajph.aphapublications.org/doi/abs/10.2105/AJPH.2017.304043.

McNeely, Clea, Brian K. Barber, Carolyn Spellings, Rita Giacaman, Cairo Arafat, Mahmoud Daher, Eyad El Sarraj, and Mohammed Abu Mallouh. "Human Insecurity, Chronic Economic Constraints and Health in the Occupied Palestinian Territory." *Global Public Health: An International Journal for Research, Policy and Practice* 9, no. 5 (2014): 495–515. https://doi.org/10.1080/17441692.2014.903427.

Spellings, Carolyn R., Brian K. Barber, and Joseph A. Olsen. "Political Activism of Palestinian Youth: Exploring Individual, Parental, and Ecological Factors." *Journal of Marriage and Family* 74, no. 5 (October 2012): 1084–1100. https://doi.org/10.1111/j.1741-3737.2012.01002.x.

Published Abstracts

Barber, Brian K., Clea McNeely, Chenoa Allen, and Robert F Belli. "Adult Functioning in the Occupied Palestinian Territory: A Survey and Event History Calendar Assessment." In "Research in the Occupied Palestinian Territory 6." Special issue, *Lancet* 390, no. S1 (August 2017): S2. https://doi.org/10.1016/S0140-6736(17)32073-1.

Barber, Brian K., Clea McNeely, Joseph A. Olsen, Carolyn Spellings, and Robert F. Belli. "Effect of Chronic Exposure to Humiliation on Well-being in the Occupied Palestinian Territory: An Event-History Analysis." Special issue, *Lancet* 382, no. S4 (December 2013): S7. https://doi.org/10.1016/S0140-6736(13)62579-9.

Barber, Brian K., Clea McNeely, and Carolyn Spellings. "Role of Political Factors in Wellbeing and Quality of Life during Long-Term Constraints and Conflict: An Initial Study." In "Health in the Occupied Palestinian Territory 2012." Special issue, *Lancet* 380, no. S1 (October 2012): S17. https://doi.org/10.1016/S0140-6736(13)60199-3.

Barber, Brian K., Eyad El Sarraj, Clea McNeely, Mahmoud Daher, Rita Giacaman, Cairo Arafat, William Barnes, Carolyn S. Spellings, and Mohammed Abu Mallouh. "Contextualised Suffering in the Occupied Palestinian Territory: A Mixed Methods Study." In "Research in the Occupied Palestinian Territory 5." Special issue, *Lancet* 390, no. S1 (August 2017): S29. https://doi.org/10.1016/S0140-6736(17)32030-5

McNeely, Clea, Brian K. Barber, Carolyn S. Spellings, Robert F. Belli, Rita Giacaman, Cairo Arafat, Mahmoud Daher, Eyad El Sarraj, and Mohammed Abu Mallouh. "Long-Term Effects of Political Imprisonment on Men in the Occupied Palestinian Territory: A Retrospective Cohort Study." Special issue, *Lancet* 390, S1 (August 2017): S30. https://doi.org/10.1016/S0140-6736(17)32031-7.

McNeely, Clea, Brian K. Barber, Carolyn Spellings, Rita Giacaman, Cairo Arafat, Eyad El Sarraj, Mahmoud Daher, Mohammed Abu Mallouh. "Prediction of Health with Human Insecurity and Chronic Economic Constraints in the Occupied Palestinian Territory: A Cross-Sectional Survey." Special issue, *Lancet* 382, no. S4 (December 2013): S25. https://doi.org/10.1016/S0140-6736(13)62597-0.

Authors' Reply

Barber, Brian K., Clea McNeely, Joseph A. Olsen, Carolyn Spellings, and Robert F. Belli. Authors' reply to Janice Halpern, "Health of Palestinians and Chronic Humiliation" (correspondence). *Lancet* 383, no. 9924 (March 29, 2014): 1206–07. https://doi.org/10.1016/S0140-6736(14)60598-5.

About the Author

BRIAN K. BARBER, PhD, is a non-resident senior scholar at the Middle East Policy Council, a senior fellow at the Institute for Palestine Studies, and professor emeritus at the University of Tennessee. He currently lives in Washington, DC. Barber's work has addressed how context—from parenting to political systems—impacts individual and social development. Barber is the editor of *Adolescents and War: How Youth Deal with Political Conflict* (Oxford University Press, 2008), among other books. For the past thirty years, he has researched more than ten thousand Palestinian families in the West Bank, East Jerusalem, and the Gaza Strip. His published articles have appeared in *The Lancet, Social Science & Medicine, Global Public Health, PLOS ONE, Child Development,* the *Journal of Adolescent Research*, and other journals. Barber's commentaries have appeared in *Haaretz*, CNN.com, *Informed Comment, Counterpunch*, and *Middle East Policy*.

WWW.BKBARBER.COM

JACKET DESIGN BY BRIAN K. BARBER

Made in United States
North Haven, CT
09 April 2025

67782053R00186